D0731531

SHADOWING THE ANTHROPOCENE

BEFORE YOU START TO READ THIS BOOK, take this moment to think about making a donation to punctum books, an independent non-profit press,

@ https://punctumbooks.com/support/

If you're reading the e-book, you can click on the image below to go directly to our donations site. Any amount, no matter the size, is appreciated and will help us to keep our ship of fools afloat. Contributions from dedicated readers will also help us to keep our commons open and to cultivate new work that can't find a welcoming port elsewhere. Our adventure is not possible without your support.
Vive la open access.

Fig. 1. Hieronymus Bosch, *Ship of Fools* (1490–1500)

SHADOWING THE ANTHROPOCENE: ECO-REALISM FOR TURBULENT TIMES.
Copyright © 2018 by Adrian Ivakhiv. This work carries a Creative Commons
BY-NC-SA 4.0 International license, which means that you are free to copy and
redistribute the material in any medium or format, and you may also remix,
transform and build upon the material, as long as you clearly attribute the work
to the authors (but not in a way that suggests the authors or punctum books en-
dorses you and your work), you do not use this work for commercial gain in any
form whatsoever, and that for any remixing and transformation, you distribute
your rebuild under the same license. http://creativecommons.org/licenses/by-
nc-sa/4.0/

First published in 2018 by punctum books, Earth, Milky Way.
https://punctumbooks.com

ISBN-13: 978-1-947447-87-5 (print)
ISBN-13: 978-1-947447-88-2 (ePDF)

LCCN: 2018959823
Library of Congress Cataloging Data is available from the Library of Congress

Book design: Vincent W.J. van Gerven Oei

HIC SVNT MONSTRA

SHADOWING THE ANTHROPOCENE
ECO-REALISM FOR TURBULENT TIMES

ADRIAN IVAKHIV

To Auriel

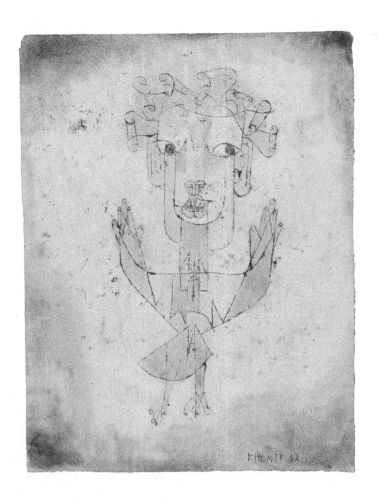

Paul Klee, "Angelus Novus" (1942), oil transfer and watercolor on paper, 31.8 × 24.2 cm. Current location: Israel Museum.
© 2018 Artists Rights Society (ARS), New York.

PRELUDE

The spectre

A spectre is haunting humanity. Or rather, it is haunting every human effort to establish humanity as central, foundational, and of ultimate consequence in the world. That spectre is reality itself, a reality that supersedes, trumps, and outwits all our ideas about it.

This spectre of reality is not exactly humanity's shadow. It is more the other way around: reality has become shadowed by a humanity, an *Anthropos*, that thinks itself real and reality a mere shadow. As the fossil-fueled sun that has powered the rise of this entity begins its long descending arc, this humanity-shaped shadow lengthens, and the Anthropos finds itself taken aback, thinking: what spectre is this, in a world we thought had no more spectres?

"The Anthropocene" is an attempt to name this situation — this reversible shadowing of humanity and reality — while, at the same time, maintaining the centrality of the humanity that is haunted by it. In thinking it can perform this double task — to recognize the realism of a reality that will overcome and bury it, as the Anthropocene will sink one day beneath the next layer of geologies to come, and to simultaneously name itself, humanity, the *Anthropos,* as the central actor in its drama — the Anthropocene is a contradiction.

The task for a true *realist* in Anthropocenic times is to unveil this contradiction, to expose it for what it is. The realist's task in the shadow of the Anthropocene — the task *of* the shadow of the Anthropocene, for those who align with that shadow — is to *bury* the Anthropocene, if not literally, then at least conceptually. It is to develop a conception, and an accompanying attitude and emotional stance, through which the empire of the Anthropocene can be undermined by the larger reality that undergirds it, makes it possible, and will ultimately overtake it. The only question for the undertaker-realist is how best to do that and what quality of compost to leave behind with that burial.

"The Anthropocene" names an event that is ultimately not an event at all. It is an ~~Event~~ of the highest, or deepest, order — an order of a burial, a burial that already knows its future as a layer among layers on a planet of sleepy layers, and in a universe that forgives, forgets, and subsumes them all. This is the geological truth that is harbored within the ~~Event~~ of the Anthropocene. (I'll have more to say about ~~Events~~ soon enough. But for starters, let us say that an ~~Event~~ is a momentous occurrence that has not quite occurred, and perhaps cannot occur, yet which displaces reality even in its non-occurrence.)

Why is Anthropocenic burial a task for *realists*? Who is a realist today?

Realism, in the way I will use the term, is not a belief that one knows the nature of reality and that it is such and such. Nor is it even a belief that the nature of reality is knowable at all. Rather, the realism I propose is a belief in a reality that outwits and exceeds us, and a belief that it always will. It is a tempered and humbled belief in a crossed-out ~~Real~~, a Real under erasure. Such a ~~Realism~~ acknowledges its own incapacity to specify the reality in which it believes, and to thereby account for its own realism. It is the belief of an optimist who cannot name the reason for her optimism, nor even be certain that it isn't folly. She can only speculate, knowing full well that the end of her speculation is likely to be quiet and inconsequential. No tragedy, no comedy. No grand finale or victorious homecoming. Just something beyond. Such is Speculative ~~Realism~~ for our time.

What follows is a series of philosophical engagements, conceptual proposals in effect, that proceed from such a realism — engagements with the challenges of the Anthropocene and with certain philosophical efforts to address those challenges. The realism I propose is an eco-realism because, like the science of ecology, it engages with the relations between things (and between humans and other things) in their thickly entangled and interdependent complexities. And it is an *immanent* realism, one that finds the tools for unmaking the master's house already present, all around, in the master's house. As I will explain, however, the house is not really a house, the master not a master, and objects not really objects. We live in a world of events within which we find ourselves always already poised to act; the question is how to do so.

The philosophical efforts with which I contend and engage include the object-oriented ontology of Graham Harman, the transcendental materialism of Slavoj Žižek, the critical post-secularism of Charles Taylor, the immanent naturalism of William Connolly, and the ontological pluralisms of Isabelle Stengers and Bruno Latour. The tools I apply are those from the philosophical tradition I identify as "process-relational" — a tradition that harkens back to ancient Greek, Indian, and Chinese metaphysicians, and that winds its way through history to the processual pragmatisms of Charles Sanders Peirce, Alfred North Whitehead, and Gilles Deleuze, among others.

The philosophical positions are less important than what they offer for living. That is what this book, and especially its second section, attempts to outline.

The first part presents the basic contours of a process-relational understanding of reality, a view that takes reality to be ceaselessly creative, semiotic, and "morphogenetic" in the sense that its forms are perpetually being generated through the relational acts of its constituent members.

The book's second part, aided and abetted by a practical psychology developed from Buddhist and other sources, offers a guide for slicing into a moment of reality so as to be able to genuinely *act* in it. The point of that section is to help us develop an attitude appropriate to our historical moment, and especially to address the crisis of agency that is very much a part of that moment — an attitude that would allow us to "slice through" this moment of the Anthropocene so as to act in ways that would bury it effectively and lovingly.[1] Burial is, of course, never only a matter of covering over, or of overcoming; it is always also a matter of rearranging and of mixing together into a larger, deeper, and more mysterious set of vital substances. The question, then, is *how* to contribute to *what kind* of rearrangement.

The third and final part fills out the picture by examining the role of images and meanings — the sorts of things that cultural beings like us spend our lives debating, negotiating, and fighting over, as we collectively constitute our common worlds. If, as I will argue, we are cultural beings who dwell in and through images and the meanings they carry, then the Anthropocene is for us also a crisis of imagery, meaning, and culture. There is no way to bury it — together, lovingly and mercifully — without recognizing the diversity of relations humans have with their images, their icons, and their gods. This part proposes an "iconophilic" approach to the diversity of those gods and other entities that serve as the vehicles or mediators of creative agency in times of crisis.

Together, these three efforts follow a triadic structure whose rationale is articulated early on in the book and developed throughout. The parts need not be read in sequence. Readers more interested in philosophical debates around the process-relational perspective and its alternatives may find the practical "tool kit" of Part Two distracting. Others who find the overall theoretical armature difficult to follow, but who are seeking for a practical "therapeutics" — what I call a "logo-ethico-aesthetics" to apply in one's daily life — may find Part Two of particular interest (and may wish to supplement it with the exercises found

---

1 I take this idea of the eco-crisis as a "crisis of agency" from my co-conspirator, artist, engineer, and eco-visionary Natalie Jeremijenko. See Jeremijenko, "The Art of the Eco-Mindshift," TED, https://www.ted.com/talks/natalie_jeremijenko_the_art_of_the_eco_mindshift/transcript.

in Appendix 3). Those more interested in debates over culture, "post-secularism," and the messy world of "multiple moderni-ties" and hetero-globalizations may find the arguments of Part Three more provocative. In any case, it is okay to skip around between the parts, getting enough of a foothold in one before moving on to another. But each part yields the most when read from start to finish.

Taken collectively, the three parts of this book make up my attempt at a manual for living, thoughtfully and reflectively, in the shadow of the Anthropocene.

1

ENGAGING OBJECTS: A TREATISE ON EVENTS

Space junk

The signs are there for those who pay attention to them. Reports of melting glaciers and impending crashes. Crashes of the ocean's fish stocks, mass extinctions on a scale not seen in 65 million years. Stock market crashes, internet seizures and data breaches, doomsday viruses online and off. Plane crashes and mysterious disappearances in Indian or Mediterranean seas. Rising sea levels and strengthening storms, with tag-teamed hurricanes battering and flooding coastal areas. Hundred-year droughts arriving in back to back years. Swirling accumulations of trash in the middles of the world's oceans. Accumulations of toxic particles, radioactive dust, and microscopic plastic pellets in the bodies and bloodstreams of every living thing on Earth. Accumulations of space junk in the atmosphere. Mountains of waste, electronic and otherwise, building up to WALL·E-like scenarios, but without Disney/Pixar's (or the Buy-N-Large corporation's) interstellar cruise-ship escape.

Sooner or later, the trash will hit the fan, the crash will burst the dam, the supercollider will hit with the full force of its impact. The mad rush for land, for survival, for salvation, will begin in earnest, even for the most protected of us.

These are among the material ecologies that make up the era tendentiously and contentiously called the Anthropocene, the New Era of the Human. There are other kinds of ecologies besides these material ones: social ecologies, and perceptual ecologies. I'll explain why it's better to think in threes than in twos, and why the social, the material, and the perceptual make a useful frame for thinking of the ecologies that constitute the world.

Our social ecologies work the same way as our material ecologies, with blowback to widening inequalities and horrific injustices coming in the form of movements of growing refugee populations — economic refugees, climate refugees, refugees from wars fought over the stakes of all these crashes and the political violence and terror that accompanies them.

Between the material and the social are the fleshy, intersensorial dynamics from which the material and the social, or the "objective" and the "subjective," continually emerge. Drawing from the ecosophies of Félix Guattari and Gregory Bateson, I will call these our *mental* or *perceptual* ecologies. Blowback there comes as guilt, bad dreams, ghostly observances fracturing our sensory perceptions, inarticulate rage against those who question the tacitly held consensus. This is the hauntedness of the present by the abyss of an ungraspable and inconceivable future. It is these affective undercurrents that are our responses to the eyes of the world haunting us from out of the corners of our vision. (More on those eyes later.) They are what makes us feel that things aren't right — a hint at the traumatic kernel of reality that both psychoanalyst Jacques Lacan and, with a different inflection, Buddhist philosophers have placed at the origin of the self, but which in a collective sense is coming back to haunt us globally.

We misperceive the nature of the world for the same reasons that we misperceive the nature of our selves. Every social and linguistic order interpellates its members — it shapes and hails them into existence with a call of "*Hey you!*" Each does it differently. But over the course of the storied history of humans — not the meta-narrative of the Anthropos, just the patchy tale of humanity in its quiverings and coruscations — most such orders have incorporated into that interpellation some sense of responsibility to more-than-human entities or processes. In whatever way they were conceived — as spirits or divinities, or as kin, or in terms of synthetic narrative or conceptual metaphors like life-force, the Way, the path, *li* and *ren,* 礼 and 仁, the four directions, *Muntu* and *Ubuntu, Buen Vivir, Nepantla,* some gift-giving and life-renewing sacrifice, and so on — these have typically borne a central connection to the kinds of relations we now categorize as *ecological.* (At least for those social orders that worked.)

Modern western capitalism has fragmented these relations, setting us up *individually* in relation to the products of a seemingly limitless marketplace. But it has left us *collectively* rudderless. So if scientists, the empirical authorities of our time, tell us we are fouling our habitat, we have yet to figure out how to respond to that, at least at the global scales where most of the problems become manifest.

This is why it is the *relational,* more than the substantive or "objectal," that humans, especially westerners, need to come to terms with. That is in part the argument of this book. Commodity capitalism has been profoundly successful at encouraging us to think that objects are real, and at projecting value into those objects so that they serve the needs of individuals, even if they never manage to do that (which is, of course, the point). The effects of our actions, on the other hand, are systemic and relational, and we won't understand them unless we come to a better appreciation of how systems and relational ecologies work and of how we are thoroughly enmeshed within them.

At the same time, it is the *objects* that haunt us: the refuse swirling around in the middle of the Pacific, the mountains of excreted e-waste, the *stuff* we send down our chutes, out our drains, off to the incinerator, the river, the ocean, the atmosphere — the black holes, out of sight and out of mind, from which we hope they never re-emerge. When they do re-emerge, in our fantasies and nightmares, we reify them as the Thing, a Demon, a *Host* — as in Bong Joon-Ho's thriller of that name, about a river monster embodying the legacy of industrial pollution in South Korea's Han River. The objects become sublime.

If our consumptive, commodity-captivated and spectacle-enraptured society has privileged the object over the process, the thing at the center of our attention over the relations that constitute it, this thing-centeredness should not surprise us. In part, it is an effect of the human perceptual apparatus, with its heavy reliance on vision, a sensory modality that shows clear edges to objects and that facilitates distanced observation and predation. Where traditional cultures de-emphasized the visual in favor of the auditory or multisensorial, the narrative, and the relational, societies like ours — fragmented and individualized, intensely visually mediated, and ecologically and historically disembedded societies (in the sense described by Karl Polanyi in his paradigm defining *The Great Transformation*)[1] — push the ontological objectivism, literally the "thing-ism," about as far as it can go.

An object flies out the window

Two earlier working titles of this book were *Why Objects Fly Out the Window* and *Against Objects*. The second one was not intended to be taken literally. How could I be *against* objects if, as will become clear, my argument is that objects are not real, at least not in the ways we tend to think they are? Or, as the founder of Tiantai Buddhism, sixth century Chinese master Zhiyi, would put it: they are real, and they are not real, and both of those are equally true at the same time and could not be otherwise. (More on him below.)

The point is not the *objects,* but nor is it what they *mean*. There is a current philosophical fashion for objects — a celebration of the uniqueness and distinctiveness of everything one might happen upon — that posits itself as a critique of human meanings, or at least of the idea that it is human meanings alone

---

1   Karl Polanyi, *The Great Transformation: The Political and Economic Origins of Our Time,* 2nd edn. (Boston: Beacon Press, 1944/2001).

that count, or that human meanings are central to whatever does count. In the debate between these object-loving ontologists and the human-meaning lovers they critique, it is reality itself that is at stake — a reality that I will argue is not one of objects, but of something more elusive than that.

The objects of my title, then, are sneaky little things that have come to populate a world where their underside — their actual reality — has become invisible. They are also a not-as-sneaky reference to the object-oriented metaphysics that have been gathering adherents in the world of popular philosophy. Many of the ideas in this book were initially developed in conversation with leading proponents of those metaphysics — conversations that took place on blogs and web sites more often than in print. Those interlocutors included Graham Harman, Levi Bryant, Tim Morton, and Ian Bogost, all of whom have identified as "object-oriented" philosophers (though Bryant has recently shifted camps somewhat), alongside tangentially connected observers like Peter Gratton and Ben Woodard.[2] And they have included many allies on the "relational" or "processual" side of this debate such as Steven Shaviro, Christopher Vitale, Leon Niemoczynski, Adam Robbert, Jason Hills, Matthew Segall, and many thinkers to whom I am indebted including Bruno Latour, Isabelle Stengers, William Connolly, Jane Bennett, Karen Barad, Brian Massumi, Erin Manning, Donna Haraway, Tim Ingold,

---

2 For a sampling of relevant works, see Graham Harman, *Object-Oriented Ontology: A New Theory of Everything* (London: Penguin, 2018); Graham Harman, *Tool-Being: Heidegger and the Metaphysics of Objects* (Peru: Open Court, 2002); Timothy Morton, *Being Ecological* (Cambridge: MIT Press, 2018); Levi R. Bryant, *The Democracy of Objects* (Ann Arbor: Open Humanities Pres, 2011); Ian Bogost, *Alien Phenomenology, or What It's Like to Be a Thing* (Minneapolis: University of Minnesota Press, 2012); Peter Gratton, *Speculative Realism: Problems and Prospects* (New York: Bloomsbury, 2014). For an iteration of my critique of object-oriented ontology in their most influential form (Graham Harman's), see Adrian Ivakhiv, "Beatnik Brothers: Between Graham Harman and the Deleuzo-Whiteheadian Axis," *Parrhesia* 19 (2014): 65–78. Others can be found at http://blog.uvm.edu/aivakhiv/p-r-theory/.

Anna Tsing, Arturo Escobar, John Protevi, Nigel Thrift, Eduardo Kohn, and Marisol de la Cadena.[3]

The short answer to the question implied in my original title — why *do* objects fly out the window? — is *not for any reason of their own.* They fly because they are the sort of disconnectibles that can fly under the right conditions. Typically this occurs when there is a sufficient difference between two atmospheres encountering each other for the first time: as when a high-speed vehicle opens its window to the outdoors, unleashing a wind capable of carrying away many objects-suddenly-become-paper-airplanes. Objects gain their ability to fly when *other* objects (or subjects) induce those conditions around them. Objects are precisely the kind of thing that can be *removed* from their processual contexts and made to enter into new ones. And in a highly artificial world, where such disconnectibles proliferate, and where the zone of encounter between environments produced by one disconnectible (say, a moving vehicle, or a moving national economy) and the connective network in which it moves disconnectedly gets amped to the max, objects fly all the more quickly. They fly all around.

There is, I will posit, an important difference between the world of disconnectibles that has flourished since the emergence and spread of carbon burning industrial civilization — the world marked by the dawning of the singular ~~Event~~ named the Anthropocene, or, as I prefer, the AnthropoCapitalocene, or A/Cene — and the world of connectibles that preceded it and that continues to support, encase, subtend, and resist it. There may be no clear line demarcating the pre-industrial from the industrial eras, the pre-A/Cene from the A/Cene; these terms overgeneralize from a long and densely tangled set of lineages. But there is value in distinguishing between these variants based on the simple fact of the sheer production of objects: that is, based on the rapid and dramatic proliferation of objects, the extent of

---

3   Steven Shaviro has been particularly active in the "object-processes" debate; see Shaviro, *The Universe of Things: On Speculative Realism* (Minneapolis: University of Minnesota Press, 2014). For other relevant titles, see Appendix 1.

their dissemination, and the breadth and depth of impacts they have on the world that burbles, thrums, and hisses alongside them.

In other words, there is value in distinguishing between disconnectibles — which this book will call *objects* — and the processes out of which those disconnectibles arise, within which they move, and to which they return.

Those disconnectibles are one kind of object. This book will propose a second and more precise definition of *object*, one which does not last longer than a moment. The things that do last longer than a moment I will call entities or things. In contrast, real objectness, objecthood, object-being, is something that arises in a flash of relationship with an equally elusive subjectivity. Objects in this second sense — let us, in an irreverent nod to psychoanalyst Jacques Lacan, call them *objects-a* — are defined by the relationships they have with subjects, or *subjects-a*. And vice versa, *subjects-a* are defined by the relationships they have with *objects-a*. These relationships arise for the moment that they arise — a flash of experiential reality — and then they are gone, subsumed within the substance of a universe that can scarcely be sighted before it is something else. Encountering an *object-a* is one move within a circle, or rather a circulation; it is something that a *subject-a* does. The next moment that object is no longer there, and neither is the subject. Both objects and subjects are winking in and out of existence all the time; what continues in and around and beneath them is *process*.

A world full of disconnectibles, however, encourages us to see objects everywhere, and nothing but objects. What you hold (if you are reading this from a book) is an object, but it is an object intended to perform a certain work upon you and upon others. As it does this work, it enters into processes that preceded it, parallel it, and have existed independently of it (more or less) until now. Process-relational thought is the thought that is intended to redirect thought toward the contexts, the relations, and the processes that surround, subtend, and inhabit objects.

Process-relational thought is not new; it is in fact ancient. This book is an attempt to articulate it in terms of recent debates over objects, processes, events, images, and the meanings of recent global events and developments in particular. It is not a philosophical treatise. Its spirit is more of an animated restaurant conversation than a systematic legal case. It is intended less for philosophers than for those it might reach through its sheer, object-like ability to fly out of windows. It is a paper airplane, and where it lands is anyone's guess.

Things (scribbled on a restaurant napkin)

1. Things are always already in process. More complex things are more in process, or in more (and different) processes, than simpler things.
2. Growing/developing things tend to become more complex; their trajectory, when they are on a roll, is uphill, which takes effort and builds capacity. Other things tend to become less complex; they roll downhill. But these tendencies are contingent on complex interactions with their environments, and on habits enfolded out of previous such interactions.
3. Being in process, things elude capture. Those that are captured become other things, and generally simpler things, than they were before.
4. You can never do only one thing.
5. You can never isolate one thing from the rest. When you try, that thing ceases to be what it is, or it drags other things with it.
6. Knowing is doing; doing is knowing. But neither of them is only and fully the other.
7. Mind and matter go hand in hand; facts and values dawdle together. Separating them is possible only at the expense of a diminution of each.
8. The present is all that there is; how you respond to it is all you can do.
9. Every action feeds a relation, tweaks a process, builds (or un-builds) a network.
10. A world full of things made by the AnthropoCapitalist Thing makes it seem that things are *merely* things, simple things,

physical things, dead things. Even *those* things aren't that (because the mental and physical always go hand in hand). But *other* things certainly aren't that.

Thing-notes

1. "Things" is a generic term for bits and pieces of world and universe. They are related to matter, but are never matter alone (mind or form are always part of them). Things do; things are done. There is no such thing as still life. Complexity and simplicity are relative.
2. Entropy and negentropy are general trends. In reality, most things don't just move all in one direction.
3. Everything becomes different from itself anyway. The question is always *what to become.*
4. But you can try.
5. Form is substance; substance is form. But... same story.
6. Epistemology and ontology are never fully independent of each other.
7. Segregating them commits the error that Whitehead called "the bifurcation of nature." More on that soon.
8. The past is what is no longer present, though its effects may remain and continue to shape future possibilities. The future is what is not present yet. Absences are present as absences; they, too, shape what is present. The present that you can respond to is not the entirety of the present. One cannot respond to things that one is not sensitive to; they don't make a difference, so they cannot make a "difference that makes a difference." But in general, this point #8 summarizes most of what we need to know in life. Everything else is extra.
9. Or many at once.
10. The AnthropoCapitalist Thing (henceforth, A/C Thing) includes humans, ruminants, cereal grasses, fossil fuels, combustion engines, cities, techno-economic networks, and a proliferating array of things made *for* the Thing and things made to *make* other things for the Thing. Even things made by the A/C Thing seem to be getting livelier and more com-

plex: digital life, nanotechnology, online worlds. We are building a complex meganetwork atop a complex meganetwork, but with relations between the two — Terra 1.0 and Terra 2.0 — growing ever more tenuous and fragile.

Metaphysical entry point

Metaphysics is the philosophical field that studies the general nature of reality. Ontology is its sub-field that focuses on the make-up of reality, or the kinds of things that exist, and on how they do that.

One of the recent efforts to develop a realist metaphysics adequate to the world in which we live is that called "object-oriented philosophy," or "object-oriented ontology." The starting point of OOO, or OOP (its representatives have occasionally been lampooned as OOPs), is the premise that the best description of the world is one that attends closely to the objects that make it up. This is its realism more broadly, and its "objectivism" more specifically.

While this premise sounds, at first blush, not unlike phenomenological philosopher Edmund Husserl's call, a century earlier, "back to the things themselves," the difference is that Husserl approached those "things" through the human perception of them. To that perception, later phenomenologists like Martin Heidegger, Maurice Merleau-Ponty, Jean-Paul Sartre, Paul Ricoeur, Luce Irigaray, and Jean-Luc Marion added an emphasis on interpretation, language, discourse, decision, embodiment, gender, and other dimensions of human experience.

Object-oriented philosophers reject this interest in correlating human perception to reality, which Quentin Meillassioux has labeled "correlationism."[4] They are interested in decentering human perception and experience so that it is no more valued in principle than any other kind of experience, or indeed than anything at all. In part, this is out of a desire to account for a world

---

4   Quentin Meillassioux, *After Finitude: An Essay on the Necessity of Contingency,* trans. Ray Brassier (London: Bloomsbury, 2010).

that, as Levi Bryant has put it, "far from reducing the number of existing objects as alleged by reductive materialisms, has actually experienced a promiscuous proliferation and multiplication of objects of all sorts."[5]

Let's name a few of these objects. In fact, let us borrow a list of such objects from one of eco-radical Derrick Jensen's polemics against industrial civilization. Jensen and his co-author, Aric McBay, ask us to consider whether life would be worth living "without CDs, plastic pacifiers, plastic wrap, sandwich bags, syringes, bottled water (and soda bottles), single serving packets of potato chips, automobiles, straws (and crazy straws!), plastic grocery bags, freezer bags, ice cube trays, bubble wrap and packing peanuts, carpet-backing, Styrofoam life preservers and take-out trays, disposable pens, disposable diapers, hairspray and plastic hair brushes, plastic toothbrushes (and toopaste!), milk crates, packing tape, plastic forks, telephones, computers, hair clips, billiard balls, shower curtains, beach balls, balloons, latex condoms, and polyester pants?"[6]

One thing all these things have in common is that they exist — they are as real as you and I, and for object-oriented ontologists that it enough: they need to be accounted for.

But there is something more specific shared by the objects on Jensen's list. It is their plasticity — a plasticity that, for all its malleability (by definition) and intended disposability, presents an obduracy that comes closer to permanence than to the kind of usable life that, for centuries, carried the day among objects. What they have in common, in other words, is that once they are used by people for the limited time of their intended use, they all become space junk. They are thrown away, with the ca-

5   Levi Bryant, "Onticology—A Manifesto for Object-Oriented Ontology, Part 1," *Larval Subjects*, January 12, 2010, par. 1, http://larvalsubjects.wordpress.com/2010/01/12/object-oriented-ontology-a-manifesto-part-i/.

6   Derrick Jensen and Aric McBay, *What We Leave Behind* (New York: Seven Stories Press, 2009), 113.

veat that, globally speaking, there is no "away." So they pile up around us, and inside us.[7]

This desire among philosophers to acknowledge the proliferation of objects is a valuable step insofar as it returns philosophy to a concern for the world, and not merely for humanity. Yet it is important to recognize that this proliferation results, in large part, from the tremendous proliferation of commodities in a capitalist world-economy — the most productive economy the world has seen, whose productivity relies on the extraction of substances from their processual relations to produce things that appear to have no such relations — objects that are simply there, for us to admire, desire, purchase, use, and in the end discard. The "objectivity" of these objects is a product of a set of relations; it is illusory, or partial in any case, to the extent that these objects are not simply objects as such, but that they, for all their specificity, arise out of certain kinds of processes (extractive, productive), give rise to others (consumptive, waste-producing), and entangle their owners in relational ecologies that are morally imbued, materially generative, and dramatic in their effects on the world that is passed on to future generations of humans and our planetary co-inhabitants.

The approach I advocate in this book shares object-oriented philosophers' goal of a metaphysical realism — which puts us all into the newish category of "speculative realists."[8] But it approaches this goal from a direction that is in certain respects their polar opposite. It begins from the premise that, in an ultimate sense, there are no objects, only events, and that what defines those events is a relational encounter in which subjectivity is central. Seeking subjectivity in the world of plastic objects

---

7   For an insightful and varied set of responses to the "plastic ocean" that has been accumulating around humanity, see Julie Decker, ed., *Gyre: The Plastic Ocean* (London: Booth-Clibborn, 2014).

8   Levi Bryant, Nick Srnicek, and Graham Harman, eds., *The Speculative Turn: Continental Materialism and Realism* (Melbourne: Re-Press, 2011); Peter Gratton, *Speculative Realism: Problems and Prospects* (London: Bloomsbury, 2014); Leon Niemoczynski, *Speculative Realism: An Epitome* (Leeds: Kismet Press, 2017).

may be counter-intuitive, but that is the whole point. If we cannot find it there, we might as well not find it anywhere.

This does not mean that my approach begins as a "revolt against substance," for the world of events — a world of relational process — is as substantial as any world of objects can be. It begins, however, from the subjective encounter. It begins, following the work of philosophers like Charles Sanders Peirce, William James, Alfred North Whitehead, John Dewey, Martin Heidegger, Isabelle Stengers, Bruno Latour, Donna Haraway, and Karen Barad, from "matters of concern," and it does this because it is such matters that we are always in the midst of. It begins with a refusal to extricate the "knowing self" or "subject" from the relations that constitute it.

More specifically, the ontology I propose in this book — one of a series of variations that a process-relational ontology can take — is one that brings together two powerful insights from two of modern philosophy's most original voices, Alfred North Whitehead and Charles Sanders Peirce.

From Whitehead, I take his turning inside-out of Cartesian dualism and of the two philosophical faces it brings together — one being idealism (or rationalism), the other being materialism (or empiricism). Rather than the subject and the object, or mind and matter, or value and fact, being two kinds of substance or quality that either interact in some form of dualism, or that subsume each other — into an idealism or a materialism — Whitehead takes subjectivity and objectivity to be active poles within a single, dipolar relational process. That process is the process that makes up every real entity in the universe, which is an entity of *occurrence,* an event, a becoming. Every being is a *becoming,* characterized by what Whitehead called *prehension.* Every becoming is a response to things given. As such, it involves emergent subjectivity taking account of, or "prehending," what has become objective for it. Once that response is completed, it becomes material for the next response.

By rendering subjectivity and objectivity internal to all things, Whitehead gives us a universe that is alive and filled with experience. The things that appear to us to be "just there" — objects to be measured, handled, or otherwise kicked around, but not to be negotiated with or granted the respect with which one might honor, say, a companion or a divinity — are not *things* at all, except insofar as they are figments of our perception. Their reality — their experiential *interiority,* or rather the specific mixture of interiority and exteriority, the same kind of mixture that constitutes all real things as processes of subjectivation and objectivation — this reality eludes our experience except insofar as something of it — its objectivity or "outsideness" — is accounted for in our own subjective experience. And crucially, the same goes for them. We are all inside-outnesses winking into existence moment by moment through prehensive encounters, with stability achieved through the complex movement of masses of such winkings. What that means should become clearer as we go.

From Peirce (pronounced "purse"), I take his revolutionary reframing of the logical categories found in Aristotle, Kant, and Hegel (among others) into a tri-categorial schema according to which everything in the universe is composed of triadic, "semiosic" process: the firstness of things in themselves, the secondness of things in relation, and the thirdness of relations in relation. This parsing results in a triadic ordering whose fruitfulness will, I hope, become evident over time. But listing some of its variations might begin to give a flavor of it. There is potentiality (a firstness), existence (a secondness), and meaning (a thirdness). There is chance, actuality, and necessity; vagueness, singularity, and generality; quality, relation, and representation; feeling, reaction, and thought. By means of these categories, Peirce was able to define meaningfully ordered relations between everything else: aesthetics (the Beautiful), ethics (the Good), and logic (the True); phenomenology (the study of what appears), normative science (the study of how we ought to respond to it), and metaphysics (the study of what it all means); and so on ad infinitum.

Far from being merely an ordering principle, Peirce took this triadism as an insight into the order that underlies all things (not over and above, but in and through), and as a way of ensuring that one of the three does not subsume or outflank the others (as Peirce thought occurred with most philosophies that preceded his). Peirce was a fierce logician and a brilliant mathematical mind, so these categories didn't come cheaply with him; he worked on them his entire life. And because that life was marred by professional failure and much of his writing remained, and still remains, unpublished (and difficult to make sense of), his prime discovery remained unsung and underutilized. This book attempts to sing it.

This marriage of Whitehead and Peirce is purely my own and no doubt deviates from other presentations of either philosopher. It is an experimental proposal, still in the process of being worked out, and is inspired for me by the spirit of Gilles Deleuze, who deeply admired both philosophers, even if he did not write much about either. Marrying these powerful concepts from Whitehead and Peirce creates a theoretical engine that I believe can help us out of numerous intellectual quandaries that mark our time of social and ecological crisis.

There are two other, larger and more diffuse, players I will bring into my philosophical machine at certain moments. The first is a particular variant of Mahayana Buddhist philosophy, which will make its distinct appearance in Part Two. The second is a more general ally whose presence I would like to open a path toward, but which I feel largely unable to speak for in these pages: this is a "decolonial" movement in the worlds of non-western and indigenous thought, and in anthropological efforts to dialogue with those forms of thought. I hope the influence of the latter is felt in Part Three, but its full development (and recognition) requires another book.

Let us, then, begin with some matters that concern us.

Matters of concern

Everything begins with matters of concern.[9] Such matters are always, as they have ever been, matters that involve us, touch and brush up against us, envelop us, or otherwise call on us to respond to them.

By "us," I have in mind not only humans, the collective "we" who have become the default in-group of philosophical thinking in the western tradition. I do not exclude humans; they constitute a relevant and useful category. But neither would I circle my philosophical wagons around them. This "us" is more like a call, an appeal, a network-building probe or vector. Sometimes the extent of that network has been taken for granted: members of a tribe or nation, philosophers, citizens, humans. But in times like ours, the "us" ought to be much more open than that, and this opening-outward is the vector I would like to pursue in what follows, even if the tools I use — language, of a philosophical kind — will not reach all of us directly. The "us" is the coming-into-being of responsiveness, in its many forms.

As for the "matters," they are such because they matter, they make a difference; so we call them to mind, we pay them attention. Mattering, they come to mind; minding, we come to matter. Matter and mind are nothing of themselves except as they come, and in the time that they come, to each other. The same can be said of subjects and objects: they are nothing except as they arise with respect to each other. "Concern" is precisely that "with respect to" that brings them together.

It has been argued that "concern" sounds too distant and paternalistic, that "care" is more direct and exposed.[10] The terms are somewhat interchangeable. Karen Barad puts it beautifully

9 Bruno Latour, "Why Has Critique Run Out of Steam? From Matters of Fact to Matters of Concern," *Critical Inquiry* 30 (2004): 225–48; Bruno Latour, *What Is the Style of Matters of Concern?* (Amsterdam: Van Gorcum, 2008). See also A.N. Whitehead, *Adventures of Ideas* (New York: Free Press, 1933/1967), 135 on "concernedness" as "of the essence of perception."

10 Maria Puig de la Bellacasa, "Matters of Care in Technoscience: Assembling Neglected Things," *Social Studies of Science* 41, no. 1 (2011): 85–106.

when she writes that "matter feels, converses, suffers, desires, yearns and remembers."[11] Even so, matter *alone* does little without, say, processes of form-building. A wave crossing an ocean contains no matter, but it shapes and moves the matter in its path, moving molecules up and down as it moves; its substance is its form, which is always related to the other waves of which it is a vector. To speak of the "mind" of a wave is of course also presumptive. Its internal energy is a part of larger movements whose full extent we have some trouble grasping because of the limits of our own imagination.

Let us, then, eliminate the terms "matter" and "mind" in their usual meanings — as, respectively, mindless stuff and immaterial agency — and refocus the words on the *how,* or the *minding* of *matterings.* To engage with matter is to mind what matters, to care for it, to "take a concern" — which for Quakers is to take something as an obligatory call to action. (More on those Quakers in Part Two below.)

To be sure, there are things, things that happen. There are matters, matters that come to mind. The sequence I will posit, considered as an ideal or logical progression, *not* a chronological one (this is important), follows the triadic phenomenology laid out by Peirce: there is, first, the *thing,* then the *happening,* then the *matter* of which the happening is a sign, a reminder, a call, a prompt, an issue, a problem, a pattern, or a law.[12] There are, in other words, spontaneously generated qualities — not Platonic Ideas, but simply the potentials inherent in anything, structured by their forward movement coupled with the play of chance. Peirce calls these *firsts;* taking a hint from Deleuze, we might call them *virtuals,* which means that they are *effectively*

11   Rick Dolphijn, Iris van der Tuin, and Karen Barad, "'Matter Feels, Converses, Suffers, Desires, Yearns and Remembers: Interview with Karen Barad," in *New Materialism: Interviews and Cartographies,* eds. Rick Dolphijn and Iris van der Tuin (Ann Arbor: Open Humanities Press, 2012).

12   Charles S. Peirce, "The Principles of Phenomenology: The Categories in Detail," in *Collected Papers of Charles Sanders Peirce,* eds. Charles Hartshorne and Paul Weiss, vol. 1, 148–80 (Bloomington: Indiana University Press, 1958).

(causally and generatively) real. Then come the relations, as certain of these potentials become actualized in real encounters, real *events,* in a multiplicitous universe. These are *seconds,* or *actuals.* Finally, there arise the mediated consistencies, habits, patterns, regularities, laws, generalizations, and meanings — these are the *thirds,* generals, or relationals (as opposed to mere relations).

This dynamic of firsts, seconds, and thirds is always at work. Peirce insisted on its universality: if any of the three is ignored or de-emphasized — the bursting forth of chance, connective causality, significance and generality — we will be drawn up one or another philosophical rabbithole. This triadism constitutes the heart of the worlding of the world (any world). In this way things become, and in this way they come to signify.[13]

But to call the things "objects" is already to suggest too much about them. There are, from this perspective, neither subjects nor objects at the outset, just things in their singularity. This is the world of virtualities, differential fields on the cusp of breaking into something: a wave, a motion, an event. They are not yet a world, but they enable worlding. Breaking, those virtualities become happenings: they intervene into the times and spaces of other things, each imposing itself on another, each resisted by others. This is the world of relational events, which is the world in the process of being made, of being woven into tangles of force and counterforce. This is the world that scientific analysis likes to probe, methodically and systematically. Finally, there is the world of significance, the world that is now fully a world, inhabited. Humanists prefer to start here, analyzing our *significances* as things not to be taken for granted, but always produced, negotiated, and lived. But where humanists often stop short is in recognizing that neither the happening nor its significance is peculiar to humans. Humans do it, but so do

---

13 Peirce's triadic outline of the logical categories of all experience was an obsession throughout his philosophical career. It took many forms, and in the end was the single contribution he felt was most original and significant in his philosophy. For one version of it, see Peirce, "The Principles of Phenomenology."

many others: we make sense of things, which thereby become signs, meanings obtained about a world through the things, the images, the objects we encounter. We feel, and respond, to that which happens, and in responding we generate a world.

I am describing here a view of the world as made up of relational processes, events of encounter, acts of experience, and nothing else. Everything there is *takes place*; which is to say that it gives *place*, it *places*. Its taking place is what gives it existence, but its specific kind of existence comes from what constitutes it at the outset, as the thing that it is, the thing in its firstness; the dynamics of its prehensive encounter with other things; and the subjective aim that is realized in the encounter. In coming to exist and relate to others, the origins of both are selectively taken up and turned into potentialities for the next set of existents. As Whitehead described things — that is, events — these are constituted by the encounter of an emergent subjectivity, a mental moment of pure feeling, with some *matter* that is there for it to behold and to respond to. The occasion is dipolar: at one end mental or subjective, at the other physical or objective. But the subjectivity lasts as long as the moment, which begins with a "prehension," a taking into account, and rounds off with a satisfaction, a "concrescence," at which point the subject becomes an object, a datum, for the next set of moments that may emerge. And so on, ad infinitum.

With Peirce, what becomes clear is the semiotic and triadic (or "depth") nature of prehension — that is, the fact that any meaning created (which he called an *interpretant*) is performed through an intermediary, a *representamen* that stands in for something else, that "something" being the distant and withdrawing semiotic *object*. There are two movements going on in such a triad: there is the prehensive grasping of the object(s) of one's concern; and there is the withdrawal (for instance, by differing and by deferral) of the original object from that representamen, and thus from the grasping. It is the prehension, or the act of "possess[ing] or intuit[ing] a datum, a given," that provides the openness, the forward motion or evolutionary momentum at the heart of things. And it is the withdrawal, the deferral and *différance* (to use Jacques Derrida's term, but applying it not only to language but to everything without exception), that provides for the elusiveness and opacity of the universe.

Peirce's triadic account of signs — which are moments or events of signification — insists on the rootedness of those signs *in* the world, their connection to and dependence on things that preceded them and that are there in the virtual-processual chance-structure of the universe. What constitutes a "sign" can be something as basic as the way a sequence of nucleotides is decoded in the synthesis of proteins, or something as complex as the idea I have of my self or of "democracy."[14]

In this way the world proceeds, an "advancing assemblage" of "processes of experience," a simmering ocean of becoming, subdivisible into streaming, temporal, relational vectors.[15] None of these processes is exactly alike: there are different kinds, varying in texture, in extent, in stability, in rate of change and style of movement, in manner of organization. In the encounters between emergent processes, the organization of such processes folds over, takes on a layering of surfaces and depths, of outwardness and inwardness, and interacts to create larger processes, larger networks, whose consistencies give us the world, or worlds, that we and others perceive and inhabit. Perceiving, we respond, and responding we come to inhabit; we habituate. The world, in the end, is a world of evolving habits shot through with chance and with novelty, which seed it with further novelty, further habituation, further evolution.

Between Whitehead and Peirce and the other thinkers who have variously contributed to a process-relational account of things, there are discrepancies, gaps, and divergences one could spend lifetimes lumping, splitting, splicing, or smoothening over. The list of such thinkers might include Heraclitus, Zhuang

---

14 Mine is only one of multiple ways of potentially reconciling Peirce and Whitehead. On a few others, see Adrian Ivakhiv, "Peirce-Whitehead-Hartshorne and Process-relational Ontology," *Immanence,* June 9, 2010, http://blog.uvm.edu/aivakhiv/2010/06/09/peirce-whitehead-hartshorne-process-relational-ontology/.

15 Whitehead, *Adventures of Ideas,* 197.

Zhou, Nāgārjuna, Śāntarakṣita, Zhiyi, Fazang, Suhrawardi, Dogen, Mullā Sadrā, Bruno, Spinoza, Leibniz, Schelling, Goethe, Nietzsche, Haeckel, Bergson, James, Dewey, Aurobindo, Nishida, Nishitani, Hartshorne, Bateson, Merleau-Ponty, Souriau, Simondon, Deleuze, Guattari, Deely, and many still among us — Michel Serres, Nicholas Rescher, David Bohm, Robert Cummings Neville, Robert Corrington, Isabelle Stengers, Bruno Latour, Sandra Rosenthal, Michel Weber, Roland Faber, Jason Brown, William Connolly, Catherine Keller, Freya Mathews, Karen Barad, Christian de Quincey, Jane Bennett, John Law, Manuel DeLanda, Brian Massumi, Ken Wilber, and others.[16] Between them one can find debates over the constitutive weight of continuity versus discontinuity, novelty versus habit, unbounded creativity versus a mere choice between options, relational symmety versus asymmetry, structural topographies and "levels" of reality with their respective forms of emergence, and other themes. A wall built with the materials these thinkers together provide might not withstand the spring's first flood. But a life-raft built from them could carry us far from where we started. And since nothing stays in place for long (at least if what they tell us is true), it is the carrying that counts, not the flood control.

Having laid out this set of primary constellations to orient us, we must eventually return to what we have in our midst, which are always those matters of concern. Projects, in other words, but projects that take their start from situations.

Projects in the making

An ant colony builds itself from the actions of its members: gathering leaf litter, sticks, bits and pieces of the environing world, tunneling, communicating, building, nursing. None of these ant "individuals," not even the queen herself, could act in this way without the rest of the colony. Both the body and

---

16 For an introductory bibliography of contemporary process-relational thought and its close relatives, see Appendix 1.

the mind of the colony — its "objective" or material parts, those we can see, describe, dissect, and measure, and its "subjective" parts, which are the moments of felt decision that turn an ant this way rather than that way in its crossing of a trail in a forest, or those that bring a team of ants together to haul a large leaf or dead grasshopper — these are all dispersed in space, they are *spaced*, detached from each other physically (or so it appears when we observe them), but *mentally*, in terms of the interactive processing of signs and relations, they are networked together into a coordinated collectivity, a form that seemingly aims to reproduce itself. That aim may be dispersed across many arising subject-objectivities, which are its actual occasions, but its global coordination is something, not nothing.

The networked form of the colony is not only made of those ant bodies, but also what they are *capable* of and what they *do* with things — with soil, leaves, sticks, pieces of food. By most measures, anthills are cities: they include complex systems of transportation, communication (pheromone-based), ventilation, sewage disposal, food production (the farming of plants, the growing of fungus, the raising of aphid cattle), cooperative labor, warfare, and slavery. As entomologist Mark Moffett details in his comparison of ants and people:

> Both alter nature to build nurseries, fortresses, stockyards, and highways, while nurturing friends and livestock and obliterating enemies and vermin. Both ants and humans express tribal bonds and basic needs through ancient, elaborate codes. Both create universes of their own devising through the scale of their domination of the environment. [... Both] face similar problems in obtaining and distributing resources, allocating labor and effort, preserving civil unity, and defending communities against outside forces.[17]

---

17 Mark Moffett, *Adventures Among Ants: A Global Safari with a Cast of Trillions* (Berkeley: University of California Press, 2010), 223.

In the worlds of ant colonies, what are the "objects" and what are their "relations"? An individual ant could hardly exist on its own, though a lost ant might be able to find food and maneuver its way into another colony. (What will happen to it there is another matter: if it is an Argentine ant from San Francisco being dropped off in San Diego, it will fit in seamlessly within its new host group, which is of the same colony or "nationality," as Moffett calls these groups. But if it is dropped off in Mexico, or in one of the other three colonial territories of Californian Argentine ants, it will likely be quickly murdered.)

A colony could hardly have emerged without its environment, such that the colony-landscape network, the subterranean city with its above-surface hinterlands and the patterns and relations holding them together, is itself an object of sorts. But if one is to say that the reality is made up of "objects" engaged in "relations," one would have to draw lines (around ants, or colonies, or something) that, like light waves and particles, are sometimes there and sometimes not. The result would be little better than acknowledging that reality includes textural lumps and nodes in the networks that make it up.

Lumps, nodes, and networks are descriptions of things from their outside. A process-relational view insists that there is also an *inside* to everything, an interiority, but that this interiority is not normally evident at the level of the everyday distinguishable object. Such distinguishing will vary depending on the thing doing the distinguishing; ontology and epistemology, in this way, are tightly interwoven within each fragment of existence. Rather, the interiority is of the moment, the event, the act of prehension and concrescence. The reality of the ant metropolis, then, is one of events of feeling and decision, acts in response to those matters of concern, the entanglements of subjectivation and objectivation that are occurring everywhere in their own time. What we — non-ants observing ants — see is not the real events themselves, but only what our own subjective grasp makes available of them to us.

A process-relational ontology takes the world to be dynamic and always in motion. Its fundamental constituents are not objects, permanent structures, material substances, cognitive representations, or Platonic ideas or essences, but relational encounters or events, moments, or acts of existence which take on formal properties as they interact. An actual occasion, as Whitehead calls such an act of existence, is a "drop" or "throb of experience," a process of "actualization of potentiality" that is inherently "emotional" and "prehensive" in nature. Whitehead revises Descartes' claim that "the subject-object relation is the fundamental structural pattern of experience" by disentangling this relation from enduring substances (and from the knower-known relation) and placing it instead in the momentary arising of each actual occasion.[18] Each such occasion is characterized by a mental pole set against a physical pole, a subject emerging momentarily in relation to an object, which is the datum or data set that comes inherited from the immediate past and from its immediate outside.

"The basis of experience," Whitehead writes, is "emotional" (Peirce refers to it as one of "feeling").[19] Its "basic fact" is "the rise of an affective tone originating from things whose relevance is given."[20] A subject emerges *in concern* for an object, with each defining the other in the process. "An occasion is a subject in respect to its special activity concerning an object; and anything is an object in respect to its provocation of some special activity within a subject."[21] Individual subjectivity, for Whitehead, or "our consciousness of the self-identity pervading our life-

---

18 A.N. Whitehead, "Objects and Subjects," *The Philosophical Review* 41, no. 2 (1932), 189.

19 Whitehead, "Objects and Subjects," 189; Peirce, *Collected Papers*, 7.364, 6.265 (1931). For further comparative insights on Whitehead and Peirce, see Charles Hartshorne's chapters on each in *Creativity in American Philosophy* (Albany: SUNY Press, 1984); Sandra Rosenthal's "Contemporary Process Metaphysics and Diverse Intuitions of Time: Can the Gap Be Bridged?" *Journal of Speculative Philosophy* 12, no. 4 (1998); Robert C. Neville, "Whitehead and Pragmatism," in *Whitehead's Philosophy: Points of Connection*, eds. Janusz Polanowski and Donald Sherburne (Albany: SUNY Press, 2004); and the writings of Robert S. Corrington.

20 Whitehead, "Objects and Subjects," 130.

21 Ibid., 131.

thread of occasions, is nothing other than knowledge of a special strand of unity within the general unity of nature," a unity in which the "general principle is the object-to-subject structure of experience," the "vector-structure of nature," "the doctrine of the immanence of the past energizing in the present,"[22] "the transference of affective tone, with its emotional energy, from one occasion to another."[23] "Each occasion has its physical inheritance and its mental reaction which drives it on to its self-completion."[24]

These quotes address the microscopic or molecular level of the view I am presenting. There are other levels, including a level of complexity in which the universe can only be conceived as a tumbling forward of such interrelated and interacting, differentiating and coming together, moments of experience. Whitehead's descriptions of "nexus" and "societies" — constellations of mutually coordinating occasions, which enjoy a relative persistence over time, over space, or both — begins to account for the more stable entities making up the universe. The human organism is such a society, at least insofar as it works in a unified way (which it does far from perfectly). The self that thinks "I" is little more than a kind of superintendant of an apartment building, as Jim McAllister puts it: "I hear the complaints [...], I have to feed the furnace, put out the garbage, sweep the hallways, but I have no experience of the lives of the apartment dwellers," who happen to be the trillions of cells, bacterial assemblages, and all the rest that makes up the grand assemblage I call myself.[25] Other relational descriptions — dynamical and emergent network theories, assemblage theories, actor-network theories, and others — are better at accounting for the different ways that *different* things come together into patterned networks, with

---

22 Ibid., 143.
23 Ibid., 144.
24 Ibid., 146.
25 Quoted in Dorion Sagan, "Coda: Beautiful Monsters: Terra in the Cyanocene," in *Arts of Living on a Damaged Planet: Ghosts and Monsters of the Anthropocene*, ed. Anna L. Tsing et al. (Minneapolis: University of Minnesota Press, 2017), M172.

agency (subjectivity) and givenness (objectivity) distributed in divergent ways through those networks.[26]

A process-relational ontology that attempts to provide a realistic depiction of the world must take note of distinctions between different sorts of relational processes. Such processes can be fast or slow, thick or thin, complex or simple, opaque or translucent, extensive or intensive, linear or multilateral, smooth or stratified, hierarchical or egalitarian. Relational processes have unfolded historically in ways that have given the world its complex and variable textures: its folds and forms with their relative thicknesses, speeds, durations, movements, rhythms, consistencies, patterns, and trajectories. The universe, in this view, is continuous (for the most part), but the continuities are pleated and enfolded, inflected with waves, currents, undulations, and vortices. It is a generative and open universe governed by intensifying, differentiating, and habit taking tendencies. And it is within these habit-formed folds and pleats that we, human "subjects," typically find ourselves.

No thing alone

If there are discontinuities in this account of the universe, there is no thing alone, none that is capable of remaining itself under every set of conditions. Because it is in process, there is always an interdependence between a thing and its environment (which means, other things that preceded it and with which it has been in recurrent, complex, prehensive or semiotic contact). An organism and its environment mutually shape each other, not only in the evolutionary history that the organism has in-

---

26 See, for instance, Gilles Deleuze and Félix Guattari's assemblage theory, Bruno Latour's actor-network theory, and the many variations that build on their work, such as Manuel DeLanda's, John Protevi's, and others'. More generally, biologists study a variety of forms of relations — mutualistic, commensal, parasitic, et al. — between species, organisms, and other entities. On the virtues of a process metaphysics in the biological sciences, see Daniel J. Nicholson and John Dupre, eds., *Everything Flows: Towards a Processual Philosophy of Biology* (New York: Oxford University Press, 2018).

herited, but in the active life-history of that organism.[27] And where there are many organisms mutually shaping themselves and their environments, there is, to misquote Jerry Lee Lewis, *a whole lotta shapin'* going on.

In Graham Harman's evocative account, in *Circus Philosophicus,* of the world as a giant ferris-wheel filled with things, being observed and responded to by people and other respondent things, Harman describes an object that becomes his example of a "dormant object" — an object that is and remains itself *apart* from any relations with other objects. This object happens to be a flag, "a purple lozenge on a field of amber," which used to be celebrated by a union of arrowsmiths, but the guild was disbanded long ago, and now the flag merely flaps in the wind, unrecognized.[28] "Yet there is a certain reality possessed by this flag," Harman writes, "no matter how cruelly ignored, and someday a new throwback union or sarcastic artist may arise to adopt it as an emblem once more."[29]

The flag's dormancy, in Harman's account, consists in the fact that it no longer means what it used to mean for anyone, and that it therefore no longer triggers celebration — but that it one day might do that again. The implication is that the flag's meanings, or at least the flag's flagness — what makes it what it is — is all still there, hidden away in some withdrawn essence, and that it can at some future point re-emerge in its glory. But what Harman does not acknowledge is that in order for that "throwback union or sarcastic artist" to retrieve the flag's forgotten meanings, they would need more than just the flag. They would need access to some retained memory of what the flag meant, or at least what flags in general mean: history books, web sites, rediscoverable underground archives, storytellers passing on stories to other storytellers, memories of attention-rapt bodily postures

---

27 See Richard Lewontin's classic argument in "Organism and Environment," in *Learning, Development, and Culture,* ed. Henry C. Plotkin, 151–70 (New York: Wiley, 1982).

28 Graham Harman, *Circus Philosophicus* (Washington: O-Books/John Hunt, 2010), 8.

29 Ibid., 9.

as flags were raised or lowered, national or cultural identities, eyes that can perceive and distinguish colors. Each of these requires ongoing relations to keep the information — the social significance, the bodily held posture, the words and syntax, the ink on paper or data on disk — from deteriorating to the point that it becomes illegible and unreconstructible. If it is the flag's meaning, and not merely the fabric and the colors, that constitutes its inner essence, then that meaning was never found in the material of the flag alone; it always required recording and decoding instruments of some kind, instruments that have persisted in some form *elsewhere,* beyond the actual lozenge on its field of amber flapping in the wind of Harman's ferris wheel.

In his effort to privilege the object — the flag as a piece of the ferris-wheel — Harman has apparently forgotten the relational networks within which that object becomes what it is, networks that include *practices* and *experiences.* The flag, after all, is not a flag unless there are flags in the world, or the memory of them, or the possibility of them — by virtue of there being social solidarities that group together under symbols like flags, names, or identifiable howls or other calls. As long as those relational networks persist, the flag is never dormant because it is never alone.

In contrast to Harman's account, what is real for process-relationists is always what is *happening.* (Of course, for any complex entity there are usually many things happening, at different speeds and involving different relata. There is no reason to assume that what I *see* happening is all that *is* happening.)[30]

Experience, in other words, is as real as anything gets. Not only does this accord with our own experience of the importance of experience (without which we may as well be in a coma), the assumption it elicits — that all things have something akin to ex-

---

30 Harman has more recently shifted to the view that objects can undergo "symbioses" in their "lifespans" — "turning-points" that mark "genuine points of irreversibility" which "transform" the "realities" of those objects, but leave their identities intact. While this concession to process thought is a welcome one, its implications for his ontology are hardly followed through. See Harman, *Immaterialism: Objects and Social Theory* (Cambridge: Polity, 2016), 47–48 et passim.

perience, some kind of interiority that gives them what is their own — suggests a need to respect those things whose experience we are not privy to. It is not because they are alone with themselves that they are important; it is because they are connected to many others *through* their experience, and ultimately to everything else in the universe. But let us leave ethics aside for now and focus on what the *doing* and *mutual shaping* might be for some of those others.

With living things, the case is fairly straightforward: all such things consume, produce, and metabolize other things. In the process, both the thing and its environment change, even if certain sets of formal relations are conserved over time. Individual organisms maintain a structural coherence; humans maintain a recursive sense of identity over time. Such sets of persistent formal relations make it possible for us to recognize certain things as "individuals" or "persons." But any such designation is a social, context-dependent designation; it applies conditionally and relationally to selected kinds of things and not to others.

A human, for instance, is an individual to *another* human, or to a dog, but probably not to an ant, a bacterium, a quark, a fungal growth, a corporation, or a star. Its individuality is a matter of its location within a set of relations where its individuality counts, where it makes a difference, where it matters. Mattering, in this sense, is what makes a world. What matters is what is significant, what is to be taken into account; it is *material,* but what is material is always also processual, relational, formal, and energetic, always a mix of the subjective or mental (viewed from the "inside") and the objective or physical (viewed from the "outside"). And by the same token, what to us appears individual, an object in its own right, to another sort of entity may be nothing of the sort. Each in its own domain defines its world, perceives and orders its world. Here is the Kantian correlation, the mind-world relationship that Meillassoux identified as the crutch at the heart of philosophy since Kant. But it is not an exclusively *human* crutch, separating an "us," those who think, from a "them" who do not. It is spread through all things, an opening that takes root at the heart of each thing, each event, each occasion of which the universe is made — and which comes to pass itself on to others at the end of that event, and so on and so forth.

But that world, the *Umwelt* of the thing in question — the term is ethologist Jakob von Uexküll's for the experienced or lived world of any organism — is never merely that organism's own. It is built of signs, of things standing in for other things, where the signs, or the meanings they carry, are not merely conceived "in the mind" of that thing. The meanings emerge out of a set of dependent, triadic relations, as Peirce described them. For something to carry meaning there must be, in his terms, a *representamen*, or sign vehicle, which carries the meaning by standing for something else; an *object*, which is the inaccessible "something else" being referred to; and an *interpretant*, which is the meaning created for a beholder at a given moment.[31]

Signness happens; it is a process of becoming. But it is anchored within the universe, and once it has happened, that sign, the vehicle of meaning, becomes datum for the next instance of semiosis. As the subject of an occasion (in Whitehead's sense) takes another as its object, prehending and responding to it, so that other (the object) is always connected to a more distant otherness, a withdrawing otherness that lies beyond the given occasion. It is that which ties that occasion to the rest of the universe.

There are, then, the moments that move together in various ways to create the patterned regularities of the world we know.

---

31 Like Peirce's sign, Whitehead's prehension involves three factors: "There is the occasion of experience within which the prehension is a datum of activity; there is the datum whose relevance provokes the origination of this prehension; this datum is the prehended object; there is the subjective form, which is the affective tone determining the effectiveness of that prehension in that occasion of experience" (Whitehead, *Adventures of Ideas*, 176). Peirce's description of the sign as the elemental process making up the universe stresses interpretability or the generation of meaning as the core of that process. Whitehead's emphasis is on feeling or affective tone, which he elsewhere relates to "appearance" as opposed to "reality." In both cases, novelty arises in the subjective form — Whitehead's "affective tone," Peirce's "interpretant" — that emerges in each prehensive or semiosic occasion.

And this world is unique to the "we" who "know" it, though it is always connected to the worlds of the other *we*'s who know their worlds in their own ways. For humans, this world is made up of distinct objects: persons, cats, cars, and cans of soup, each performing the activities that makes them what they are. But for many unlike us — ants, amoebas, bacteria, electrons, oxygen molecules, biospheres, stars — things may be quite different. We share the same universe, however, and so we may as well use our imaginative abilities to describe that universe in a way that might apply as well to amoebas and stars. A process-relational ontology differs from an object-centered ontology, then, in its belief that the best first step toward a more cosmopolitically *common* ontology — a common world, whose members will always remain somewhat elusive to each other — is the claim that subjectively-experienced events and processes, and not enduring objects, are primary.[32]

That world has a relational complexity that eludes a division into objects. There are boundaries — firewalls, as Harman calls them — between the internal and external, or "domestic" and "foreign" relations of an object, an entity or set of relations that persists over time and external change. But even a firewall requires maintenance, and its activity is a matter of doing, of behavior, or at the very least of habit. A wave builds or recedes as it merges with the contours of other processual trajectories in its crossing of an ocean. A bear or tree goes into hibernation for the winter, then re-emerges into action when spring comes. A caterpillar recedes into a larva, which one day is shed by a butterfly. I learn how to consume vast quantities of alcohol, or become a heroin addict, or learn to spend most of my time in online gaming worlds, surfacing for food or drink only once or twice a day but dramatically affecting the features of the game world. My partner grows a fetus within her body, which is born and, in intimate interaction with her and other humans, becomes a child and eventually an adult. The Earth begins to convert carbon dioxide into oxygen, leading to the emergence of aerobic

---

32 Isabelle Stengers, *Cosmopolitiques*, 7 vols. (Paris: La découverte, 1997).

organisms. Each of these is a transformation, which may be patterned over time in relation to its environment, or which may be singular and irreversible. Among the irreversibles is the point at which a body we call *living* collapses in its vital circulations, those that maintain it with a certain integrity of structure and allow for an integrated engagement with its outside, and restabilizes at a reduced level of activity, at which the hair becomes mere hair, the bones mere calcium compounds, the body mere body, no longer social, no longer person. At this level, too, molecular and electrochemical life continues.

Topographies of morphogenesis

Another way to get at the firewalls is by thinking of them as force-fields between form-takings. Let us build up the description of a moment as such a series of form-takings.

A dog is walking to a park. That park exists — it is its own thing, a park-thing, a first (for the purpose of our analysis). It consists of a particular layout and boundaries, of grass, mounds, ditches, and play structures, all of which can serve as affordances — for dogs, or for kids, or for other creatures. It is, of course, in process and never quite the same as yesterday's park, just as Heraclitus's river is never yesterday's river, despite the similarities that are maintained through formal relations with other processes — traffic flows, city ordinance makings, lawn watering schedules, weather patterns, sunrises and sunsets, squirrel foragings, ant crossings and mound-buildings, and so on.

At night, the park retains the scents of the day that has ended. The next day, it adds the scents of those who were there this morning, or who run around in it now. It is different today, but not altogether different. Today there is that pooch I like to run after, to sniff and play with, and those hounds I better keep away from, or growl back if they get mean. I know the etiquette of encounter and the territorial affordances for running; none of that is much different from yesterday's park adventure. *My* interaction with *this* particular Tuesday-afternoon-park is a *second,* a real encounter. The interaction of *that* dog with the very same

Tuesday-afternoon-park is a different second. Our meeting is yet another second. Time is not measured in seconds here; it explodes with them — with real events, with actual instances by which one set of processes, one wave, meets and meshes with another to produce something novel, a new disturbance pattern.

Accompanying all these seconds, these real interactions, is the sense that is made of them — their significance and meaning. One such significance for dog-me might be "going for a walk with my human," or "going to *that* park again, *woohoo!*" The park visit is in this way akin to my human's reading of a daily newspaper (though I might not know that) — it's how I learn that foul-smelling Rover was here recently, having eaten some pig fat, and that someone has blotted out my own scent markings beneath this lamp post. (Sometimes I see Rover still there, or back again, as if the characters in the newspaper articles have come to life. Don't I love going to the park!) Any particular significance and meaning I get from any of this — any particular thirdness — is likely to have been somewhat anticipated but also somewhat surprising, which means that it is part of the shaping of the interactions (the secondnesses) and of the thing itself (the firstness/es). The thirds cannot be disconnected from the seconds or from the firsts; they are all there in any *eventing* that occurs.

For analytical purposes, then, we are calling the thing itself — whatever we are bracketing out from the rest of the universe — a *first*. In this case, it is the park-world. (There's no assumption that the park-world "subjectivates" in any way; it's more likely to be an aggregate of subjectivating things, but that's immaterial to this exercise. Inasmuch as it is a real, "encounterable" thing and *is what it is,* it is a first. It firsts.) My doggish interaction on this day with that park-world is a second, or rather a long string of seconds. It takes place during a specific duration of time which has a beginning (*Hey, there's the park! Woohoo!*) and an ending (*See y'all later!*), rounded off by anticipatory preludes and more or less satisfactory *dénouements*.

How this park-experience relates to my larger world and the impactful significances it generates in that world, or in any world, is a *third,* or (again) a string of thirds. The visit to the park may put me into a better mood (*Mmm, yes!*), make me stronger (*Lookit here!*), strengthen my appetite (*Yumm…*), lead to new friendships or enmities. My going to the park has also allowed my human to make new friends (or enemies), fertilized the grass, added to the pile of dog-poop-filled plastic bags going into the landfill or the incinerator, and even generated a little demand for more urban green space (or at least demonstrated that demand for a city councilor who had been previously unconvinced). These are all "upshots" or "realizations," significances *for someone* of the dog-in-the-park experience.

This sort of analysis can go on indefinitely, stringing along firsts to seconds to thirds in concatenations that, at their maximum extent, include everything in the universe. In *Ecologies of the Moving Image,* I analyzed the experience of viewing a film.[33] There was, first, the *film-world,* which is the world of a film that exists in its thingness, if one could separate it from its viewing — the film in its qualitative distinctiveness, with its internal structure of unfolding, intersecting lines of potential relation and tension, and so on. This was the film as a viewerly accessible object. Second, there was the *film-experience,* which is what happens to any particular viewer when they allow themselves to be taken into that film-world while watching it unfold. Third, there was the relation between this film-experience (the second-world) and the world at large (the third-world) — the way my viewing of this film interacts with and changes the world I had brought to it and, in aggregate, the world other viewers bring to it.

These three — film-world, film-experience, and film–real world relation — can be broken down in turn into three other triads. The film-real world relation is the largest, or most higher-order, of the set. It unfolds within three dimensions, which are roughly equivalent to the three "ecologies" I described earlier: the *material ecologies,* or the relations involving "stuff" that is there in and around the production and consumption of the

---

33   See Ivakhiv, *Ecologies of the Moving Image,* chs. 1 and 2.

film, which are materialities insofar as they are "stuff seen from its outside"; the *social ecologies,* or relations involving agency and its recognition — the interplay of recognitions of *interiority* or subjectivity in and around the production and consumption of the film; and, between them, the *mental* or *perceptual ecologies,* which are the actual, causally connective, prehensive (or sensory-perceptual) relations involved in the generation of social and material ecologies.

Why distinguish between these three sets of ecologies? Because the two poles, the mental and the material — which means the interiority or "subjectivation" and the exteriority or "objectivation" — are part and parcel of every relational event. This means that in a world where relational events accumulate and take on forms, interiorities and exteriorities come to define the perception of those forms. When we view the things of the world from their "outside," we see material objects, things in their givenness. When we view those same things from their "insides" — which we can only do for ourselves, but which we can adduce is doable from multiple perspectives — we see mental subjects, or active *doings.* Each of them is part of the reality of the world of our experience, though the reality itself is fully definable only in their interplay. Science has come to masterfully describe the materiality of the world along with some of the apparent forces governing action, but ultimately the method of studying external relations alone breaks down. A fully coherent explanation can only come from acknowledging both the internalities and externalities as they are shaped in and through prehensive, or triadic, encounters.

Now if we take these encounters — these *doings* or seconds, these events of prehension — and analyze them triadically, we get something similar. There is, first, the "stuff" that is experienced, which serves as object to our subjective responses: the other dogs in the park, the trees or bushes, and so on. In the viewing of a film, there is the audio-visual stuff that shimmers on the screen in front of us (which, in my film volume, I called film's "spectacle"). Second, there is the response itself — the subjective, prehensive encounter: my bark, the gleam of fear in the other dog's eyes, the running to and fro, and so on. (With film viewing, there is the sequential connectivity in my following the stuff happening on the screen in front of me.) And third, there are the subjective significances generated within these encounters: "mean dog," "watch me as I run around the bastard," "next time I'll get him," and so on.

The basic formula for parsing these components might be summarized very simply:

1. Stuff →
2. Stuff Happens →
3. *So that's what's happening!*

The first is virtual (in Deleuze's sense), the second actual, and the third semiotic. The second mostly covers the causalities, though meaning always infuses (and helps to shape) the actions of world-dwelling agents. (More on who qualifies as such an agent soon.)

Finally, we can take the things themselves, the firsts — in our examples, the park-world and the film-world — and analyze them likewise. With the park-world, there is the apparent stuff that is out there as it is, in its objectness: the park as such, as an object-entity, a set of specifiable relations and boundaries. There is the interactive to-and-fro of the running, sniffing, looking, barking, biting, listening, interacting, pretending to be mean, being mean, and all of what makes up "parkness" in my dog-experience of it. And there is the agency that drives it forward — my desire to run around with those other dogs, our sheer dogness — which is always in process, always becoming-dog, never quite finished or sated in its dogability, its canimorphism. These are all morphisms, all becomings.

For animal-ish entities of a certain size on a certain planet's land surface, the objectification might as well be called *geomorphism*, where the "geo-" refers to the ensemble of things in the background of our activities that we can rely on for their *being there* for us, in support of our active worlds. The subjectification, the becoming-dogness, is its own kind of thing, which we (humans) might as well call *canimorphism*. And the middle-ground, where all the negotiation occurs — where the objects and subjects are parsed out to render things somewhat understandable, moment to moment — let's call that *biomorphism,* since it is the kind of interactive, dynamic thing we recognize as definitive of the living.

With the film-world, we get a similar kind of "geomorphism" in the ways that things take on the character of being there, given and accessible but mostly in the background, and the ways they are spaced or distributed in particular ways. Classical Hollywood westerns are grounded on assumptions about wilderness (that sandy, rocky, spacious stuff) versus civilization (the homes and ranches and towns that have been laboriously carved out of the latter). We understand that division or distribution of meanings; it's taken for granted. It is the geomorphism of the film, at least until it gets disrupted and renegotiated.

Since making, watching, and interpreting films is a human thing, the *subject*omorphism of the film-world is best categorized as *anthropo*morphism (we'll unpack this a bit more soon). In a film-world, this is the way in which the becoming-subjective of things takes on its own distribution of agency — who gets to be an agent, a hero, an effective challenger to the villain or problem faced by a community, and so on. Geomorphism is the givenness; anthropomorphism is the capacity to do.

But it is in between the two where the real negotiation always takes place — the interactive to-and-fro between becoming-object and becoming-subject. All the *real* activity is always here, driven forward by the aim embodied in the subjectivation, yet held together (and resisted) by the objectness of what is given. The creativity in the response is not infinitely open, but nor is it random. It is motivated in a particular direction chosen from the array of potentialities available to the act (and the momentary actor).

Everything in the living universe is like that, ceaselessly (if pulsatingly) moving forward. Peirce's triadism helps us understand three things. There is that which is driving these movements forward: the emergence into thirdness, or the way in which all things move toward taking on meaning for other things *and for themselves,* subjectivating as they semiotically flourish. Then there is the stuff is that provides the fodder (or the matter) for that movement: the firstness, or qualitative "stuffness," of things. And there is how it all happens, which is the secondness of interactive co-responsiveness. There is the pulling toward the world, the world-that-becomes (the "thirding"); there is the world being pulled, the world that had been and that is being tugged forward (in its firstnesses); and there is the pulling itself, in its specific shapes, feels, contours, and stretchings (the "seconding"). There is subjectivation, objectivation, and prehension.

"Anthropomorphism," in this redefinition, has little to do with the traditional definition of this word. That definition was representational: the bird sings, just as I sing; it is *like* a human, so maybe it also *means* the same things as I mean when I sing. The bird resembles the human, but the human itself is taken for granted. My redefinition of the word is *anti*-representational: whatever the bird, or the human, *becomes* will be the form (the morphism, the morphology) that it takes. The human itself acts as *if* it were human, but this "as if" is left open, referring not to what is known (and past) but to what is potential (and future). It is the forward pull of subjectivation. Canimorphism is the same for dogs, avimorphism for birds, corvomorphism for crows, amoebomorphism for amoebas, and so on. Since we can never be sure what a body is capable of doing (*pace* Deleuze and Spinoza, but to be explored more soon), we are never sure where this subjectivation will lead.

Humans just may canimorph — and presumably have, to some degree, from millennia of co-evolving with dogs. Chimpanzees just may anthropomorph, as those brought up in captivity and learning American Sign Language to some degree do. (Others, retained in zoos, become little more than signifiers of chimpanzeeness, ossified chimpanzomorphs.) Or a human can strive to "become bear," as "grizzly man" Timothy Treadwell apparently tried to do; or to become computer, to become virtual, to become cyborg. Success at any becoming-other will not likely result in a human-bear hybrid (or another kind), but it will expand the capacities for humanness, or bearness, or machineness. The point is that there is no essence to the *future* or the *capacity* of a thing, only to its past. Essentialism weds us to the past, while radical constructivism disavows it, but a process-relational view simply recognizes the past as past, carried forward in novel and creative ways into the open, ever-becoming present. The degree of creativity an "eventity" is capable of introducing into a given moment may vary, but it is always somewhere between none and all. It is never nothing. And in that span is the openness of all things.[34]

The soul(s) of things

Let us return to the question of agency. Martin Heidegger rather famously (or infamously) declared rocks to be "worldless" and animals to be "poor in world"; for him, only humans qualified as rich in our worldhood. Biological aliveness and mortality play a role in these distinctions, but object-oriented ontologists have resisted them, for philosophically valid reasons.

Even as I have mostly resisted thing-language, I have suggested that only things that *prehend* — only unities that are centers of subjectivation, that relate to objects in their surrounding world, translating those objects (as data) into a newly concrescent unity — can be said to harbor agency. Most forms of panpsychism (a school of metaphysical thought that has recently been gaining adherents) agree that there is mental activity, or mentation, in all things, but then they specify the criteria for what qualifies as

---

34 Distinguishing triadically between *geo-*, *bio-*, and *anthro-* is not original. It can be found, for instance, in soundscape ecologists' distinction between the acoustic worlds specific to landscapes, living things, and the human world, respectively called "geophony," "biophony," and "anthrophony." See Bryan Pijanowski et al., "What Is Soundscape Ecology? An Introduction and Overview of an Emerging New Science," *Landscape Ecology* 26, no. 9 (2011): 1213–32.

such a "thing."[35] If a thing is biologically alive, then of course it qualifies. Beyond that, it may as well; let's talk.

Whitehead innovatively suggested that the subatomic world consists of such mentating, psychically active things. But that can only ever be speculation on our part. With larger entities, things get a little more clear. Whitehead distinguished between aggregates, such as a rock, and genuine "societies" such as a human, a dog, or a flower. Rocks may *include* some semiotically active doings (at the molecular or subatomic levels, for instance), but they may not be semiotically active in the unified or coordinated way that humans and other organisms are.

This is the kind of claim that object-oriented ontologists dislike. Timothy Morton has suggested, for instance, that, ontologically speaking, a pencil lacks nothing that a human or a flower possesses. It may not be *aware* of the ways it maintains its form, but it does maintain its form, and it is its own thing: it retains some mysterious underside that will never be known by anyone else.[36]

If there are only objects that are "real" and objects that are "sensual" (perceived but not real), as object-oriented ontologists claim, then the pencil is certainly as real and as substantial as you or I, or as the spider descending in front of me as I write. The challenge for a process-relational account is to specify in what its reality lies. We can easily anthropomorphize a rock (in the traditional sense of the word) by imagining that it acts, rather like us. This is what animists have always been accused of doing (and animism is really just another, more loosely deployed word for panpsychism). There are animists for whom humans, and bees, and possibly rocks and clouds may be "persons" (though it may depend on the specific rocks and clouds), but for whom pieces of paper, electric backscratchers, and numbers may not

---

35 On panpsychism, see David Skrbina, ed., *Mind That Abides: Panpsychism in the New Millennium* (Amsterdam: John Benjamins, 2009), and David Skrbina, *Panpsychism in the West*, rev. edn. (Cambridge: MIT Press, 2017).

36 See Timothy Morton, "Anthropomorphism," *Ecology Without Nature*, December 22, 2010, http://ecologywithoutnature.blogspot.com/2010/12/anthropomorphism.html.

be. There are neo-animists who go further, acknowledging the personhood of their backpacks and laptops and business cards and fingernail clippings and thoughts and shadows.[37] But do they all *act,* or are they merely involved in processes of inter-action within which they play an active but not *agential* role?

One of the solutions to this quandary is to speak of *distributed agency.*[38] For instance, as I sit writing, my shadow — which my body casts on the part of my office that it blocks from the sun's rays — darkens the space around the flower sitting on the coffee table behind me. The flower, being a flower, presumably senses the presence of sunlight nearby and slowly twists its way over toward it. To say that the shadow is an agent here in its relationship with the flower is going too far, as it doesn't act of its own accord on the flower. The shadow could be called an *actant* — something that "could be said to act" (in Bruno Latour's non-committal phrase) — but it is more reasonable to say that the system of relations "sun-body-shadow-flower" incorporates a kind of distributed agency.

The shadow, however, is fully formed by the interaction of my body and the sun (and any other nearby light sources). Those relations exhaust it; apart from them, it is nothing. Tim Morton's pencil, on the other hand, has more going on than the "external" relations that affect it. It has a structure of capacities that is its own. It has been shaped to do certain things — to be used for writing, primarily — but its form and structure give it additional capacities that may not have been intended by its makers: the capacity to roll off a desk, hit the floor, and cause a lead marking on that floor; to collect dust on a shelf; to be poked into an infant's eye or nose; and so on. This certainly makes it an actant, a thing that affects the processes within which it is involved. But it is a stretch to say that it interacts *creatively* with the world around it, as an active agent interacts with its *Umwelt.* It does

---

37 On animism and some of its novel varieties, see Graham Harvey, ed., *The Handbook of Contemporary Animism* (London: Routledge, 2014).

38 See N.J. Enfield and Paul Kockelman, eds., *Distributed Agency* (New York: Oxford University Press, 2017).

not *enworld,* though it may be *worlded* by others who do. It does not *pencilmorph* in the sense that pencilmorphing is either (definition #1) responding to others as if they were (like) pencils, or (definition #2) becoming (open-endedly) pencil — pencil*ing.*

Unless we define "morphism" more broadly. The pencil is part of a morphogenetic network within which its pencilness plays an active, co-constituting role. Pencils, pens, and similar writing implements have made it possible to keep track of large numbers of tradable items, to write poems and books, to doodle in a way that made boring school lessons tolerable, and to add to one's hair-do when placed behind the ear. They *did* change the world — so much so that we live today in a "pencilmorphed" world.

So in this sense Morton is correct: pencils *do* pencilmorph. But this is a different definition of morphing than the usual one, and different as well from my revised definition. Viewed through a Whiteheadian lens, the subjective agency of the pencil may reside in the molecules and other "actual occasions" making up that pencil, not in the pencil *qua* pencil, since it has no central, regnant unity directing the way in which it responds creatively to its environment. But even the fact that it is humans who have done most of the writing *with* pencils doesn't take the penciling away from the pencils; it is their pencilness that enables that penciling to occur.

This is where it is helpful to bring a very different tradition of thought into the conversation, one that traces itself to the psychodynamic ontology of Carl Jung. James Hillman, Edward Casey, Thomas Moore, Susan Rowland, Robert Romanyshyn, and others in the Jungian line of descent have argued for a revival of the idea of "soul" and for an acknowledgment that *things have soul.* This can be thought of in a purely relational sense — that soul or soulfulness is a quality of relations, for instance, between me and my pencil, or the painting in front of me, or the garden I have been patiently cultivating for several summers. In this sense it indicates a capacity for objects to trigger responses in others, and thereby to make us (humans and other subjects) shimmer and vibrate alongside them in ways that are not "of our own making." Or it can be thought of in an object-oriented sense, such that the soul of an object refers to its capacity to withdraw from relations. In this sense, "soul" is a way of indicating the ways in which things withdraw to their fathomless depths — the depths of the pencil, of a hammer, of a pair of peasant's shoes (such as Van Gogh's famous pair), a lotus flower, a sunset, and so on. In that sense, the shadow cast by the mountain whose side I live on clearly also has soul.

The two kinds of soul may be reconcilable, in fact, if we take soul not as a possession of the pencil, but as a quality of the relationship between myself and my pencil. Soul in this sense *deepens* the middle-ground between two (or more) entities. It is a "depth of field" that makes images — that is, particular kinds of relations — *possible* while making sure that they are never *exhaustive*. In this way, the concept of soul defers and disperses the question of agency (and of subjectivity) into the depths of matter — depths in which subjectivity might reside, but need not. It shimmers and hums within and around those things, setting off circulations of energy made possible by them. This, at least, is one way we might posit a sort of "object-process ontology."

Soul, in this sense, refers to the depth — potentially fathomless — of objects as perceived by subjects, and at the same time of subjectivity in its captivation by objects. It is a quality of relations (which makes it relational) that is indicative of the *recessive* character of objects (which makes it object-oriented). It points toward objects' withdrawal from relations, but is produced relationally, through networks in which it circulates. Soul can expand or contract, and there may be objects or relations or practices that lead to the expansion and deepening of soulfulness, and others that lead to its constriction. That would mean we could come up with ethical criteria or at least suggestive indicators for *how to act* and *how to live* (more on those in Part Two). In this sense, a pencil may have soul, but a world full of pencils, rulers, papers, and abacuses may be a little less soulful than a world full of old-growth forests, streams full of salmon, Japanese gardens, and whalesong. And it is the larger world of relational networks through which agency circulates that evokes questions of *how to act* in relations involving pencils, salmon, and other loci of soulful action.

Earth jazz

To further evoke the enactive nature of soulful, circulating agency, consider musical improvisation. The universe gives rise to wondrous entities in its long history of spontaneity, relational responsiveness, habit-formation, and form-building. The habits start as rhythms, melodic chirps that turn into territorial refrains and calls, and that gradually maneuvre their way into verse patterns, melodies, harmonies, and polyrhythms. Distinct songs develop for particular purposes and gradually get released from those purposes, taken up into improvisational routines and performances, some of which crystallize into larger-scale structures, but only ever temporarily.

There is a tendency to think that certain musical traditions — the classical European, Indian, or Chinese, for instance — are more "highly evolved" than others. But there is no height involved here, just distance: they may be more *distantly* evolved, in the sense that they are more professionalized, specialized, and extracted from any relationship with the rhythms of everyday labor (save for that of the musicians). That professional distance is something that genres like rock, folk, and blues have historically rebelled against, and in the process have helped to maintain a broader scope for musical ecology.

In their references to music and to the semiotic ethology of Jakob von Uexküll, Gilles Deleuze and Félix Guattari are penetrating guides into this musical-ecological-philosophical territory. Territories, for them, are built from a refrain. But so are openings to novelty: "One launches forth, hazards an improvisation. But to improvise is to join with the World, or meld with it. One ventures from home on the thread of a tune."[39]

---

39 Gilles Deleuze and Félix Guattari, *A Thousand Plateaus: Capitalism and Schizophrenia*, trans. Brian Massumi (Minneapolis: University of Minnesota Press, 1987), 313.

An analogous, if more straightforward, account of ecology as a kind of "earth jazz" is found in Evan Eisenberg's *The Ecology of Eden*. Eisenberg writes:

> All life plays variations on the same few chord changes. Each taxon improvises, following certain rules but obeying no pre-determined destiny. Each responds to the riffing, comping, noodling, and vamping of those around it. Life makes itself up as it goes along. [...] How do you collaborate with Gaia if you don't know exactly how she works, or what she wants? You do it, I think, by playing Earth Jazz. You improvise. You are flexible and responsive. You work on a small scale, and are ready to change direction at the drop of a hat. You en-courage diversity, giving each player — human or nonhu-man — as much room as possible to stretch out.[40]

That is as good a summary of adaptive management, one of the key principles of systems-theoretical ecological management, as any. Eisenberg's Earth Jazz is about process and relationality.

An objectologist may reply that even an improvisational outfit as perversely relational as the Grateful Dead is not im-mune to the reality of objects: their song "Dark Star" is still "Dark Star," "El Paso" is still "El Paso" and not "Morning Dew" (which it almost transmogrified into in one performance, ac-cording to the Deadheads commenting on YouTube), and Tom Verlaine's band Television is still Television and not the Grateful Dead. (Verlaine once lamented the repeated comparisons made between his punk-ish "Marquee Moon" and the Dead's "Dark Star," a song that Jerry Garcia and company amphibiously wove into a meanderingly delightful half-hour improvisation.) Or, to put it into more cashable terms, that "Stairway to Heaven" is still "Stairway to Heaven" and not Spirit's "Taurus," as a Califor-nia jury decided in June of 2016 despite the two songs' similari-ties. And that rejoinder would be appropriate. But each of these

---

40 Evan Eisenberg, *The Ecology of Eden* (New York: Vintage Books, 1998), 293–94.

songs can be traced to their origins, to the processes that gave rise to them, crystallized them, and carried those crystallizations forward temporally and spatially. And those origins would be messy.

This is something that is relevant to blogger Skholiast's meditation on "Buddhism, objects, and eternity," which captures a few key points in the objects-processes debate. Skholiast's defense of the idea of eternity is daring: "The 'eternal objects' of the sort I have in mind," he writes, "are the aspect of any object, the "side" if you like, that faces away from us in time. Within time, things come into being and pass away; they are determined by the churning or flow of a fractal interdependent causality. But eternally, in what one might not hesitate to call the World Soul, things are themselves, alone with the alone."[41]

Skholiast is hewing close to Whitehead here, with the latter's "eternal objects" and his God who suffers with the sufferer and thereby redeems that suffering for eternity. Referring to the task of "re-enchanting the world" — a theme we will pick up in Part Three of this book — Skholiast contrasts the "religions of the book," with their Platonist presuppositions, against recent eco-Buddhist efforts to forge such a re-enchantment "out of interdependence alone." "The eternal object," he writes, is "precisely the face of the object in the sense Levinas uses the term," which is something ignored by the more fully relational forms of Buddhism. Then he cites an epiphany related in G.K. Chesterton's "The Man Who Was Thursday," when the protagonist has a glimpse into the double-sidedness of human beings:

When I see the horrible back [of a man], I am sure the noble face is but a mask. When I see the face but for an instant, I know the back is only a jest. Bad is so bad, that we cannot but think good an accident; good is so good, that we feel certain that evil could be explained... Shall I tell you the secret of the

---

41 Skholiast, "Eternity and objects," *Speculum Criticum Traditionis*, June 10, 2010, http://speculumcriticum.blogspot.com/2010/06/eternity-and-objects.html.

whole world? It is that we have only known the back of the world. We see everything from behind, and it looks brutal. That is not a tree, but the back of a tree. That is not a cloud, but the back of a cloud. Cannot you see that everything is stooping and hiding a face? If we could only get round in front...

This could be taken as a response to Paul Klee's "Angelus Novus," the painted angel (pictured as the frontispiece of this book) about whom Walter Benjamin wrote:

This is how one pictures the angel of history. His face is turned toward the past. Where we perceive a chain of events, he sees one single catastrophe which keeps piling wreckage upon wreckage and hurls it in front of his feet. The angel would like to stay, awaken the dead, and make whole what has been smashed. But a storm is blowing from Paradise; it has got caught in his wings with such violence that the angel can no longer close them. The storm irresistibly propels him into the future to which his back is turned, while the pile of debris before him grows skyward. This storm is what we call progress.[42]

Benjamin's angel, turned toward the past, sees only the backs of men and the wreckage they produce. Were he to turn toward the future, he may see more wreckage, but beyond it he may see its redemption by the World Soul, the *anima mundi* whose soul and intelligence contains all sin, all forgiveness, all continuity. Chesterton's protagonist concludes, in defiance of Benjamin: "One might say, for shorthand: objects have souls."

Skholiast's use of the Chesterton passage provides a redemptive twist to the objectologists' notion of the perpetually withdrawing object, the object whose soul remains firmly and finally

---

42 Walter Benjamin, "Theses on the Philosophy of History," in *Illuminations: Essays and Reflections,* ed. Hannah Arendt, trans. Harry Zohn, 253–64 (New York: Schocken Books, 1969), 257–58.

unknown, which also, they argue, makes it as worthy of respect as any other. But it also suggests that much depends on *how* we know things at all, and that the *how* is a variable we can learn to play with. Earth Jazz, of the relationalist sort, does not presume to ever *know* the others with whom and with which it plays along. But it maintains that play we must, whether this means muddling forward (as the Dead do through much of that version of "Dark Star") or attaining peaks and plateaus (as Deleuze and Guattari urge us to, and as Television manages toward the end of "Marquee Moon") that settle into further and different plateaus, never retracing their steps but always finding rhythms to lock into for a while, and then to release into another set.

Earth Jazz in this sense recognizes that objects have souls — this is the precondition of living in an ensouled world — but it perceives those objects as players, relational processes, whose souls work their way into the playing, and which continue to develop, soulfully, in and through the playing. Soul, in this sense, is not the *possession* of objects; it is the way in which those objects *are possessed* (and prepossessed). It is their very nature.

Skholiast, like the objectologists, opts for an idea of "eternity" (or in their case, withdrawal) that is a little too separate from the playing itself. Instead of Eternity — or a side of things locked away into a realm where it can never truly encounter others — I will opt for what Whitehead and especially Deleuze proclaim a *virtuality,* a space where the unmanifest and unactualized continues to churn, while remaining intimately interfolded with the manifest and actualized. This virtuality is neither *present* as actuality, but nor is it *separate* from actuality. It is folded through, but there are many folds and pleats to choose from in its patterns. If this is an eternity, it is a changeable one consisting of "back sides" that are not the eternal dark side of a unrevolving moon, but the mobile and ever withdrawing arcs of a moon that revolves in its relations with us and with others. And if the temporary "back sides" include some that are cosmically scaled, then there is no need for an Eternity to lure us toward new possibilities. That, perhaps; is why Whitehead himself replaced his "eternal objects" with the lure of "Eros," which, he wrote, "endows with agency all ideal possibilities."[43] And it is why his student and influential interpreter, philosopher Charles Hartshorne, insisted on the non-predetermined nature of those "eternal objects," rendering them as "universals" that were "emergent" in an open and indeterminate universe.[44]

Meanwhile, improvisations degenerate, their elements getting whipped into commercial formulas, national anthems, or martial hymns. And new ones emerge out of our efforts to engage with their provocations, and to invent new and contrasting ones.

Where we find ourselves

The point, for a process-relational philosophy, is to develop a vocabulary sensitive to the various kinds of relation, interaction, inhabitation, flow, change, emergence, network-building, and system-maintenance that make up a dynamic world, a world that develops new habits and actualizes new potentials at every step of its way. We find ourselves amidst those relations, tied to things, material densities, in specific ways, and come up against the challenges those ties, habits, and tendencies conspire to generate.

Our questions, our matters of concern today — such as how to satisfy the requirements of seven and a half billion humans, how to balance these against each other, and how to manage our activities so they remain within an allowable basin of error, rather than bifurcating through an irreversible shift in global climate systems to something unseen in millions of years — these are all questions of relational design (where *design* is a verb and not a noun), questions of *composition*. Habits and patterns of interaction have developed over time. Alliances have

---

43 Whitehead, *Adventures of Ideas*, 270.
44 Charles Hartshorne, *Whitehead's Philosophy* (Lincoln: University of Nebraska Press, 1972), 32. And see Steve Odin, *Tragic Beauty in Whitehead and Japanese Aesthetics* (New York: Lexington, 2016), 144–45.

been built — between humans, photosynthetic processes we call grasses, and herbivorous processes we identify with sheep, cows, and the like; and between humans and flesh-compounding processes that have given us fossil fuels. Interactions have intensified, but knowledge of the sustainability of those interactions has lagged behind their novel production. Humans, like other animals, are experimental and pragmatic modes of functioning for whom error follows trial, learning follows error, and innovation, where it occurs, follows or accompanies learning.

There are, in all such relations, matters of concern. There are things that happen, and that provoke a response. Observing the many things that happen, relational processes all, we note a scale of complexity and differentiation, of pattern-making at variable levels of order. There is feeling, feeding, oxygenating, reproducing, socializing, swarming, migrating, erupting, quaking, thinking, dramatizing, road- and city-building, boundary-maintaining and boundary-crossing, warring and peacemaking, atmosphere-carbonizing and ocean-plasticizing, and much more. These relational events, these networkings, are always and everywhere temporal, dynamic, interactive, effective, and affective. They are verbs rather than nouns, processes rather than objects; they are verbs connecting nouns or nodes, which are temporary congealments, eddies in the stream.

An amoeba responds to an object in its environment by moving toward or away from it, or by ingesting a part of it. The molecules of a slab of metal mingle with oxygen to produce rust. The slowness of the latter, and the minimal amount of agency compared to what we humans are used to, in no way eliminates the structural parallel with our own activities. Neither does the magnitude and impact of a much grander scale of event: a lake's damming by a family of beavers; a gathering of world leaders upstream from the dam (say, in Bretton Woods, New Hampshire, in 1945, agreeing on an international financial architecture that will shape the world for the next forty-five summers); a volcano's erupting 28 million years previous to that, extinguishing many of the life forms on the planet's surface. Where in that range future geologists will place the Anthropocene is, as yet, uncertain.

There are events, which become matters of concern, and that is where we find ourselves. Mattering, they come to mind. Minding, we come to matter. And in the moment of contact there is a feelingful act, a decision, a choice, which is the hinge on which all things (perpetually) turn. It is where the action is. And with each turn of the wheel, each point of decision, each feelingful response to the world, a next world, with its new arrangement of possibilities, comes into being.

Time's arrow is in this sense asymmetrical, with novelty entering into every moment, changing the equation for the next moment and the next. As Whitehead put it, "[t]he creativity of the world is the throbbing emotion of the past hurling itself into a new transcendent fact. It is the flying dart, of which Lucretius speaks, hurled beyond the bounds of the world."[45] In the process, the world is continually renewed, and we are invited to be part of its renewal. How we, all of us — subatomic particles, organisms, suns — follow our invitations determines the trajectory of its further renewal. It is this matter of *how* we take up those matters of concern that matters most of all. (That will be the topic of Part 2.)

Slice of time

This model of time is worth contrasting a bit further with the more usual one. When we think of slicing into time to depict a moment of it, we typically picture it as a linear flow. Slicing into time, in this view, is like slicing into bread: on the left of the slice is the past (for those who read from left to right), on the right is the future, and the cut itself is where we are right now. The world as it appears to us is a cross-section of the loaf. Or, since we are in motion, we might conceive of ourselves as a train moving forward on the track of time: the tracks ahead of us are the future, those behind are the past, and we are the train.

---

45 Whitehead, *Adventures of Ideas*, 177.

Physicists, at least since Einstein, complicate this with the notion of spacetime as a container that we are caught within. The tracks may move forward ahead of us, but on some level it is assumed that future and past are also in motion — that they make up a curved continuum within which we are caught, unable to step out of (and thereby to become truly free), but somehow aware of the tension between the fact of our imprisonment *within* time and the desire to be able to act in it.

A process-relational slice of time — which means a slice of the universe, or pluriverse, since time is not a container but only the durational dimension of the things that actually make up the pluriverse — is not like this. It looks more like a circle or a sphere, the outside perimeter of which is expanding, and the inside of which is being sucked into a black hole at its center. If we like the idea of time as a train, this train is one that is going in countless directions at once, spreading outward from a center and laying down its tracks, while swallowing those behind it, as it goes. It is a spherical train, a train as chaosmos.

The expanding edge of the sphere consists of virtualities — firstnesses, in Peirce's terms — emerging into actuality, or secondness, and actualities emerging into significance, organization, pattern, habit, law, or (together) thirdness. It is these that give shape to the universe. The secondnesses are its outer form, its exteriorities, or what Gregory Bateson (drawing on Carl Jung) called "Pleroma," which is the empty, asignifiying "fullness" of what is observed and studied, say, by science. The thirdnesses are its felt meanings, its interiorities, its meshes of distinctions, or what Bateson (and Jung) called *Creatura,* that is, the meaning-laden *Umwelten* that creatures like us live.

Since we are there at the outer edge, we see only what is within our perceptual-semiotic orbit, where our *Umwelten* meet the world; but this is true for all actual entities. (That orbit expands with recording and decoding mechanisms of various sorts such as oral and textual literacies, optical and archaeological technologies, and so on; but let us leave that aside for now.)

If there could be a seer who was able to see everything, he or she would only see that outer edge of the universe, where the expanding circle is continually becoming new. In Whitehead's best known systematization, in *Process and Reality,* this seer, who is also a feeler and a sympathetic experiencer, is God. Opting for a non-theistic language (as do some of Whitehead's interpreters), I prefer to think of it as *Rigpa,* the Dzogchen Buddhist term for the subjectless subjectivation that is "empty in essence, cognizant in nature, and unconfined in capacity."[46] Or *Satcitānanda,* the Advaita Vedanta word for the subjective experience of all that is, "existence-consciousness-bliss." It is the background luminosity of the universe that surrounds the circle we are describing, bathing it in a sympathetic cognizance. Perhaps we can agree to call it God and leave aside the question of what kind of relationship one might have with it (for the moment).

The firstnesses emerge out of the differential structure of virtualities that makes up the interior side of the outer rim of the circle. This structure changes moment to moment alongside the processes of actualization that are its exterior side.

The sucking that occurs in the middle of the circle is that of unactualized virtualities sinking into oblivion. Actuality is, in effect, always escaping away from the great sucking at the heart of the universe, the "dark flow" speeding into nothingness. Some virtualities escape into *being,* the rest escape into *nothingness.* Which of them go one way and which go the other is something that is determined by the decisive acts occurring all around at the outer perimeter of the sphere. And insofar as we act decisively, we contribute to the forward motion. For Whitehead, it is at the circumference of the universe where everything happens, where the darkness of virtuality emerges into the light of actualization. At the same time, the actualized world is ceaselessly passing over into objectivity: it becomes object, which means it becomes virtuality, potentiality, stuff from which, or in response to which, other stuff emerges. For Whitehead, any-

---

46 See, e.g., Tsoknyi Rinpoche, *Fearless Simplicity: The Dzogchen Way of Living Freely in a Complex World* (Hong Kong: Rangjung Yeshe Publications, 2003), 88ff. For another non-theistic interpretation of Whitehead's metaphysics, see Donald Sherburne, "Whitehead without God," *Process Studies* 15, no. 2 (1986): 83–94.

thing that has died to its own subjectivity—become object (or "superject")—in this way becomes available for the creativity of subsequent arisings.

It is here, at the circle's edge, that the world that *has* been, the brute objectivity of the world that has concresced from previous acts, meets the spontaneously arising spaciousness of Rigpa, the emergently responsive luminosity of naked, subject-less subjectivity. In countless acts at this Edge of Things, this luminous subjectivity—which is neither mine, nor yours, nor anyone else's, except that it is the becoming of each of us, sub-jectlessly subjectivating—selectively takes up the data arriving from the past, the virtual potentialities that are to shape the next moment, and the next, and casts aside those that will *not* shape it except by their absence.

At this edge, then, is where the universe constantly folds out into new orchestrations, improvising along a million lines of feelingful decision. In his exegetical account of Whitehead's "pancreativism," Michel Weber explains why it is that concres-cence, which means the becoming of actuality, "does not hap-pen *in* the World, but *at the edges* of the World." It is there that novelty germinates, in and through the decisions that are part of every actual entity coming into being. "When [novelty] enters the World, it is fully integrated within its existing structure *and* modifies it."[47]

Weber continues: "Subjectivity, i.e., existence of actuality *per se* [i.e., *becoming*], is articulated with objectivity, i.e., being or potentiality. The former is the locus of (free) final causation; the latter of (deterministic) efficient causation. The durational pre-sent (i.e., the existence outside physical time) of the free con-crescing 'actual occasion' is bound with the past experiences sheltered by the transitional actual entities."[48]

Subjectivity arises in intimate embrace with the objectivities that it responds to, which are the bodies cast off by the men-

---

47 Michel Weber, *Whitehead's Pancreativism: The Basics* (Frankfurt: Ontos, 2006), 26.

48 Ibid., 27.

tal potencies of other subjectivities. Put otherwise, *"existence,"* which is "actuality in the strong sense of the term — i.e., subjectivity as redefined by Whitehead independently of conscious experience [...] — takes place in an immediate present that does not belong to physical temporality and to its deterministic order. It belongs instead to the durational temporality that has been eminently explored by Bergson and James. Consequently, *being,* i.e., the World, is always already potential, past, determined, temporalized."[49]

To say that existence takes place *outside* the World while *being* is both "past" and "potential" may sound paradoxical. Past is potential in that it is virtual; it is no longer real except insofar as it provides the conditioning determinations, the differential structures, with which *becomings-subject* contend with. Existence itself is the *contending,* the *subjectivating,* the feeling–responding–doing that constitutes all that is really real at any given moment. It is the World in its openness, its freedom, yet it is outside the World-as-already-there, because it is always what World is in process of becoming. "When the actuality-subject is satisfied," Weber writes:

> [I]t topples into objectivity — it is *released into* the World *in solido* —, and becomes available as material for further concrescences (i.e., it starts exerting causal efficacy). There are thus two ways of speaking of the "after" of a concrescence: to speak of 'actuality-object' is to emphasize that it is the outcome of a concrescence; to speak of "actuality-superject" (as *Process and Reality* does) is to underline that it is itself at the root of further concrescences.[50]

The "secret of the Whiteheadian ontological reform," Weber continues,

---

49 Ibid., xv.
50 Ibid., 27–28.

is quite simple: the actuality-subject grows, concresces, at the edges of the World — *beyond the bounds of the world* —, buttressing itself on the determinism materialized by the actualities-object. "When" its organic growth is terminated, it topples into objectivity and becomes an actuality-object fully integrated in the mundane plenum.[51]

Everything in the universe follows this movement, each in its own way, with its own degree of freedom or creativity and its own durationality. The percolating rhythm by which actualization occurs, one concrescence after another — a rhythm which differs for everything that is actualizing, but which congeals into patterns *across* differentiations — is the composite heart-beat of the universe.

Another way of saying all this is that *the only reality is the present moment.* In the present moment we respond, feelingly and effectively, to things that affect us, and those responses create the conditions for the next present moment. What was possible a moment ago is no longer possible (in quite the same way) in this moment. "Virtualities" in this sense are possibilities or potentialities present to this moment. They are real in their presence, which shapes the moment; they are virtual in that they have not been actualized. Most of them pass, they go down the black rabbit hole. Some get cashed, or actualized — like winning lottery prize tickets that get redeemed for $5 and turned into quarters for the next set of slot machine calls. (This is the universe as Las Vegas.)

All of this happens everywhere at once, for everything from quarks to neurons to rhizomes to people to nebulae (or, at least, for anything that's thinging, for *anythinging*). At any given moment, the range of possibilities for action is determined by everything that led up to this moment, but the actual decision of what happens is left up to us to the extent that we (quarks, people, nebulae, whatever) are capable of acting on it. This capacity

---

51 Ibid., xv.

is the capacity for freedom in every moment, and it is present in every real thing going.

The only "cash" carried over from one moment to the next is made of the effects of what we do, which is what in South Asia has been called *karma* (and which has been repeatedly misunderstood by westerners, and maybe by easterners, too). If we carry less of it around with us — less gluey wanting-things-to-be-this-way-or-that-way — and instead receive and respond, go with the rhythm, doing what's best in a world of shared experience among entities that recognize their solidarity with each other — that makes for the best jazz. What this looks like, if we could slice into the whole thing at once, is a circle that keeps expanding (on the outside) and contracting (on the inside), on and on. Or so it appears to the knife-edge that is doing the slicing. (To us, when eyes are most open, it is much richer, more divergent, and more beautiful.)

Eventology 1

For an object-oriented ontologist, an important question to answer is: *How do things enter into relation with other things? And what happens (in the world) when they do?* For a process-relational eventologist, on the other hand, there is no question of entering into relations, since they are always already entered into. The question is always how to *alter* existing relations, how to move them and shape them, how to respond to what is given. What are the different ways of moving with and against existing relations so as to reshape them, enhance them, enlarge them, soften them, tweak them, beautify them, link them with others?

If everything is an event, the question is how to distinguish between different kinds of events. Events can be defined as new relations arising somewhat unpredictably from the encounter of previously unconnected processes. If all things are taken to be organized sets of processes, bounded or unbounded, open or closed in varying degrees, then events would be occurrences that do not merely *repeat* cycles of activity, but that bring new things — new relations — into existence. They always feature the setting-off of processual action into a new direction, or into many. The general parameters of an event may be more or less predictable, but there is always an element of unpredictability, because of the creativity instantiated in the "creative advance into novelty," as Whitehead termed it, that constitutes that event.

To an eventologist, an archaeologist of what happens in the moment after it has happened, there are at least three kinds of events: events, Events, and ~~Events~~. The first is the class of any and all events. "Wherever and whenever something is going on," Whitehead wrote, "there is an event."[52] Events are things that happen — hyper-forms of relational enactment, consisting of assemblages becoming something other than themselves. What is required for something to be an event is a doing and a being-done-to: a bipolar passage between a becoming-subject and a becoming-object (or several such). An event is, in this sense, any smallest movement or shift in the structure of the universe, a universe that is made up precisely of such movements.

The second kind, the Event, is an event that wraps far more into itself than a typical observer (if there were such a thing) could have predicted. There is a certain confluence of trajectories and flows, and then suddenly, a manifold of new events has arisen. Things have shifted, dramatically. A set of relational systems finds itself suddenly spun into a higher orbit. One might as well call this a Hyper-Event — analogous to Timothy Morton's "hyperobject," but that capital "E" saves us from the questionable suffix. Such an Event encompasses not a single prehensive occasion, but a meeting of processual consistencies out of which arises an unpredictable set of distinctly *new* processes, which in turn expand the circle of affective horizons by which their effects reverberate into the universe.

Uprisings and political revolutions are examples of such Events, and their causes are always somewhat mysterious.[53]

---

52 A.N. Whitehead, *The Concept of Nature* (New York: Cambridge University Press, 1920), 78.

53 Alain Badiou's conception of "the Event," which is always unpredictable and radically contingent, yet which always ruptures a given social order, would seem to qualify as a form of "the Event" as I am describing it. While all

Historians may reconstruct some of their contributing streams and may come up with theories to account for them, but these almost always remain contestable. They are moments when suddenly much more is at stake than is normally the case.

Of course, there is no universal measure for distinguishing a mere "event" from an "Event." The Events of interest to me will be different from those of interest to the ant crawling on the window in front of me. Epistemology in this sense always impinges on ontology; categories are affected by the perceptual capacities of those for whom they are relevant. In a process-relational view, *all that there is* consists of events, which we can take as open moments — relational alignments opening up onto particular sets of possibilities, of which some become actualized and others do not, through the activity of the singular points of agency woven into each of them. But revolutionary moments are *big* moments, those in which many highly dynamic processes converge to create possibilities for radical change spanning layers and levels of activity that rarely get aligned all together in one fell swoop.

Moments like these take a lot of groundwork to become possible — preparation such as the various action plans drawn up by Egyptian activists in the lead-up to Tahrir Square in 2011, or the manifestoes and years of agitation leading up to the Russian or Chinese revolutions. But they also arrive very much of their own accord, a re-alignment of stars and planets (or class formations and technological capacities) as much as of anything else. In the midst of such moments it is impossible to tell where things will end up. What will be the shape of the new constellation that emerges once the dust is settled? Which social and political groups will take power into their hands, and what kind of redistribution of power (and of its shadow, exclusion) will oc-

---

of Badiou's primary examples of such "Events" are of political revolutions (the Paris Commune, the Russian and Maoist revolutions, and May 68), his secondary examples range more freely across human (but always human) experience: for instance, falling in love, or Schoenberg's invention of 12-tone seriality. See Badiou, *Being and Event,* trans. Oliver Feltham (New York: Continuum, 1995).

cur? Which figures, and which slogans and ideas, will rise above others? Which elements (military, police, churches, intellectual groupings, and so on) will turn against their traditional allies or masters, and which will not? Or will it all slide back into a hardened and more brazen authoritarian grip for another few years or decades?

When there is so much in play, the possibilities for change — for high-amplitude remodulation, quantum leaps, and unpredictable reconfigurations — reach the level of a chaotics that cannot be controlled by any single player. This is when the cosmos is really and truly a *chaosmos,* a fluctuating order that is generative of novelty on such a scale as to be out of anyone's hands. Agency is splintered along a million points of light, points that can only be coordinated through an affective resonance and a momentum that is notoriously difficult to shape and direct.

There are moments that combust (Berlin and Prague 1989, Egypt 2011, Kyïv 2014, Chiapas 1994) and those that fail to combust (Tehran 2009, the protests at COP-15 in Copenhagen, the attempted coup of July 2016 in Turkey). There are moments whose combustion is partial and symbolic, more a redistribution of what is already burning than a combustion of the total field (as with the first public declaration of the Zapatistas on New Year's Day, 1994). Each such moment consists of potentialities emerging out of a mega-constellation of processes and turning in a certain new direction — launching into a different orbit — which resuscitates the set of conditions that gave rise to it, in an altered yet loosely related form. What is time if it is punctuated by swirling moments, some of which leap into a new orbit and some of which fail to do so? It is a cyclical yet always differentiating space.

The larger the constellation, the less predictable its aftermath. The East European revolutions of 1989–90 left behind a mixed legacy, but only a die-hard Bolshevik or authoritarian centralist would argue that they did not open up possibilities that, whether realized so far or not, are better left open than bottled up as they had been under Soviet rule. Ukraine's 2004 Orange

Revolution changed a few things for the better (making media more pluralistic, and giving people a taste, at least, of radical democratic action) but merely realigned others (such as the oligarchic clan formations that had carved up power since Ukraine became independent) in ways that ensured their pliability for larger powers-that-be. Iran 2009 merely slid back into a more hardened authoritarian rule. Iran 1979, on the other hand, catapulted a reserve of seething energy into a form of totalistic authoritarianism that was entirely different from, yet not distinctly better than, what it replaced. Michel Foucault wasn't the only one enthusiastic for that revolution at the time, and many have harkened back to that outcome in warning against enthusiasm over current events.

Eventology 2

The events mentioned so far are cast against the background of a stable, more or less unified human subject. They are events of Humanity. None threaten that subject thoroughly and completely. Which leads us to posit a third kind of event, an Event *sous rature*: not a non-Event, nor (exactly) a non-event, but an ~~Event~~.

Let's take the ~~Event~~ of *La Soufrière,* Werner Herzog's 1977 film about the anticipated eruption in 1976 of an active volcano on the island of Guadeloupe. As in his quasi-science-fictional films — *Fata Morgana* (1971), *Lessons of Darkness* (1992), *Wild Blue Yonder* (2005) — Herzog affects a tone of tender and lyrical, apocalyptic beauty, a resignation in the face of what appears to be humanity's passing. Like *Aguirre, the Wrath of God* (1972), *Heart of Glass* (1976), *Grizzly Man* (2005), and several of his other films, it is also about the human encounter with an indifferent but powerful (capital-n) Nature.

The same elements that later appear in *Lessons of Darkness,* a film about the burning oil fields of Iraq, and in different permutations in several other films — moving vehicle and helicopter shots of a landscape emptied of humans, orchestral music including the Prelude to Act I of Wagner's *Parsifal,* and the feeling of a *waiting,* as if something momentous is about to occur, or has already occurred, or both — are already present in *La Soufrière,* though without the cinematographic intensity of *Lessons of Darkness.* At times the film is like an archaeological dig through an abandoned city, or a devastated one (the town of Saint-Pierre in Martinique). At others it is about sheer contact — between the camera and the world — and about its embarrassed failure, the "inevitable catastrophe that did not take place." This is the failure that, Herzog seems to be suggesting, haunts the *cinéma vérité* desire to be there when *It,* whatever It may be, occurs.

Like most of Herzog's films, *La Soufrière* blurs several sets of lines: between documentary and fiction (a line that Herzog prides himself on dissolving, though here he hews closer to the first pole), between observation and performative enactment (in that his own persona is ever-present — here taking his crew up to the caldera to poke their camera inside the steaming volcano, as if to dare nature to scald them with some smoke and ash), and between the hilarious and the deadly serious. The film highlights the barbed irony that when, in 1902, the inhabitants of neighboring Martinique were preparing to leave before an anticipated volcanic eruption, their governor persuaded them to stay; 30,000 died. Now, seventy-five years later, the inhabitants left (except for the few that Herzog's crew finds and interviews, and of course, Herzog himself, attracted to the volcano like a moth to the flame). And the volcano... balked.

Herzog notes an "embarrassment" in this, "something pathetic for us in the shooting of this picture," in that the film becomes "a report on an inevitable catastrophe that did not take place." Catastrophe here, however, is accompanied with pathos and wry comedy, as with the schmaltzy, orchestral rendition of Eric Carmen's pop hit "All By Myself," its melody taken from Rachmaninoff's Second Piano Concerto, adding a layer of surreality to the camera's panning across the island's vacated landscapes. (Anyone who has heard the Carmen song — "All by myself,/ Don't want to be/ All by myself/ Anymore" — knows it is the kind of melody that can never be unheard, even if the chorus isn't actually heard in the film.)

Or take *Lessons of Darkness,* a film composed of documentary images of the burning oil fields of Kuwait in the wake of the First Gulf War of 1990–91. Herzog shows little interest in the film in helping us understand why the war occurred or who should be held responsible for it. Instead, he presents us with just the images themselves clothed in the quasi-science-fictional, apocalyptic garb of his occasional voice-over narration and subtitles: "A planet in our solar system," "A Capital City," "The War," "After the Battle," "Finds from Torture Chambers," "Satan's National Park," "And a Smoke Arose Like a Smoke from a Furnace," and "I am so tired from sighing; Lord, let it be night." The result is an ironic apocalypse of a hell on earth that is visually sublime but politically intangible — "a requiem," as he has called it, "for a planet that we ourselves have destroyed."[54] Like an extraterrestrial visitor to the post-apocalypse, Herzog is vulnerable here to the same critiques that followers of deep ecology have faced for years: that by identifying the perpetrators of the ecological crisis with an all-embracing "us," we lose the political precision necessary for understanding how it came about, who has benefited from it, who has suffered most, and how to challenge the institutional actors responsible for it.

Yet Herzog's artistic decisions can be defended on the grounds that we already knew enough about the war. Viewers at the time had already seen the videogame-like images that characterized American media coverage of the war, and they were likely to already have well-formed opinions about the justifications for the war. With its "stubborn refusal to contextualize itself," as Nadia Bozak puts it, the film intended to present the images *differently.* Bozak writes that in contrast to the frenzy of cable television coverage of the war, *Lessons of Darkness* "slows down and even fossilizes the events of the war, turning fire-fighting machinery into dinosaurs, abandoned weaponry into ancient bones."[55] Such aestheticization had long been Herzog's response to the politi-

---

54 Paul Cronin, ed., *Herzog on Herzog* (London: Faber and Faber, 2002), 249.

55 Nadia Bozak, "Firepower: Herzog's Pure Cinema as the Internal Combustion of War," *CineAction* 68 (2006): 18–25, at 24.

cal violence of the world. In a 1979 interview, he stated that "we live in a society that has *no* adequate images anymore" and that "if we do not find adequate images and an adequate language for our civilization with which to express them, we will die out like the dinosaurs." Referring to the environmental issues of the time, he continued: "We have already recognized that problems like the energy shortage or the overpopulation of the world are great dangers for our society and for our kind of civilization, but I think that it has not been understood widely enough that we absolutely *need* new images."[56] If this was true in the 1970s, one would presume it no less true in the 1990s, and perhaps much more so in the second and third decades of the twenty-first century.

The newness of Herzog's images can be disputed. They are, after all, a reiteration of well-known western tropes: apocalypse, humanity's decline, and the futility of hope, all set to a soundtrack of Wagner, Mahler, Prokofiev, Verdi, Schubert, Grieg, and Arvo Pärt. My interest in these images is that the event they point to is not an event that has actually happened, but nor is it an event that *can* happen — to a subject that experiences events, that *lives through* them, that survives them. The ~~Event~~ can never be witnessed fully insofar as it undermines the very subjectivity, the very witnessing capacity, of those for whom it is an ~~Event~~. It can only be ever gestured at, only witnessed through its before and its after, its ominous, rumbling premonitions and its decisive yet ambiguous aftermath, an aftermath that remains ever fictional, virtual, ever on the horizon, but never fully present.

Unlike Alain Badiou's "Event,"[57] the Herzogian ~~Event~~ is not historical. It is not a lightning streak that marks history with the shadow of its exposure — as with May '68, or the Russian or French or American revolutions, or the messianic event that initiated the history of Christendom (alongside its Pauline recognition, from which the historical event of "Jesus of Nazareth"

---

56 Werner Herzog, Roger Ebert, and Gene Walsh, *Images at the Horizon: A Workshop with Werner Herzog* (Chicago: Facets Multimedia, 1979), 21.

57 Badiou, *Being and Event.*

can hardly be separated). Rather, the ~~Event~~ is one before which humanity pales into insignificance, even if our creative capacity to reach out to that ~~Event~~ is worth celebrating (as Herzog does). The ~~Event~~ is closer to an anti-Event, a form of anti-matter to the matter of human events (or Events). And Herzog, sublime ironist that he is, takes this Derridean absence of Eventness to be part of the ~~Evental~~ structure.

Introducing his translation of *Feu la cendre* (*Cinders*), Jacques Derrida's poetic meditation on time, loss, language, and trauma, Ned Lukacher asks, "At what temperature do words burst into flame? Is language itself what remains of a burning?"[58] Derrida's reference point is the Holocaust, but it is also the entry into language, which resonates with Jacques Lacan's notion of a gap between the Real and the Symbolic. With its implied reference to the cultural memory of Pompeii — Western civilization's archetypal reference point for volcanically cataclysmic trauma — Herzog's *La Soufrière* dwells on the signature of the ~~Event~~. Like a nuclear explosion that leaves its radioactive shadow splayed across everything, the traumatic Event leaves everything askew, haunted by a spectre and ringing with inaudible or incomprehensible sounds. The vacated city, the empty landscape, the city frozen in time, with its illegible ciphers, the ~~Event~~ is an Event we can never return to because it has not yet happened, but which we can nevertheless perpetually circle around. Something at its core eludes us like a black hole that sucks its own reality away from our efforts to find it.

That ~~Event~~ today goes by the name of the Anthropocene, if only because that name projects forward to a time when the present will have become covered over, one layer sandwiched between others in a past that is only accessible through its cinders. A time when time as we know it (or don't, rather) will have overcome the us who know it, along with the time in which it was known.

---

58 Ned Lukacher, "Introduction: Mourning Becomes Telepathy," in Jacques Derrida, *Cinders*, ed. and trans. Ned Lukacher (Lincoln: University of Nebraska Press, 1991), 3.

The eruption of Eyjafjallajökull as seen from Þórolsfell on May 10, 2010. Photo by David Karnå/Wikimedia Commons.

It eludes us because it is no longer there: once we have recognized it, it is gone. That, after all, is the nature of dwelling in a universe of perpetual becoming that is also a perpetual perishing.

Glimpses of the ~~Event~~ have been around forever; we like to call them "sublime." In modern times, science has brought many to us. Geology in its emergence portended a vastness that threatened common conceptions of humanity's centrality to all things. In recent years, there has emerged a veritable industry of such posthuman Events, found in books like Alan Weisman's *The World Without Us* and media productions like National Geographic's *Aftermath: Population Zero* and The History Channel's *Life After People* (both partly inspired by Weisman's volume).[59] Many of these make use of real places, such as Chernobyl's Zone

---

59 Alan Weisman, *The World Without Us* (New York: St. Martin's Press, 2007); *Aftermath: The World After Humans* (National Geographic/Cream Productions, Canada, 2008); *Life After People* (dir. David De Vries, History Channel, USA, 2008).

of Alienation (the roughly 1000-square-mile zone evacuated after the 1986 nuclear accident, to which I will return in Part 3), to depict this rendering of human absence. In this sense, there are real places that have become emblems, reminders, of this ~~Event~~ of our extinction.

There is, in all of this, a dialectic between Events and ~~Events~~. What better name, one might wonder, for this dialectic than Eyjafjallajökull? As an Icelandic tourist site put it in 2010, under the redundantly emphatic heading "No reason for travelers to worry":

> There are no reasons for travelers to worry about their trip to Iceland. This is a small volcano. Yet immensely beautiful and uniquely situated in stunning surroundings. The lava waterfalls tumbling down hundres of meters are a lifetime memory for all that can behold it! [...] It is difficult to predict how long the volcanic eruption will last. It could end tomorrow but it could also last for days, weeks or even months. All the more reason to COME NOW and see nature at its finest!"

Come. See. Nature at its finest. Unlike Herzog's Soufrière, Eyjafjallajökull blew...

Humanity's extinction, like the end of the world and the end of the self, is the primal extinction that defines us (to the extent that there is an "us") in our finitude and our ultimate emptiness. This posthuman gesture is toward a beyond that is familiar to the tradition of apophatic mysticism, which has carved out a less than comfortable home within Buddhist, Christian, and other mystical traditions (and to be explored more in Part Two).

In the words ascribed to the bodhisattva Avalokiteshvara by the Buddhist text known across East Asia as the "Heart Sutra," we are exhorted to go altogether beyond: *Gate gate pāragate pārasaṃgate bodhi svāhā!* "Gone, gone, gone beyond, gone altogether beyond. Oh what an awakening, all hail!"[60] Going be-

---

60 This translation of the famous mantra from the Heart Sutra, the most renowned of Buddhist sutras (teachings) in much of the East Asian world, is

yond humanism, beyond anthropocentrism, and even beyond the possibility of a world that is knowable to us or to anyone who identifies with our "us."

This is its impossibility, and thus its Reality. As Tweedledee remarked to Alice in response to her protestations that she was real: "You won't make yourself a bit realer by crying." Perhaps he meant: you, humanity, will only make yourselves a *bit* realer by crying. But a bit realer is not quite ~~Reality~~ itself, which is, and will remain, forever inaccessible. Always beyond.

But then so is humanity itself. Ever beyond our reach. Which is ~~Reality~~.

Edward Conze's; see Conze, *Buddhist Scriptures* (New York: Penguin, 1959), 164. On the Heart Sutra, see Kazuaki Tanahashi, *The Heart Sutra: A Comprehensive Guide to the Classic of Mahayana Buddhism* (Boulder: Shambhala, 2016).

2

ENGAGING THE ACT:
WHAT A BODYMIND CAN DO

Returning to immanence

Going beyond, or remaining here: that is the decision-point of every decision, the openness at the heart of every becoming, the difference that differentiates each repetition from the same. How to *remain* here and go *beyond* at the same time.

Here we come to the paradox of the immanent. The word "immanence" has become a slippery signifier in continental philosophy. In a work examining four currently influential French philosophers of immanence — Gilles Deleuze, Alain Badiou, Michel Henry, and François Laruelle — John Mullarkey notes that "Immanence is everywhere, but its meaning is completely open: that is our problem." He then provides four "lexical definitions" of immanence: "'Existing or remaining within'; being 'inherent'; being restricted entirely to some 'inside'; existing and acting 'within the physical world.'"[1]

Immanence here, and most commonly, is counterposed against transcendence: either the world accounts for itself, needing no further explanation, or we must appeal to larger forces — God or gods, spirits, the Cogito, Being, Ideas, the tran-

---

1 John Mullarkey, *Post-Continental Philosophy: An Outline* (London: Continuum, 2006), 20.

scendental consciousness, non-material forces of one kind or another, and so on — something that transcends the world and gives it its dynamism, its reason, or its meaning. In religious, and especially monotheistic, thinking, a theology of transcendence provides the background of all thinking. (Which, ironically, makes it immanent to all thinking.) By contrast, a theology of immanence is one that posits that god(s) or spirit(s) are not relegated to some heavenly realm from which access is closely guarded, but that, if they are to be found at all, they will be found in the world, in matter, and at the heart of every moment. (In the reaching.)

Putting it this way suggests the terms are always relative: if there is transcendence, it is because we have restricted the immanent to a certain domain — materiality, or physical law, or something else — and thereby rendered it insufficient. But if the world is unbounded, then its immanence is always open. That is the leap of faith in the philosophies of Deleuze and Whitehead, to name two philosophers of "immanent transcendence." At the heart of the world, and of things, is an openness that breaks apart the causal dependencies that would otherwise lock the universe into stasis.

All four of Mullarkey's thinkers of immanence are process philosophers of a sort: they seek "process truth (for Badiou); process vitalism (for Deleuze); process theoretics (for Laruelle); process phenomenology (for Henry). In each case," Mullarkey continues, "there is a focus on how immanence relates to change."[2] Deleuze differs from the others in his insistence that there are two "worlds" within the immanent: an actual world that is conditioned by a virtual world, for which repetition always comes with difference. The immanent, for Deleuze, is itself the source of novelty. Creativity, or creative repetition, as it is for Whitehead, is at the core of becoming; and becoming is all that there is. This suggests not that there is no transcendence, but that transcendence is *of* the immanent, that it is the openness at its heart. Or as Deleuze puts it in one of his last writings, entitled

---

2   Ibid., 21.

"Immanence: A Life," the transcendent precedes "the world of the subject and the object,"[3] and immanence is itself a "transcendental field," an activity that can only be ascribed to the sheer indefiniteness of "a life":

> A life is everywhere, in all the moments that a given living subject goes through and that are measured by given lived objects: an immanent life carrying with it the events or singularities that are merely actualized in subjects and objects. This indefinite life does not itself have moments [...], but only between-times, between-moments.[4]

Whitehead, likewise, writes:

> The only intelligible doctrine of causation is founded on the doctrine of immanence. Each occasion presupposes the antecedent world as active in its own nature. [...] We are in the world and the world is in us. [...] The body is ours, and we are an activity within our body.[5]

Taking issue with the common translation of Descartes' "Cogito, ergo sum" as "I *think*, therefore I am," Whitehead writes:

> I find myself as essentially a unity of emotions, enjoyments, hopes, fears, regrets, valuations of alternatives, decisions — all of them subjective reactions to the environment as active in my nature. My unity [...] is my process of shaping this welter of material into a consistent pattern of feelings.[6]

There are three elements making up this "unity":

---

3 Gilles Deleuze, *Pure Immanence: Essays on a Life,* trans. Anne Boyman (New York: Zone Books, 2001), 25.
4 Ibid., 29.
5 Alfred North Whitehead, *Modes of Thought* (New York: Free Press, 1968), 226–27.
6 Ibid., 228.

If we stress the role of the environment, this process is *causation*. If we stress the role of my immediate pattern of active enjoyment, this process is *self-creation*. If we stress the role of the conceptual anticipation of the future whose existence is a necessity in the nature of the present, this process is the teleological *aim* at some ideal in the future. This aim, however, is not really beyond the present process. For the aim at the future is an enjoyment in the present.[7]

Life, he continues, "is the enjoyment of emotion, derived from the past and aimed at the future. [...] Each occasion is an activity of concern, in the Quaker sense of that term. It is the conjunction of transcendence and immanence."[8]

In a time of AnthropoCapitalist turbulence, how might we take this enjoyment of the present and hurl it into an objective engagement with the things that concern us deeply?

A time of suffering

There will be death and dying and weeping there, and gnashing of teeth. There will be suffering.

To point to something like this today is to risk discrediting the finger one points with. Suffering is, suffering will be: such was the message of Siddhartha Gautama, the Buddha, twenty-five centuries ago. Saying that in a world of apparent plenty sounds quaintly doomish. Is the universe a universe of (only) suffering? Does the extent and quantity of suffering outmatch

---

7   Ibid., 227–28.

8   Ibid., 229–30. For other articulations of "immanent transcendence" see Patrice Haynes, *Immanent Transcendence: Reconfiguring Materialism in Continental Philosophy* (New York: Bloomsbury, 2012); James Williams, "Immanence and Transcendence as Inseparable Processes: On the Relevance of Arguments from Whitehead to Deleuze Interpretation," *Deleuze Studies* 4, no. 1 (2010): 94–106; Kenneth Inada, "Immanent Transcendence: The Possibility of an East-West Philosophical Dialogue," *Journal of Chinese Philosophy* 35, no. 3 (2008): 493–510; Jan Engberts, "Immanent Transcendence in Chinese and Western Process Thinking," *Philosophy Study* 2, no. 6 (2012): 377–83; and the work of Japanese Kyoto School philosopher Nishida Kitaro.

the extent and quantity of hope, of joy, or of the satisfaction (however temporary) of desires, projects, and pursuits? On a cosmic scale, how could we even begin to know the answer to that calculus? Is it not a bit comical to ask it today?

In times of catastrophe, the only genuine question is what to do now. This is not because of the catastrophe. If the calls of catastrophe turn out to be false alarms, the question will still be what to do now. To an eventologist, that is always the question.

When Siddhartha Gautama developed an analysis of the fundamental dissatisfaction at the heart of human existence, he (or his followers) characterized it according to a medical model, with a diagnosis, an etiology, a prognosis, and a prescription for treatment. His Four Noble Truths denote four fundamental facts attested to by the Buddha: the fact of *dukkha,* or existential suffering; the cause of it, which is craving for and attachment to that which passes; the possibility of eliminating that cause; and the path toward that elimination.[9]

Following a similar model today, we might try to diagnose something that is specific and unique to our time. Let us call it the *excess* suffering attributable to the processes of the AnthropoCapitalocene. Its four truths run roughly parallel to the Buddha's.

1. **The Existence of Excess Suffering:** We all hunger, thirst, experience misfortune, get sick, witness others' deaths, and die ourselves. But some get sick more often, experience more misfortune than others, and die more often (metaphorically speaking, but also statistically) for reasons that are not "natural," but that are political and economic in origin. While such suffering has gone on for as long as humans have had the polities and economies that generate it, its quantity has taken a measurable upward curve in

---

9   Buddhism includes a vast philosophical tradition, and even summarizing something as simple as its "Four Noble Truths" is tricky territory. For those interested in Buddhist philosophy's intersections and differences from major western philosophical positions, I strongly recommend Jay Garfield's *Engaging Buddhism: Why It Matters to Philosophy* (New York: Oxford University Press, 2015).

recent times. In conditions of the A/Cene, it is likely to continue increasing. It constitutes a new turbulence within the fabric of socio-ecological relations on this planet.

2. The Cause of Excess Suffering: This uneven distribution of environmental benefits and risks is produced by a particular system of relations, a system that works through *extractive capitalization,* or the rendering of more and more of the world into ownable resources, tradable commodities, exchangeable labor markets, and opportunities for economic profit. (Capitalization can proceed comfortably even under labels that reject the term "capitalism," as in so-called Communist China or the Soviet Union.) By rendering buried and stored carbon deposits into industrial fuels, this system created the most productive and, at the same time, most destructive civilization in human history. Fossil fuel capitalism in its various forms has created great abundance, but at the price of high health risks, toxic by-products, large-scale disruption of ecosystems, and impending global climate change, with potentially suicidal intensification of risks to humans and nature.[10]

These costs have usually been deflected outward, off-loaded, rather than being accounted for internally. This is a kind of misrecognition by the system of its own nature, a misrecognition Nicholas Mirzoeff has called "auto-immune climate-changing capitalism syndrome," or AICCCS (which rhymes with "aches" and is accompanied by pains).[11] It is a state of "dis-ease," but also

---

10 This argument has been made (with numerous variations) by an expanding cadre of sociologists, geographers, economists, and others. For a few perspectives on it, see Jason W. Moore, *Capitalism in the Web of Life: Ecology and the Accumulation of Capital* (London: Verso, 2015); Tim di Muzio, *Carbon Capitalism: Energy, Social Reproduction and World Order* (London: Rowman & Littlefield, 2015); and R. Scott Frey, Paul K. Gellert, and Harry F. Dahms, eds., *Ecologically Unequal Exchange: Environmental Injustice in Comparative and Historical Perspective* (Cham: Palgrave Macmillan, 2019).

11 Nicholas Mirzoeff, "Autoimmune Climate-Changing Capitalism Syndrome: AICCCS," http://www.nicholasmirzoeff.com/O2012/2012/08/25/autoimmune-climate-changing-capitalism-syndrome-aicccs/.

a form of self-protection for the system as it slowly destroys the basis on which it thrives.

This self-protective deflection of reality has been aided by two "bubbles." The first is a very long-term real estate bubble: the 12,000 year Holocene Bubble that humans and our companions have flourished within, but which now is bursting. As it bursts, the "established patterns and regularity of Holocene phenology" are "unraveling," in Glenn Albrecht's words. They are likely to be followed by a "new abnormal" in which "life will be characterised by uncertainty, unpredictability, genuine chaos and relentless change. Earth distress, as manifest in global warming, changing climates, erratic weather, acidifying oceans, disease pandemics, species endangerment and extinction, bio-accumulation of toxins and the overwhelming physical impact of exponentially-expanding human development will have its correlates in human physical and mental distress."[12]

The second bubble is a shorter term, more intensive perceptual (and political-economic) bubble, a Bubble of Willed Ignorance. This is the real or pretended ignorance about interdependency and global injustice that is perpetuated within systems of media paid for and dominated by the classes that benefit most from the A/Cene regime.

3. The Healing of Excess Suffering: It is possible to eliminate this excess socio-ecological suffering in at least two related ways: by internalizing the costs, or the "bads," so that they are factored into the production of the "goods"; and by spreading the goods and bads much more justly and evenly. The first is a form of *industrial ecology,* requiring the transformation of systems of production and consumption from open and debt-bearing ones into closed-loop, regenerative ones; it is mostly a technical task. The second is a form of *economic* (but not only economic) *democ-*

---

12 Glenn Albrecht, "Exiting the Anthropocene and Entering the Symbiocene," *Minding Nature* 9, no. 2 (2016), https://www.humansandnature.org/exiting-the-anthropocene-and-entering-the-symbiocene.

racy: it would democratize decisions over what to produce and how to produce it; this is a mostly political task.

Astrobiologist Adam Frank has suggested that energy-intensive planetary civilizations like ours can expect to face a "sustainability bottleneck" once we begin to use up the stored carbon of millennia.[13] The fact that the universe apparently generates the conditions for the emergence of such civilizations (we are, in fact, here) tells us that, to the best of our guesses, we are part of a game of chance and of skill, a kind of cosmic evolutionary process, which in turn gives us a realistic hope that we might make it through. (Or not.) Realistically speaking, our chances are somewhere between abysmal and possible. So it makes sense to try.

4. The Path Forward, or the Nimble Path of Liberation: Pooling together what we know from a range of efforts to understand environmental issues scientifically, social-scientifically, and humanistically, it is reasonable to conclude that the path forward requires at least the following four elements.

Technical knowledge: We need scientific data gathering, which remains the main source for our knowledge about the state of the Earth's biogeophysical systems. We also need the engineering know-how for addressing specific technical challenges — in energy production, food production, infrastructure, ecology, and many other areas. Where scientists often consider this knowledge to be the main requirement, humanists would respond that we have plenty of it to work with, but that it alone is simply far from enough.

Institutional Capacity: Addressing problems requires having the organizational, institutional, and functional mechanisms for doing that at all levels, from the local to the regional, national, and transnational. We are beginning to develop institutional capacities locally in select places, and globally through interna-

---

13 Adam Frank, "Is a Climate Disaster Inevitable?" *New York Times Sunday Review,* January 17, 2015, http://www.nytimes.com/2015/01/18/opinion/sunday/is-a-climate-disaster-inevitable.html.

tional institutions. There are examples of communities, cities, and nations taking the lead on developing policies to facilitate transition to a more just and sustainable relationality. But there is a long way to go. If, on a scale of 1 to 10, with 10 as the goal, our knowledge (the first of these four elements) has achieved a 7 or 8, our institutional capacity is hovering down somewhere around a 3 or 4 at best.

Coherent, integrative, and motivating images and narratives: We need images and narratives that could reframe people's awareness of their place in time and in space toward one that is more enabling of the radical actions that are called for. While scientists often think of the arts and humanities as a handmaiden for communicating scientific knowledge (the first element) to the broader public, humanists and artists insist that there be a two-way movement between the two realms, and that working with image, discourse, and narrative is both more complicated and quite autonomous from anything generated by science. This area is, rightly, where the critical and creative work of the eco-arts and humanities is focused; its lessons frame the background of this book.[14] But it, too, is not enough.

Affective preparedness: No matter how much information, institutional capacity, and "storied imagery" there is, people will not move into action until they are *affectively prepared* for doing that. And until circumstances create an opening for it. Those circumstances tend to be rapid events: eco-disasters, political shock waves, or revolutionary situations that emerge unpredictably, revealing business-as-usual to be inadequate and calling forth rapid and responsive action. They tend to be Events, which

14 On the eco-arts, see, for instance, Linda Weintraub, *To Life: Eco Art in Pursuit of a Sustainable Planet* (Berkeley: University of California Press, 2012), and T.J. Demos, *Decolonizing Nature: Contemporary Art and the Politics of Ecology* (Berlin: Sternberg Press, 2016). On the environmental humanities, see Robert S. Emmett and David E. Nye, *The Environmental Humanities: A Critical Introduction* (Cambridge: MIT Press, 2017); Serpil Oppermann and Serenella Iovino, eds., *Environmental Humanities: Voices from the Anthropocene* (London: Rowman and Littlefield, 2017); Ursula Heise, Jon Christensen, and Michelle Niemann, eds., *The Routledge Companion to the Environmental Humanities* (London: Routledge, 2017).

are unpredictable in their genesis and in the trajectories they make possible. Artists are often more sensitive than others to this affective level. But what needs more thinking today are the critical connections between it and the infrastructural — social media, organizational links between diverse groups around the world, and so on.

More crucially, developing a sense of agency adequate to the demands of the A/Cene requires the cultivation of a kind of engaged Anthropocenic mindfulness (or bodymindfulness, bodymind-heartfulness, bodymind-soulfulness). This means an ability to act with the full awareness of how our actions play into the aesthetic, ethical, and political-ecological dynamics of the A/Cene. Those dynamics include multiple legacies of social and ecological violence rooted in colonialism, racism, sexism and heterosexism, classism, inter-ethnic and inter-religious rivalry, and other forms of oppression and strife. But they also include multiple desires and visions for collective betterment, which are in turn rooted in real experiences of wonder, transcendence of personal limits or fears, and empathic embrace of others (including nonhuman others). The complexity of both the "negative" and the "positive" kinds of relations is difficult to come to terms with in one's own life; doing the same with one's interactions with others is all the more difficult. It requires skillful practice.

Where do we begin finding this sort of affective preparedness? In what follows, I will try to suggest a few tools for doing that. They are not meant to replace others — variations of psychotherapy, spiritual or somatic practices, or collective activities of one kind or another, from religious ceremonializing to political organizing to direct action. But I hope they can supplement the other kinds of strategies. They are intended to do that by making process-relational insights more approachable, experienceable, and "intuitive," such that the others are seen as examples within an underlying process of "process-relationalizing."

Situating ourselves

Before one can act to change anything significant, anything that requires determination and resolve, it is important to be able to account for one's situation. That means being able to take it on and embrace it as one's own, with one's full existential capacity.

If the global predicament as I have described it rings true to any significant degree, then genuine understanding of that predicament — the sort of understanding that can inform effective action — can only occur through understanding one's own situatedness within it. That means that this predicament will be a different one for a migrant farm laborer, an Asian or African textile worker, or an aids sufferer or forced prostitute than it will be for a university professor, a Hollywood actor, or a bank executive. Some have great difficulty extricating themselves from precarity; others have little direct experience of it.

If you are reading this book, you are likely to be in the class of people with the luxury to read such books — which means somewhere in the middle of the spectrum, though likely closer to the top, on a global scale, than to the bottom. This means you are either capable of *feeling* the predicament in some of its daily, embodied dimensions, or at least able to imagine those dimensions from reports, literary or cinematic depictions, or other forms of cultivated empathy. Those dimensions might include experiencing daily anxieties — ranging from eating disorders to chronic depression to lesser or greater degrees of trauma-induced stress stemming from the competitive pressures of consumer-capitalist industrialism, systemic racism and sexism, and the like.

To be sure, we may all be alienated (as Marx described) from our work, or from our places of residence, or from those around us. But many of us also feel a sense of possibility: we have career options we can choose from, products or gadgets we might buy that could enhance our enjoyment of life, physical or other kinds of practices we could try on for size, places we could visit, foods we could eat. The global middle class is that class for whom the world may be its oyster, but the oyster shell weighs more or less heavily on our backs at least part of the time (if only in our dreams and nightmares).

If we think of our personal feeling of that predicament as a form of Peircean *firstness,* then gauging our capacities for action is the entry point to *secondness*. What can I do about the world from where I am? What are the hinges or action-points from which I can act? How can I act, or who could I *become* in order to be able to act effectively? With whom, and in what contexts of collective endeavor? Effective or satisfying action is likely to involve some modification of our habits — habits of perception, of interaction, and of understanding. (Those will be explored momentarily.)

Finally, *thirdness* would relate to the larger vision that might draw forward such action, to which it would contribute and which it would enable. Some variation of the account offered in the preceding section ("A time of suffering") may suffice to provide a working understanding of the global predicament. (Consider it an example, then write your own.) To be effective, a Peircean approach would insist that any such vision be triadic: it should convey a *sense of the reality* of the day-to-day *and* excess sufferings of the A/Cene; a sense of the *possibilities for responding* to those sufferings creatively; and a *vision* of how those possibilities might figure into the longer-term crap-shoot of an open-ended cosmic process. Put differently, these are: a *feel* for the situation, a *method* for action to overcome or transform that situation, and an *aim* or rationale for why it should be bothered with at all.

A Peircean approach insists that each of those three steps is necessary. (I challenge you to propose a variation that fails to include one of the three, and then to make that variation viable.) Much of what will follow will continue to reiterate this triad, so we might as well line up some terms to help us think it:

Firstness	Secondness	Thirdness
Feeling	Action	Realization
What	How	Why
Object(ivation)	Method	Subject(ivation)
Aesthetics	Ethics	Logic
Quality	Resistance	Representation

But first, as always, we must start with the moment.

Philosophy of the moment

In the shadow of the Anthropocene, philosophical speculation is best applied to life so as to change that life. Not (necessarily) because of the possibility of doom, but simply because that is the only task allowable to a process-relational realist. This may not be the common understanding of what philosophers do today, but it has arguably been at the heart of philosophy since ancient times.

Philosophical historian Pierre Hadot has been the most articulate recent proponent of this view, finding the notion of "philosophy as a way of life" — accompanied by rigorous spiritual practices — in Plato, Aristotle, the Stoics, the Epicureans, the Cynics, the Neoplatonists, and numerous other ancient and (less frequently) modern philosophers. A similar model held among many of the philosophers of ancient India, China, and elsewhere. It has held also for many in the American pragmatist tradition of Peirce, James, and Dewey, and has been revived not only in popular books like *Zen and the Art of Motorcycle Maintenance* or in *Philosophy Now* magazine, but also in the thought of influential Continental philosophers, from the existentialists to Deleuze, the later Foucault, and Peter Sloterdijk. Michel Foucault's late focus on the "aesthetics of existence" and the "arts of the self" almost singlehandedly aimed to revive this tradition.[15]

---

15 See Pierre Hadot, *Philosophy as a Way of Life: Spiritual Exercises from Socrates to Foucault,* trans. Michael Chase, (Oxford: Blackwell, 1995); Pierre

To the extent that there is a loose consensus within the process-relational tradition on what constitutes a philosophy of life, its core would likely include two shared intuitions. The first is a *trust in life process,* or as Gilles Deleuze calls it, a "belief in this world," which he explains is also "a link between man and the world."[16] Elucidating Deleuze's phrase, Lars Tonder notes that "to believe in this world" is "to perpetuate life, to affirm its cracks and dissonances as sites of undisclosed potentiality."[17] The second intuition is a *willingness to experiment* — an openness and even eagerness to engage in things decisively so as to see where they will go, and a willingness to change directions when it becomes evident that they aren't going where they might *better* go.

These are not universally held intuitions. Among many Buddhists, for instance, life process is sometimes seen as unreliable to the point of being illusory. (Here is where it's worth distinguishing between life-affirming and life-escaping wings of the twenty-five century tradition of Buddhist thought.) But both of these views make clear why the focus of any process-relational *practice* is on the present moment.

The present moment is our most direct foothold in experience. The moment is also the basic unit of experiential coherence, and the locus of whatever agency is to be had in experi-

Hadot, *What is Ancient Philosophy?,* trans. Michael Chase (Cambridge: Harvard University Press, 2002); Pierre Hadot, *The Present Alone Is Our Happiness: Conversations with Jeannie Carlier and Arnold I. Davidson,* trans. Marc Djaballah (Stanford University Press, 2009); and, for slightly divergent perspectives, John M. Cooper, *Pursuits of Wisdom: Six Ways of Life in Ancient Philosophy from Socrates to Plotinus* (Princeton: Princeton University Press, 2012); Horst Hutter, *Shaping the Future: Nietzsche's New Regime of the Soul and Its Ascetic Practices* (London: Lexington, 2006); Edward F. McGushin, *Foucault's Askesis: An Introduction to the Philosophical Life* (Evanston: Northwestern University Press, 2007); Richard Shusterman, *Body Consciousness: A Philosophy of Mindfulness and Somaesthetics* (Cambridge University Press, 2008); Peter Sloterdijk, *You Must Change Your Life!* (Cambridge: Polity, 2013).

16 Gilles Deleuze, *Cinema 2: The Time Image,* trans. Hugh Tomlinson and Robert Galeta (London: Continuum, 1989/2005), 166.

17 Lars Tonder, "A Secular Age: Spinoza's Immanence," *The Immanent Frame,* December 5, 2007, https://tif.ssrc.org/2007/12/05/spinozas-immanence/.

ence. Analogous to what in a film would be a "scene," moments attain toward a unity within the multiplicity of elements that make them up and the ambiguity of those elements' involvement in them (since those elements usually precede the moment and continue on after it has ended). Moments occur at a mesocosmic level — they are neither the kind of entity Whitehead called the "actual occasion" nor the event that I have called an "Event." They are something more experientially tangible than either.

Understanding a moment of experience is useful for the bearer of it insofar as it allows one to get a handle on what is happening here and now and what one can do within the possibilities on offer. Isolating or slowing down a moment allows us to analyze what our range of action is. It also enables us, ultimately (with dedicated practice), to begin to see the nature of experience as a dynamic flow characterized by the mutual co-arising of subjectivity and objectivity. In turn, a more accurate understanding of the nature of reality contributes to more effective engagements with that reality.

Following our Peircean-Whiteheadian approach, we could characterize a moment in two primary ways. The first analyzes it into its *firstnesses*, or things in their "in-themselfness," their thusness; its *secondnesses*, or existential action-capacities — the living edges of firstness grappling against each other in the motion of effortful engagement; and its *thirdnesses*, or significances taking account of such encounters of secondness.

Walking in the woods with my young son on my back one afternoon, I heard sounds that struck me in their sonic distinctiveness, simply as they were; I responded to these sounds with an affective thrust — a quickened heartbeat, a prick of the ears, a sudden stop, an unpremeditated gesture to my son to listen or look in *that* direction; and I recognized some of the sounds via thoughts like "There's that thing I heard before, which sounds like a woodpecker, and I wonder what sort of woodpecker has made its way over here this week," and "It's a beautiful spring here this year, isn't it?" While my hearing the sounds was already a *second*, the sounds in themselves (apart from any perception of them) were *firsts*; the reactions were *seconds*; and the thoughts or meanings arising from and accompanying those reactions were *thirds*.

Alternatively, a moment can be characterized by the dynamic co-arising of subjectivity (which is a thirdness), objectivity (in and through secondness), and withdrawal or perishing. The first of these co-active elements, *subjectivation*, is what occurs when I recognize sounds and make some sense of them: "I wonder what sort of woodpecker that is" and "It's a beautiful spring this year" contribute to the narrative timeline I have of living where I do, in northern Vermont; of recognizing birds (as poorly as I do) and noticing their comings and goings over time; and of living (and constructing) my life in the context of seasonal changes, moments and conversations with my son, public debates over global warming, and much more. At the same time, my gesture to my son becomes an invitation for *his* subjectivation; and my stopping and listening to the bird becomes an invitation to *that bird's* subjectivation, wherein it might notice me and sing in some particular way in recognition of a new listener.

The second element, *objectivation*, is the *other* thing that happens when I recognize sounds and make some sense of them: that sound becomes "*that* woodpecker," a sequence of seeings and hearings becomes "this spring," and so on. Things become pinned to labels (verbal or other kinds) whereby they can be stitched into a fabric of habitual responses, incorporations, harnessings. They, like any commons, can be "enclosed" into the narrative fabric that comes to constitute a "self" and a world.

And thirdly, there is the *withdrawal* of these others even as I have pulled them into these semiotic arrangements. The sound ended, the bird flew off, the moment passed. All the other firsts that I failed to notice or to capture in my webs of meaning — all are gone to me, swift as a shadow disappears when a light is switched on. Withdrawal constitutes the imperceptible background of the moment. It becomes lost to experience, or to future experience (though these are not identical destinies).

Sensings

Let us now build up a more sophisticated methodology for accessing the present moment.

The easiest way to do this is to begin with the feeling of one's self: Who or what am I, you, us? *How* are we, and *where* are we? Where and how do we arise and find ourselves — in the midst of what actions, what becomings? And finding ourselves, what can we do with ourselves?

We arise at decision points, poised at new folds in the fabric of eventness. The "we" that do this are everyone: humans (sort of), mitochondria (sort of), single-celled organisms (sort of), and whatever else does anything with some sense of the doing. Generalizing about this range of doings is difficult, so it makes sense to start from our own experience and then to speculatively branch outward. What is it that *we* can do at all?

To find out how we in fact do anything, how our machinery works, it is helpful to have a rigorous practice of self-observation based on some language or map of the possibilities. Maps of the psyche are a dime a dozen, but some are more phenomenologically informed and time-tested than others.[18] To continue with our Peircean triadism, it makes sense for us, writer/readers of this book, to look for triadic models. As it turns out, there are several that fit this bill. In what follows, I will propose a map of *doings* that distinguishes between a series of three sensory modalities (because we are sensory-perceptual creatures), three relational categories, and three orientations. Because the senses provide an easy foothold into our experience, and because there exists a simple but effective model for classifying them, let us start there.

Westerners typically think of the senses as being five: seeing, hearing, smelling, tasting, and the vague and overburdened category of "feeling," which others would distinguish into more nuanced subcategories like moving or kinesthetic feeling, gut

---

18 See, for instance, Charles Hampden-Turner's dated yet informative compendium of mental models, *Maps of the Mind* (New York: Macmillan, 1982).

feeling, and others. Helpfully, a model exists that reduces these to three and that maps out well against a series of other "maps of the mind." This model happens to be a perceptive distillation of centuries of quasi-scientific introspective practice associated with Buddhism — primarily Theravada Buddhist practice (especially the Vipassana tradition of mindfulness), with Japanese Zen, Tibetan Vajrayana, and several other reference points. This is a model developed by contemporary meditation teacher and Shingon Buddhist monk Shinzen Young. (It is a model that I encountered through a series of experiential retreats that Young led in Vermont several years ago, and which he has developed into new formats since.[19] Henceforth I'll refer to Young as "Shinzen.")

Shinzen's system describes human subjective experience as phenomenologically distinguishable into three primary fields, spaces, or elements[20]: the visual, the auditory, and the bodily-felt. Each of these is characterized as either internal or external in its orientation, and is labeled with a single word when observed within mindfulness meditation practice: "See" or "Image" for the visual; "Hear," "Sound" (if it is external), or "Talk" (if it is mental-internal) for the auditory; and "Feel" or "Touch," for the bodily-felt. The last of the three includes tactile, olfactory, gustatory, kinesthetic, visceral, affective, and emotional functions, which are grouped into "Feel-Out" for those experienced as external in their source (the first four), and "Feel-In" for sensations that are "internal" to the bodymind (the last three).

---

19 Shinzen Young's websites, unifiedmindfulness.com and Shinzen.org, and his *YouTube* site contain an enormous array of material. See, for instance, the detailed explications of terms in Shinzen Young, "Five Ways to Know Yourself: An Introduction to Basic Mindfulness," 2011–16, http://www.shinzen.org/wp-content/uploads/2016/08/FiveWaystoKnowYourself_ver1.6.pdf. For more general discussion, see Shinzen Young, *The Science of Enlightenment: How Meditation Works* (Sounds True, 2016), and Shinzen Young, "What is Mindfulness? A Contemplative Perspective," in *Handbook of Mindfulness in Education*, eds. Kimberly Schonert-Reichl and Robert Roeser, 29–45 (New York: Springer, 2016).

20 He uses these terms somewhat interchangeably. The account that follows draws in particular on personal conversations and guided exercises conducted between 2010 and 2014.

These three modalities can be conceived as developing somewhat autonomously over the course of human evolution and over the course of individual ontogenesis. First, we learn to *feel* with our bodies — in the oceanic mix of feelings and sounds that occurs in the womb. Then, once born and tasked with the need to make sense of visual experience, we start to *see* things as distinct entities. Finally, we learn the words and the linguistic-discursive constructs that come to shape both our subjectivities and our conceptual worlds for us. Learning to hear is, in this sense, a two-stage process. For the infant in the womb, and perhaps for early humans in the evolution of our senses — ontogenesis and phylogenesis, respectively — distinguishing sounds evolved as part of the repertoire of feeling: kinesthesia, tactility, hapticity, and the like. So it could be treated as an element of "Feel" up until that time when it becomes distinctly linked to verbal and linguistic awareness.

In practice, of course, these three are usually thickly mixed and highly interactive. And over time the three kinds of elements become tangled and knotted into emotionally laden force fields. Distinguishing between them is, in any case, a matter mostly of convenience; they serve as hooks onto which mindfulness practitioners can hang their impressions, sensations, and perceptions as they observe them arising and passing. Sensory blurring and interaction occurs all the time in human experience, but as we are familiarizing ourselves with what our bodymind does, it makes things easier if we can bring some order to it.

There is a provocative correlation to be made between these Buddhist-derived phenomenological categories and psychoanalyst Jacques Lacan's tripartite analysis of the psyche, with its distinction between the Real, the Imaginary, and the Symbolic. For Lacan, the *Real* represents a kind of nondual state of nature, one from which we become alienated as we learn to assume the qualities of socially defined subjective experience. The *Imaginary* represents the image-based world of self-other relations and fantasies that emerge through the "mirror phase," with its recognition of the body that appears in a mirror as the same one that others see when they see "me." Finally, the *Symbolic* is the language- and narrative-based world that "interpellates" or "hails us" into being the kind of subject that finds its uneasy fit in the social world. The first is correlated with bodily feeling, the second with image, and the third with the textualized sound of language.[21] With the movement from the first to the third, the emergent human subject undergoes a rupture between the non-dual, felt-bodily experience of infancy and the subjective constitution of the "self." This rupture plays out differently in different socio-historical conditions, with the characteristic insecurities and pathologies of a society laying themselves onto the subject more or less violently (according to Lacan), but with some sort of rupture or gap being a basic condition of human social existence.

Another model that resonates with Lacan's and, albeit loosely, with Shinzen's is neurophysiologist Paul McLean's triune brain model, which subdivides the brain into three complexes: the *reptilian,* which accounts for instinctual behaviors connected to aggression, dominance, territoriality, and ritual displays; the *paleomammalian,* or limbic system, which supplies the emotion and motivation related to feeding, reproduction, and parenting; and the *neomammalian,* or neocortex, which enables planning, abstract thinking, and language. While the correlations are imprecise, one could easily connect the first with "feeling" and the Real, the second with "seeing" (insofar as it pertains to the soci-

---

21 For Lacan's tripartite description of psychic life, I am relying mostly on secondary literature. See Jacques Lacan, *The Four Fundamental Concepts of Psychoanalysis: The Seminar of Jacques Lacan, Book XI,* ed. Jacques-Alain Miller, trans. Alan Sheridan (New York: W.W. Norton & Co., 1998); Slavoj Žižek, *The Sublime Object of Ideology* (London: Verso, 1989); Philippe Julien, *Jacques Lacan's Return to Freud: The Real, the Symbolic, and the Imaginary* (New York University Press, 1994). In *Gramophone, Film, Typewriter* (Stanford: Stanford University Press, 1999), Friedrich Kittler correlated these three registers with those three technologies: the Real with the gramophone, the Imaginary with cinema, and the Symbolic with the typewriter. Others have correlated them with Peirce's index (with its traces and effects), icon (with its imagery), and symbol; see, for instance, W.J.T. Mitchell, *What Do Images Want? The Lives and Loves of Images* (Chicago: University of Chicago Press, 2005). While somewhat simplified, these correspondences remain provocative.

ality of groups) and the Imaginary, and the third with "hearing" (specifically that of language) and the Symbolic. Of course, neither this nor any other model should be taken as scientifically accurate maps of the brain, even if McLean's was originally intended that way. The carving up of this landscape is best considered somewhat arbitrary, but some kind of carving is necessary, if only to break practical experience down into more workable bits. And this particular tripartite analysis is suggestive in its evocation of sensorily-bound force fields.

Let us assume a loose correspondence between Lacan's and McLean's models. Consider the "rupture" (gap, *sevrage,* "basic fault" in psychoanalyst Michael Balint's terms) that is experienced between the felt (reptilian) Real, the phantasmic (paleomammalian) Imaginary, and/or the linguistic (neocortical) Symbolic. Freudian psychoanalysis works at mitigating the effects of such rupture through its "talking cure," a lengthy (and costly) process that comes with risks of transference and counter-transference and no guarantees of success. Wilhelm Reich built on Freud's insights to develop a physical form of therapy that worked directly with patients' bodily "armoring," that is, with psychosomatic blockages built to prevent the Real from overcoming the Symbolic and/or Imaginary self (allowing for a some hasty overgeneralizing here). Buddhist Vipassana meditation arguably works at the same "rupture" by allowing for the patient accumulation of observations and insights via trained introspection of a kind that "settles" the mind to a lower-level reactivity, such that the basic patterns might become directly evident. Zen Buddhism, in its classic form, does the same through a kind of methodically applied psychological sleight-of-hand that is highly dependent on a good teacher and setting (and subject to more particular pitfalls because of this). Tibetan Vajrayana Buddhism, in turn, works at it through a kind of "re-patterning" using various tools of sensory, bodily, emotional, and linguistic-imagistic practice; but this takes time and carries its own risks. Jungian analysis can be seen as a mix of the psychoanalytic talking cure and the Vajrayana-style multi-modal approach. Hermetic and esoteric forms of magical practice offer combinations of one type or another. Each of these takes place within a social context that, over time, can become encrusted with its own institutional misdirections and derangements, so frequent modification and renewal might be recommended in order to keep things operating more or less as they were intended.

A more modern approach like Shinzen's provides a toolbox and "playbook" that lets users experiment on their own, with guidance available but not required. The point is that through regular practice one can gain leverage points into the dynamic structure of subjective experience, and, with guidance, to work toward untangling that structure and peering "beneath" or "behind" it to the underlying nature of things. A related method, Russian-Armenian spiritual philosopher G.I. Gurdjieff's, stressed practices of "self-remembering" and self-observation informed by a similar model of a "triune brain" and a startlingly Peircean, if independently developed, "Law of Three."[22]

The first methods taught in Shinzen's system are typically those of "Focusing In," whereby one learns to note and distinguish between internally produced feelings (Feel), sights (See), and sounds (Hear), and "Focusing Out," which does the same with sensations, images, and sounds in or of the world around us. These three sets — Feel-In and Feel-Out, See-In and See-Out, Hear-In and Hear-Out — respectively make up the internal and external coordinate spaces of subjective experience.

Normally the "internal" ones come packaged in tightly woven, momentum-driven flows, and often — such as when they matter most — in rapid onslaughts. The stories we tell ourselves,

---

22 The resonances between Gurdjieff's and Peirce's triadisms are fascinating, but we must leave them for another time. The same, incidentally, goes for the Christian trinity, the Hindu *trimūrti*, and other trinitarian deities, with their diverse interpretive permutations over the centuries; comparative triadistics is yet to be developed as a serious research field. On Gurdjieff, see Jacob Needleman and George Baker, eds., *Gurdjieff: Essays and Reflections on the Man and His Teachings* (New York: Continuum, 2004); on the Law of Three, see Basarab Nicolescu's chapter in that book, "Gurdjieff's Philosophy of Nature," 37–69.

the images and internalized voices of our parents, siblings, spouses, children, friends and enemies, bosses and co-workers, all come to us wrapped in affective adornments, muscular tightenings, bodily armorings, and the like. But the practice of noticing, acknowledging, and focusing in on the pieces of these emotional entanglements allows us to build spaces between them and, over time, to begin disentangling their knotted webs. As Shinzen has put it (I'm mostly paraphrasing), it's the "undetected micro-emotional experiences" that drive the parade of horrors known as human history; and it is these that mindfulness practice allows us to observe, gain insight into, and over time begin to neutralize. Beyond that, his additional methods of "Focusing on Rest" (finding the restful states between active states, such as the spaces of silence between bits of "mental chatter," and resting in those spaces) and "Focusing on the Positive" (generating positive states) offer two more variations on traditional contemplative practices such as meditation using mantras, *Metta* or "lovingkindness" meditation, Christian "centering prayer," and the like.

It is the fifth and final of Shinzen's "Five Ways" that makes things yet more interesting.[23] This is what he calls "Focusing on Change" or on "Flow," where we watch things coming, going, transforming, scintillating, undulating, vibrating, expanding and contracting, winking in and out of existence, and ultimately disappearing down the cosmic rabbithole (and taking us with it, for a little while at least). He describes this as a way of attuning to the "wave" as opposed to the "particle" structure of reality, with the eventful winkings in and out being sourced in a "fountain of energy" out of which everything comes and to which it all returns. Shinzen's language here uncannily resembles not only the traditional Chinese cosmo-physiological tradition of Qi with its emanating energy flows and *Yin–Yang* polarities, but also Whitehead's ontology of "actual occasions," with their dipolar structure of co-related subjectivation and objectivation.

---

23   See Shinzen Young, "Five Ways to Know Yourself."

But let us first mine the riches of the model before complicating it with the fact that things *aren't things at all,* but different forms of flow. (At this point, it would be useful to spend some time practicing the exercises suggested here. Specific practices related to this and other sections of Part Two can be found in Appendix 3.)

Relatings

To put these three sensory fields — feeling, hearing, and seeing — into the context of everyday life means making them more than something to observe while sitting motionless on a meditation cushion. There is a more primary categorization of activity that should provide a better starting point, and it is directly related to Peirce's categories.

For Peirce, again, there is (1) that which there is at all, and which precedes any doing on our part (which becomes the object-pole of our doing); (2) that which we do in response (the relational prehension); and (3) that which is realized in and through the doing (which becomes the subject-pole, momentarily, only to offer itself up as object for other doings to come). And insofar as these are categories for noting what is happening — noting firstness, secondness, and thirdness — we can also add a zeroness for those things that occur without our conscious awareness. So we have four categories:

0. Free Activity: This is bodymind doing what it does, as it does, on its own. It is a kind of primordial flow — things arising spontaneously as responses or results of previous arisings — which captures the world prior to the cut made by a new agent. We could think of this as our base-zero, "nonconscious" state of functioning.

1. Sensing (See, Hear, Feel): Sometimes I see it happening. If I only saw it and resisted the impulse to act, I would be here, observing, noting. Like the trained Buddhist meditator, I can watch what arises, moment to moment, and gain a feel for what is there.

This can be aided by mentally labeling, categorizing, and classifying — at which point I have moved onto the next two phases, those of acting and interpreting, but for purpose of learning what is going on it is worth distinguishing between *passive* sensing and *intentional* acting. So, when I hear a sound — say, an airplane engine in the sky outside my window, or thumping music from a passing car — I can label this "Hear-Out," to indicate that I have noticed a sound that is "out there" in the world. Its point of origin is not just outside my window, but outside of the psycho-physical system I identify as "myself." And when I hear a sound "in my head" — say, my inner voice saying "This is boring" — I can call that "Hear-In," to indicate that it has originated *inside* my internal mental field.

The same with images, which can be somewhere in my gaze (See-Out) or inside my mind's eye (See-In). And the same with feelings, smells, kinesthetic sensations, and everything else: "Feel-Out" refers to things that originate outside of us, "Feel-In" to things that originate inside us (such as the breathless feeling when we suddenly remember something important we had just forgotten to do, or that complex mix of angry and depressive impulses that take us over when we realize the love of our life has betrayed us). Humans being complicated creatures, we probably have more of the "In" things to note than most creatures, but in principle any actual occasion is responding to something arising *outside* itself or *inside* itself. (Let us set the ambiguities aside for now.)

To be consistent with Whiteheadian, Peircean, *and* Shinzenian interpretations, this sensing or noting should also be considered a "feeling": one notes what has arisen, feels or "tastes" it, and then allows it to go on its own course without attaching anything of "self" to it. Here we have added a step to the normal course: a very small step — mere (feelingful) observation — but an important one. Most forms of the first category of meditation mentioned above fall into this category of (minimal) action. But calling everything, including a sound or an image, a "feeling" takes away from some of the precision of the analytical scalpel we are wielding with our experience. So let us instead take the words "image" and "sound" to be as emotional or feelingful as they need to be.

2. Intervening (Show, Sound, Touch): Action may be what I am doing most of the time — and what many forms of meditation aim to stop or at least slow down — but this category is meant to indicate *intended* action. Some things, and perhaps most things, I do unthinkingly. Important things — speaking significant words to a loved one, driving to the hospital in an emergency — I do intentionally. Intended action involves responding to stimuli, resisting them, replacing one stimulus (external or internal) with another, or even cultivating specific states or modes, for instance, through mental exercises with specific goals in mind. Again, we can distinguish between actions whose intended locus is outside of what we conventionally think of as ourselves — the movement of my body as I push open a door, the clearing of a throat to let someone know of my presence — and those whose locus is internal to our mental or emotional space, such as my visualizing of tomorrow's meeting with a boss or a lover. In place of the Feel-Hear-See triad, let's call these Touch, Sound (as in *sounding* or *making* a sound), and Show (for action with respect to a visual observer).

3. Realizing (Map, Convey, Move): This is the upshot of action, the result or realization of actions upon the external-sensory-bodily ("out") and internal-mental ("in") fields. The labels refer to the modalities through which the action is accomplished: seeing and showing become "mapping," hearing and sounding become "conveying" or "speaking" (as in "it speaks to me," auditorially or verbally), and feeling and touching become "moving" or "being moved." Those with a locus of realization that is internal to the bodymind are labeled "in," while those external are labeled "out."

Adding numbers here makes this schema consistent with Peircean phenomenology, at least as a first approximation. It is true that Noticing may already involve a *turning* of the mind toward the firstness of what's arising in the mental-perceptual field. To the extent that this "turning" is already an encounter between one thing and another — mental contents arising, and a mental observer that is produced through the action of observation or "turning" — it becomes, or is always becoming, a form of secondness, not a pure firstness. But the point is to try to get as close to firstness as possible. If the observation affects what is being observed (as arguably always occurs), then the injunction is simply to "observe *that*, too." It is the orientation *toward the arising firstness* that makes it "Noticing."

Analogously, Action or Intervention, in this system, is an intentional response to something, which involves a turning to what is there *and an action* upon it or in response to it. Alternatively, it may be an action *replacing* what would normally arise: for instance, the recitation and focusing of one's mind upon a mantra so that the mental field will not be taken over by other habitual activities. The goal may be to cultivate particular states of mind, as in meditative or trance states of one kind or another, or states valued for their positive valence in a particular religious or cultural tradition (such as a devotional, compassionate, or solidaritous state, identification with a deity, and so on).

Finally, Realization in the sense meant here also involves the intention of making sense of the activity in question.

Each of these has its common or "normal" forms as well as the specific, cultivated (or cultivable) forms they take within meditative, yogic, or psycho-spiritual training of some kind. Furthermore, to say that action or interpretation is "intended" is to beg the question "intended by what or by whom?" One's answer to this — for instance, "by me," "by the self," "by the process of conditioned arising that envelops a mental-bodily field," or something else — already depends on an onto-epistemological interpretation of what arises. If you believe there is an active "self" *behind* everything your mind does, then you are already committed to a subject-object duality that process-relational philosophy (and Buddhism) rejects.

How to make a bodymind flow, or, deconstructing experience with ~~Reality~~

This is where things get interesting. For most process-relation-ists (and most Buddhist philosophers), subjectivity and objec-tivity are not static conditions or polar categories holding up the universe. Rather, they are results — outcomes, however tempo-rary and ultimately insubstantial — of a less differentiated, more constructive, and more flowing activity. Shinzen Young simply calls this activity "flow," while other metaphysicians — from Na-garjuna and Vasubandhu to Whitehead, Bergson, James, and Deleuze — analyze it at more microscopic or rigorously concep-tual levels.

What this means is that our categorization of things as in-ternal or external to the bodymind is inaccurate. It doesn't hold up, at least not for long. But it feels as if it does, so we might start by paying attention to those points at which it slides into something less clear. Shinzen refers to many phenomenological "flavors" of flow — as expansion and contraction, undulation, vibration, tingliness, percolation, electricity, and so on — but also to flow as the experience of the ontological fact of imper-manence, or *anicca* (in Pali). Flow is partnered with *vanishing*, for which Shinzen uses the notational label "Gone."

So, on the one hand, "flow" is indicative of the fact that all things pass, and, on the other, of the ebullient energy of their continual arising. This corresponds with the ontology of per-colating creativity described by Whitehead, which I have built on to posit that there is a circulatory undulation — a movement between the subjectivation and the objectivation that consti-tutes every moment or actual occasion — which gives rise to all form. (There is a second movement, which is the difference and deferral I referred to as described by Peirce's semiosic process.) If we can learn to pay attention to this movement as it arises, we can get a feel for its many flavors, and as a result "subject" and "object" begin to soften and melt into dipolar acts of becoming.

When the arisings of subjects and objects come to crystal-lize around certain formations over time, getting habituated into "grooves" or "channels" dug into a socio-mental landscape through repetition, they come to take the form of—that is, to geomorph, biomorph, and anthropomorph as—stable entities such as one's "self" (seen from within), "the world" (seen from a situated subjective perspective), "selves like me," "others unlike me," and everything else that appears to exist, as seen from any perspective possible.

Each social regime produced over the course of human history digs its channels a little differently, creating different kinds of individual and collective "selves," in-groups and out-groups, networks and relations, and all manner of entities by which to populate its world. These are analogous to the "collectives" Bruno Latour has written about, some of which "mobilize ancestors, lions, fixed stars, and the coagulated blood of sacrifice," while others "mobilize genetics, zoology, cosmology and hæmatology."[24] Modern western society has come to produce specific kinds of selves and social units as well—most commonly, "rational, self-maximizing individuals," nuclear families, more or less sovereign nations, and so on, but with a wide latitude for variations in the overall mix. As Latour argues, these things aren't *social* constructions so much as they are *relational* co-productions, made up of matter/mind stuff, that is, of material and semiotic relations that are fully real in their effects, even if they are ultimately insubstantial—empty (as Buddhists insist) of self-subsistent being.

Critiquing one's own social milieu is an important part of one's liberation from circumstances. The primary goal of mindfulness meditation practice, however (in Shinzen's account), is to bring oneself into greater contact and resonance with ~~Reality~~, which means to bring one *out* of the hardened categories we have put in ~~Reality~~'s place, and *into* the flowing percolation that *constitutes* both those categories and the category-making process itself *along with everything else*. When we add this category of Flow—the rippling and percolating interactivity that constitutes and produces all things, which is also the elusive but

---

24 Bruno Latour, *We Have Never Been Modern*, trans. Catherine Porter (Cambridge: Harvard University Press, 1993), 106.

tangible background hum of the universe — we get a set of possibilities that looks like this:

	OUT	IN	FLOW
0.			(Free activity; nondual flow)
1. SENSE	Sense Out	Sense In	Sense Flow
2. ACT	Act Out	Act In	Act Flow
3. REALIZE	Realize Out	Realize In	Realize Flow

For each of these categories, we could further distinguish between feeling, seeing, and hearing, and combinations thereof, to get the following possibilities.

0. Free activity: This is simply the ongoing arising of phenomena without a "self" or watcher intervening or even witnessing. It *precedes* what a bodymind can do.

1. Noting, Sensing, or Observation: *Sensing-Out* refers to the pure awareness of external phenomena, or of what goes on in the world. It can also be the casual observation of behavior or a more hypnotic merging with the observed; or it can be the controlled merging of "absorptive" forms of sensorially-based meditation. *Sensing-In* is the pure awareness of internal mental states and phenomena. It can be done casually and without particular intention, as in the observation of dream or hallucinatory phenomena, or it can be done with meditative discipline, as in Vipassana (insight) meditation. And *Sensing-Flow* is the pure awareness of flow states, for instance, of the rippling-flowing arising of subject-object circulation as things arise and pass away. This kind of flow state can and does arise spontaneously. It is perhaps the most "natural" state of mind in some sense — a form of nondual flow where the observer and observed are more or less merged, both present and not clearly separated. This is also where intersubjectivity — the relational field encompassing oneself and others — is experienced from within (or, technically, across the border separating within from without). In its meditative form, Sensing-Flow is nondual awareness of the present moment.

2. Acting, or Intervention: *Acting-Out* is equivalent to "acting in the world," which names most of what we do when we are recognizably doing anything that affects the surrounding world. It includes speaking, moving, arguing, making love, building and destroying things, and all the rest. Technically, it means the intentional response to, resistance against, replacement of, or cultivation of, external states of activity. In its meditative or yogic forms, it includes all types of physical activities such as rituals and devotional actions performed for a particular spiritual or religious purpose, such as for the benefit of all beings or to please a deity. Its paradigm cases are Karma-Yoga (action performed *as* yoga) and the performance of "good deeds." *Acting-In* is the intentional response, resistance, replacement, or cultivation of *internal* states. This is what we do when we visualize scenes "in the mind's eye" while listening to a story or reading a novel, or when we train ourselves to learn a poem or a language. (To the extent that we are focusing on the meanings of words, they are being treated as mental objects rather than mere shapes seen on a page.) In its meditative or yogic forms, Acting-In includes all those traditional practices that involve the generation of imagery, sound, feeling, or mental and emotional activity, such as Metta or "loving-kindness" meditation, mantra meditation, and deity meditations of one kind or another. (Many and perhaps most of these qualify under Shinzen's "Focus on the Positive" rubric.) Finally, *Acting-Flow* is the realm of intersubjective action, that is, action that emerges and is carried out collectively, characterized by blurred boundaries between oneself and others — for instance, by "emotional contagion" and some degree of shared awareness. We can catch a flavor of it in special kinds of events, such as revolutionary events, which is why those events leave such a strong imprint on their participants. In its meditative form, Acting-Flow is nondual action or what Daoists call *Wu-wei,* action that effectively "does itself," effortlessly, with one's own "self" being merged with and in the action. It is what the phrase "going with the flow" is intended to convey. It is an important part of what many of the more this-wordly spiritual systems (such as Daoism, Tantrism, Mahayana Buddhism, and certain forms of Paganism) aim for.

3. Realizing, or Interpretation: *Realizing* names the process of making sense of or effecting change in the world, with a realization being a "completed event," as it were. *Realizing-Out* does this in the external, outwardly observable world. In its mental forms (See, Hear), it generates knowledge or understanding in others — which, for instance, is what all types of science and education, at their best, aim to accomplish. In its physical (feeling) forms, it generates physically felt change. *Realizing-In* is the same with states internal to the observer and actor. It includes the interpretation of the workings of one's own mental or emotional states. *Realizing-Flow* in its "normal" variants consists of the kinds of things that process-relational theory aims to do: to make sense of the process-relational, nondual nature of all things. In its meditative or yogic variant, Realizing-Flow becomes the free, unobstructed flow of subjectivation-objectivation: perceiving and being-perceived, doing and being-done-to, understanding and being-understood, all co-arising and passing in the continuous percolation of one moment after another. We can think of this as meditative or nondual *praxis,* or as a kind of "enlightened Thirdness."

If the latter sounds like the "free activity" that characterizes the zero-level (the Zeroness that precedes Firstness), that is because it is very much the same — it is a return to free, unobstructed activity — but with continuity of awareness added. That continuity of awareness, according to Dzogchen and related traditions of Buddhism, is everpresent but obscured to start with. The difference here is that now "I," the "self," has also opened up to that recognition, which means that this "self" is no longer an obstruction to the flow of recognition (clear awareness, effortless action, understanding). The arising of the self has become part of the arising of world that is being observed, acted (and acted upon), and realized.

It is tempting to distinguish this final activity of meditative praxis or "enlightened realization-flow" by granting it a further level — a "fourthness" — since it both encompasses and expands upon the previous three levels. It is a synthesis of Sensing, Acting, and Realizing, mediated over time into an ongoing recursive praxis. Peirce would have advised against calling it "fourthness," since according to his phenomenology any term beyond a third is merely a third of a third. Thirds do not exclude firsts and seconds; they include and transcend them. Realization in this sense always includes some form of both observation and action. Shinzen refers to the "complete experience," which is equivalent to the realization of a momentary "enlightenment" insofar as the latter is considered a quality of experience and not a permanent state.

There is a combination worth commenting on further. The combination of Acting-Out, Realizing-Out, and Realizing-In (or *processing* those actions and their results) — that is, of changing the world according to an analytical understanding of how it ought to be changed — is what most forms of "critical social theory" or "critical educational praxis" aim for. In less coherent forms, they are what people's lives, at their best, tend to be most *about*: doing things, reflecting on what we have done, and learning in the process to do things better. The movement between these is a continuous one between observation, intervention, and theorization.

Religious or spiritual practices usually combine more than one of these as well. The generation of positive mental states, for instance, is typically accomplished not only through mental discipline, but through physical change in the world — such as through the creation, maintenance, and use of sanctuaries, temples, meditation rooms, altars, sand mandalas and tangka paintings, retreats and spas, and the like. Political practice, in turn, can be more than mere outward "action" and "realization": it can include the cultivation of mental states and the institutionalization of practices of working, relating, and cultivating.

Rather than a set of individual options or "slots" into which observations or behaviors would be classified, all of this is understood to be a more flexible sort of tool — a game-board, as Shinzen calls it, that can be used in various ways. For instance, one could focus on one or a few sets of options at a time (such as Hear-In, Touch-Flow, or Note-Out). Or one could focus on dynamic relations or interdependent "constellations" connecting different modalities: for instance, on the ways that external sounds give rise to internal feelings, or how bodily touch elicits both internal feelings and external impacts on someone else whom one is interacting with (such as during physical or sexual play).

If taken up as "bodymindfulness practice," the choice of what to focus on can range from being fully predetermined for a given length of time — as is the case in fairly typical meditation practice where one might focus exclusively on the sound of a mantra or the feeling of one's breath — to being an open-ended, free-flowing form of mindfulness, akin to Vipassana "insight" meditation but applied to all mental, sensory, bodily, social, and interactive activities and phenomena. The goals of this practice, as with the mindfulness practice taught by Shinzen, are three-fold: they are to develop sensory, mental, and emotional clarity (a practice related to firstness); to develop attention (a practice related to secondness, as it involves the effort of attending); and to develop equanimity in the face of life's exigencies (a practice related to thirdness, involving the cultivation of an attitude and an understanding).

At its most complete, then, this becomes a fully conscious mode of living. The goal here is not necessarily to bring everything that is *un-* or *pre*-conscious to *consciousness*. Rather, it is to serve as a practice by which consciously chosen aesthetic, ethical, and logical principles are established within one's bodily and mental habits for living in the world.

The bodymind Rubik's Cube

Let us summarize what we have so far. This system of interpretive practice might best be visualized in the form of a Rubik's Cube, with three rows, three columns, and three levels intersecting with each other to create nine domains, along with the variable relations between them. The three sets classify the following strata:

1. **Sensory modes (See, Hear, Feel):** Sensations and perceptions are grouped into three modalities: the visual; the auditory; and the bodily-felt, which includes the tactile, olfactory, gustatory, kinesthetic, visceral, affective, and emotional. The latter group is further distinguishable into the "felt-out" (the first four) and the "felt-in" (the last three) based on whether the sensations refer to relata that are "internal" or "external" to the bodymind in question (see #3 below). These three sensory modalities may develop somewhat autonomously, but they get blurred and interactive in practice. Distinguishing between them does not follow any universal or essential triadism; it is just a useful heuristic.

2. **Relational categories (Sensing/Noting, Acting, Realizing):** These are based in Peirce's triad of categories: there is the sensing of firstness, the acting upon secondness, and the realization of thirdness. A *first* is something in and of itself, and perception of a first is perception of it simply as it is, a noticing of it in its purity, insofar as this is possible. A *second* is an actual, existential interaction with something. As an interaction, it is an *action,* with conscious or unconscious intent and with a resistant (to one degree or another) object of that action. A *third* involves the grasping of a second (an interaction) through some form of mediation, which generates a semiotic relationship: a meaning or significance, an interpretation, a pattern, a habit, a regularity — which we are together defining here as *realization.*

3. **Orientations (In, Out, Flow):** On the surface, "In" and "Out" distinguish between whether the second — the object perceived in the

case of perception, the object being acted upon in the case of action, and the object generated in the case of realization—is internal or external to the referencing bodymind. In sensing/ noting (firstness), they are distinguished according to their immediate source; in acting (secondness), they are distinguished according to their intended goal or destination; and in realization (thirdness), according to their *achieved* direction. Whether realization has actually been achieved outside oneself—say, in a listener, a viewer, or an audience—is a matter of speculation or approximate knowledge. In a Peircean understanding, realization is always on the move toward a truth that is logically conceivable, but practically elusive.

Distinguishing between "internal" and "external," however, implies a dualistic ontology—a separation between subject and object, perceiver and perceived—that process-relational ontologies reject or transcend in one way or another. Such an ontology corresponds to what foundational Buddhist metaphysician Nāgārjuna called "conventional truth," and what Tiantai Three Truths doctrine affirmed as the "provisionality" of existent and impermanent things. By contrast, "flow" states, where the boundary between internal and external is breached or suspended, acknowledge *nonduality,* or what Nagarjuna called "ultimate truth" and Tiantai doctrine referred to simply as "emptiness," though its understanding of this "emptiness" is not at all empty, but dazzlingly lively.

A word here on Buddhist metaphysics is in order. Nagarjuna's Two Truths doctrine underpinned Madhyamaka philosophy which, with its main sparring partner, Yogacara philosophy, informed much of the Mahayana Buddhism that spread across wide swaths of central and eastern Asia in the first millennium of the Common Era. Upon their arrival in China, these ideas met and mingled with an extant Chinese preference for a pragmatic realist metaphysics, as found in Confucian, Daoist, and related schools. The most philosophically sophisticated synthesis that emerged from the encounter was arguably the Tiantai metaphysics developed by sixth century Chinese Buddhist philosopher Zhiyi (Chih-i), with its doctrine of Three Truths, which contemporary Tiantai philosopher Brook Ziporyn translates as the truths of Provisional Positing (*jia*), Emptiness (*kong*), and the Center (*zhong*). The first two are equivalent to Nāgārjuna's conventional and ultimate truths, while the third, "Centrality" or "the Middle," insists on the necessary "intersubsumption," or mutual dependency, of the first two. In doing so, it simultaneously affirms the contingency of all things *as* the reversible and accompanying precondition of their ultimate reality. Subject-object duality is thus not denied but *realized* in nondual flow, and vice versa. Let us look more closely at Ziporyn's articulation of these Three Truths.[25]

The first truth is that of "conventional truth," "local coherence," or "provisional positing," which means that a thing really is what it appears to be: sky is sky, an arrow is an arrow, a slap on the face is a real slap on a real face. The second truth is that of "ultimate truth," "global incoherence," or "Emptiness," which understands an object alone as utterly empty of self-subsistence, meaning that it is nothing outside of the context of its relations. This also means that the object *is,* at the same time, everything that it appears *not* to be. Not only is the arrow *not* really a simple arrow — since its arrowness is but a factor of its material body, the motivations that shaped it and its present motion, and all of the things that went into producing them — which are ultimately all of the things of the universe up to this moment, and which by now (however many moments later) no longer exist as they appeared to then. The arrow is also the non-arrow that will kill (and therefore not kill) the (not) me when it pierces me through the (non-) heart. All of these are "empty" in their complete and utter non-self-subsistence. There is nothing intrinsic to them except for the directional flow that continues in and through them, which, even a second later, is already gone beyond, already something different, differing and deferring as it goes.

---

25 Ziporyn's most complete accounts of Tiantai philosophy are *Emptiness and Omnipresence: An Essential Introduction to Tiantai Buddhism* (Bloomington: Indiana University Press, 2016), and *Being and Ambiguity: Philosophical Experiments with Tiantai Buddhism* (Chicago: Open Court, 2004).

While Two Truths theory had acknowledged the validity of both of these "truths," its built-in tendency was to privilege the ultimacy of "emptiness" — that is why its second truth has come to be known as *ultimate* truth. Tiantai rejects this apparent privileging and insists on the "reversible as-ness" of the two truths, according to which it is the synthesis of the prior two that makes them *both and neither* what each of the two claim. As with Peirce's thirdness, this "both and neither" is irreducible. The latter insight is the goal of Zen and Chan enlightenment practice, where the body, the house, the arrow, and all other things are seen to *really be* all those things and, at the same time, to be *empty* of any such substance as we ascribe to them, since they really do "intersubsume" all other things in order to be anything at all. Tiantai further posits that the Three Truths are nothing if they are not *used,* and that the means of using them, in Ziporyn's translation, is by "opening the Provisional to reveal the Real." That is, once the provisional reality of any one thing is "opened" and seen clearly, it is revealed not merely as emptiness, but as simultaneously (1) provisionally itself in its uniqueness; (2) globally not itself at all, but "intersubsumptive" with everything else; and (3) irreducibly both at the same time.

Shinzen Young's concept of Flow captures an essential element of this "irreducibly *real* and *not real* at the same time" nature of things, with an emphasis on the "at the same time," which is always not "at time X" but in the perpetual time of simultaneous becoming and vanishing. Flow can be classified into a few different types. First, there is *cross-modal flow,* which crosses between the sensory modalities, as in experiences of "Hear-See Flow," "Touch-Sound Flow," "See-Sound-Move Flow," and so on. In themselves, these are not *nondual* flow states except to the degree that they also are, or become, one of the next two forms of flow. But they can be a focus for mindfulness practice, and in that context are helpful for providing a *feeling* of flow. Second, there is *cross-directional* flow, which refers to the blurring, movement between, or achieved unity of the internal ("In") and external ("Out"); by definition, this is, or includes, nonduality. And third, there is *evental–processual flow,* which is the category consisting of flow experiences characterized by change over time (*temporal* flow) or variability in nature and sensation (*textural* flow): for instance, arising/passing (which Shinzen labels "Here!" and "Gone!"), vibratory, undulating, and so on.

Considering all of these as forms of "flow" and taking them as intersecting with the other two orientations ("in" and "out"), the following set of possibilities is generated (Table 1). In each category, I am including examples taken from ordinary experience, indicated by "O," and examples taken from mindfulness/meditation or spiritual practice, indicated by "M." (See Appendix 2 for a more complete rendition of the cube.)

It is important to remember that this map tells us nothing specifically about the things encountered in life — the others, which, for humans, could include other people, animals, dream semblances, or stars. Rather, the map is intended to be used for *orienting* oneself from the inside of one's own experience. One could use it in any of the following ways: as a classification of types of experience, and of types of meditative and spiritual experience in particular; as suggesting the relations between these different types of experience; as a map of the territory traversable during insight or "open monitoring" styles of meditation, both in traditional sitting practice and during active participation in everyday life; as suggesting what a complete system of human developmental education might include; and as a mandala-like object of contemplation that would help one habituate one's thinking into a triadic, process-relational style.[26]

---

26 Overviews of research on mindfulness meditation techniques and how they affect their practitioners include Kirk W. Brown, J. David Cresswell, and Richard M. Ryan, eds., *Handbook of Mindfulness: Theory, Research, and Practice* (New York: Guilford, 2015); *Social Cognitive and Affective Neuroscience* 8, no. 1 (special issue on mindfulness neuroscience); Claire Braboszcz, Stephanie Hahusseau, and Arnaud Delorme, "Meditation and Neuroscience: From Basic Research to Clinical Practice," in *Integrative Clinical Psychology, Psychiatry, and Behavioral Medicine*, ed. Roland Carlstedt, 1910–29 (New York: Springer, 2010); and the classic study by Antoine Lutz, John Dunne, and Richard Davidson, "Meditation and the Neuroscience of Consciousness," in *Cambridge Handbook of Consciousness*, eds. Morris Mosco-

OUT	IN	≈	FLOW
–	–	≈	O: Free activity M: Nondual flow
SENSE OUT SEE–HEAR–FEEL OUT O: Absorption in sensory activity, "pure" sensing M: Sensory-absorptive meditation	**SENSE IN** SEE–HEAR–FEEL IN O: Dream states, absorption in subjective/internal activity M: Vipassana (insight) meditation; See-in, Hear-in, Feel-in	≈	**SENSE FLOW** SEE–HEAR–FEEL FLOW O: Intersubjective observation M: Nondual meditative awareness; See/Hear/Feel flow
ACT OUT SHOW–SOUND–TOUCH OUT O: Action in the world, doing (of any kind) M: Active meditation, "spirit possession"; Karma Yoga, "good deeds"	**ACT IN** SHOW–SOUND–TOUCH IN O: Visualizing scenes in "mind's eye" (e.g., while listening to a story or reading a poem or novel) M: Visualization, metta, mantra meditation; Tantra, deity meditation; "Focus-on-positive"	≈	**ACT FLOW** SHOW–SOUND–TOUCH FLOW O: Action with the world, doing-with, social/collective action M: Nondual Tantra/deity ritual; nondual action (wu-wei)
REALIZE OUT MAP–CONVEY–MOVE OUT O: Science, logical reasoning (about external world) M: Integral science?	**REALIZE IN** MAP–CONVEY–MOVE IN O: Psychology, Cartesian introspection M: Analytical meditation, Jnana-Yoga	≈	**REALIZE FLOW** MAP–CONVEY–MOVE FLOW O: Integral, process-relational ontology M:Nondual free activity, enlightened flow, Praxis, "complete experience"

Table 1

With practice, as one begins to get familiar with these modalities in one's own experience, one also begins to experience the flow that connects them, and us, to all the other sentient beings (and beyond) making up the universe. That, at least, is the promise offered by such practices.

Dark flow, or the great sucking sound at the heart of things

But all of that still sounds too smooth, too graspable and tame; it disguises the harshness of ~~Reality~~. For there is always the great sucking sound at the heart of all things: that of their withdrawal.

The image of "dark flow," described in a *New Scientist* article as 1400 galaxy clusters streaming toward the edge of the universe at blistering speed in the ongoing "afterglow" of the big bang, has haunted me ever since I first read about it. Caused "shortly after the big bang by something no longer in the observable universe," and possibly by "a force exerted by other universes squeez[ing] ours" (a force doing *what…?*), I can't help thinking that astrophysicists are arriving at the point where the known universe is being bounded and taking its place amidst a more mysterious space of otherness, where we have no clue — indeed, cannot have a clue — about what goes on.[27] So it becomes the realm of poetry, of dreams and nightmares, of haunted imaginings, like the deep sea, beyond the reach of sunlight, that still fascinates us, but even more deep, dark, and vital.

Einstein famously said that "as our circle of knowledge expands, so does the circumference of darkness surrounding it." Perhaps recent events and their reflections in popular culture — terrorist incidents, refugee emergencies, economic crises with their Ponzi schemes, bank machinations, and the West's growing interdependence with poker-faced and unreadable nations (like North Korea), gradually accumulating reports about

---

vitch, Philip Zelazo, and Evan Thompson, 497–549 (Cambridge: Cambridge University Press, 2007).

27 Quotes from Marcus Chown, "Mystery 'Dark Flow' Extends Towards Edge of Universe," *New Scientist*, November 14, 2009, 11.

climate change, and films about forthcoming apocalypses, zombies, and vampires — all are conspiring to make things seem more curious, more spooky, and more surrounded by a kind of lingering, lumbering darkness.

Slavoj Žižek's account of the Robert Heinlein novel *The Unpleasant Profession of Jonathan Hoag* includes a lovely passage where Žižek equates the Lacanian Real, the unassimilable kernel around which subjectivity is formed, with the "grey and formless mist, pulsing slowly as if with inchoate life" that emerges at the boundary of the known world and the unknown, outside a traveling couple's car window. Buddhist accounts of emptiness generally lack the Lacanian spookiness conveyed here (though it's hardly foreign to the Tibetan tantrics, with their nighttime graveyard meditations), but, to the goth-loving nature hound, these make a comforting addition. The passage is worth reproducing in detail. "At the denouement of the story," Žižek writes,

Hoag invites Randall and his wife to a picnic in the country. He tells them that he has at last become aware of his true identity: he is actually an art critic, though of a peculiar kind. Our universe, he says, is only one of several, and the masters of all the universes are mysterious beings who create different worlds, including our own, as experimental works of art. To maintain the artistic perfection of their efforts, these cosmic artificers from time to time send into their creations one of their own kind disguised as a native, to act as a kind of universal art critic. The mysterious committee members who summoned Randall are representatives of an evil and inferior divinity attempting to corrupt the work of the cosmic artists.

Hoag informs Randall and his wife that, in the course of his visit to this universe, he has discovered one or two minor blemishes which he intends to have put right during the next few hours. Randall and his wife will notice nothing; but on the drive home to New York, they must under no circumstances open the windows of their car. They set off, and the journey is uneventful until they witness a road accident. At first they ignore it and continue on their way; but when they see a patrolman their sense of duty prevails and they stop to report the accident. Randall asks his wife to lower her window a little.[28]

Here Žižek quotes from the original Heinlein novel:

"She complied, then gave a sharp intake of breath and swallowed a scream. He did not scream, but he wanted to. Outside the open windows was no sunlight, no cops, no kids — nothing. Nothing but a grey and formless mist, pulsing slowly as if with inchoate life. They could see nothing of the city through it, not because it was too dense but because it was — empty. No sound came out of it; no movement showed in it. It merged with the frame of the window and began to drift inside. Randall shouted, "Roll up the window!" She tried to obey, but her hands were nerveless; he reached across her and cranked it up himself, jamming it hard into its seat.The sunny scene was restored; through the glass they saw the patrolman, the boisterous game, the sidewalk, and the city beyond. Cynthia put a hand on his arm. "Drive on, Teddy!" "Wait a minute," he said tensely, and turned to the window beside him. Very cautiously he rolled it down — just a crack, less than an inch. It was enough. The formless grey flux was out there, too; through the glass city traffic and sunny street were plain, through the opening — nothing."[29]

"What is this 'grey and formless mist,'" Žižek continues, "if not the Lacanian Real — the pulsing of the pre-symbolic substance in all its abhorrent vitality?" This substance "irrupts on the very boundary separating the 'outside' from the 'inside,' materialized in this case by the car window."[30] Like the car window, from which "objects in the mirror are closer than they appear" (and

---

28 Slavoj Žižek, "The Undergrowth of Enjoyment: How Popular Culture Can Serve as an Introduction to Lacan," *New Formations* 9 (1989): 7–29, at 12.

29 Ibid.

30 Ibid.

through which our starting objects flew out, in Part 1), this car window creates a discontinuity between the world as known and that which is typically mere backdrop, but which here is something altogether different. Žižek writes:

> It is as if, for a moment, the "projection" of the outside world has stopped working; as if we have been confronted momentarily with the formless grey emptiness of the screen itself, with the Mallarmean "place where nothing takes place but the place."[31]

David Lynch's Red Room (from *Twin Peaks*) comes to mind as well.

> Continuity and proportion are not possible because this disproportion, the surplus of inside in relation to outside, is a necessary structural effect of the very separation of the two; it can only be abolished by demolishing the barrier and letting the outside swallow the inside.[32]

This "excess" of the inside is "the fantasy-space — the mysterious thirteenth floor, the surplus space which is a persistent motif in science fiction and mystery stories."[33] It is at this point that we wake up from our dream, like Chuang Tzu, not knowing if we are Chuang Tzu having dreamt we were a butterfly (or Žižek dreaming he was a black widow spider) or vice versa: if the spider is dreaming of this reader and viewer carried along by a text toward oblivion.

That oblivion, at the macro level, is the window out of which we ourselves disappear into the darkness, the quiet whimper of our world flushed out into the heat-death of the universe. Philosophers can debate whether the flushing out is balanced by an equivalent in-flush or "reflux" elsewhere, with the whole

---

31 Ibid., 13.
32 Ibid.
33 Ibid.

constituting a closed system, or one redeemed by God, or if it is final — an asymmetrical vector where departure is for good. Randall and his wife witness the rippling flow speeding back down the rabbit-hole, to the source from which it and their entire world arose and to which all things return in the end, or perhaps now. Spiritual traditions often color this flow as bright, full rather than empty (full of light, for instance), but it seems more reasonable to propose the image of Dark Flow as the cosmic Real, the shimmering atomic structure of things *behind* the structured object-world we (think we) see. Dark Flow is the wave-like spirit-energy that Buddhists call "emptiness" only because giving it a more substantialist term would already be a way of trying to contain and claim it. This Reality is unclaimable and uncontainable. If astrophysicists hadn't "seen" it, we would have had to invent it. (I mean ~~we~~, ~~invent~~, ~~it~~.)

The apophatic, inside-out twist

Žižek's articulation of the Real provides a nice backdrop for what we might call the Quaker, or apophatic, shift in our bodymind mapmaking. (Apophatic, ἀπόφασις, refers to something obtained through negation or denial; something like our crossed out ~~Real~~.)

Quakers, or the Religious Society of Friends, are the ones within the Christian tradition whose practices have been most shaped by the idea of silence. Quaker "silent worship" cultivates a receptivity to the "voice of God within," which is taken to precede the ability to live "in the light" of that quiet voice, a voice felt "in the heart." We could just as well refer here to the cosmic immensity of Vishnu (or Cthulhu, for that matter), where even the heart is rendered elusive in the light of what is beyond it. The point is that there is an opposite move to be made with each of the forms of *positive* noting indicated by Shinzen's system of practices. There is something, yes, but there is also the nothing that surrounds it, from which it arises and to which it returns.

If our game-board is a Rubik's cube, the apophatic game-board is that cube twisted inside out, or, better, entered into, as if we were entering the Red Room at the heart of all six sides of our triply-cubed cube. Inside out, the game-board's three dimensions appear as follows:

1. Behind all appearance — all sound, all image, all feeling — there is the void: the Emptiness beyond feeling, the Silence beyond hearing, the Darkness beyond seeing. There is that which withdraws from appearance, which is the place from which appearances arise and to which they return. It is dark matter, the ocean of being, the zero state of appearance.

2. Behind all action — all touching, sounding, and showing — is the rippling tenderness felt by the heart, from which action arises and to which it returns: the palpitating Tremor of flesh at the origin of feeling and touching; the tremulous Murmur of sound at the origin of hearing, sounding, and speaking; the radiant Flicker of light at the origin of sight and of showing. It is unbounded feeling, the ocean of becoming, the zero state of relationality.

3. And behind all realization — all movement, all communication, all mapped understanding — there is the unfathomable Mystery, the "cloud of unknowing" that precedes knowing and that engulfs it in the end: the Immovable, the Unspeakable, and the Invisible and utterly Unknowable. It is the shadowy presence that withdraws from realization, from which all realization arises and to which it returns, realization in its zero state, the realization that is non-realization.

These can in turn become focal points for one's bodymindfulness practice in three ways that reverse the terms of the previous. First, where Sensing (or Noting) practice typically pays attention to what is going on, "Reverse Sensing" involves paying attention to the background from which "what is going on" arises and to which it returns, that is, to the silence, the darkness, the emptiness, the void. Second, where Action practice typically pays attention to what one is doing (in interaction with others), "Reverse Action" involves paying attention to the background from which "what one is doing" arises and to which it returns, that is, to the heartful flicker, murmur, and tremor within and out of which all relational engagements unfold. And third, where Realization practice typically pays attention to "what is realizing" from one's actions (or from intersubjective activity), "Reverse Realization" involves paying attention to the background from which "what is realizing" arises and to which it returns, that is, to the mystery that is unknowable, invisible, unspeakable, and immovable.

Things start to sound Zen-like and paradoxical at the point that one undertakes these shifts. This triad of Emptiness, Heart, and Mystery pertains to context, or to the dark absence that surrounds what is emerging into presence. It is the shadow of the original triad (Sensing–Acting–Realizing), the Triad of Absence to that Triad of Presence. It is the penumbral ~~Real~~ that surrounds all things in their irreality and ungraspability. It is also an indicator of how *we* might shadow the "reality" of the Anthropocene. (For practices associated with this apophatic shift, see Appendix 3.)

Returning to the things themselves, differently

Maps like the one presented here make it sound as if the goal of such bodymindfulness practice is to accede to the "top," which is the level of complete thirdness, complete Realization in and as Flow. But then, you might ask, why do meditation systems most commonly gear their practitioners toward the lower levels of this diagram, especially the observation of mere internal or external experience?

The reason for this is that by the time we get to the stage in our lives at which a rigorous meditative or spiritual practice comes to seem useful, the world has for us become so pre-interpreted and predigested, its meanings and thirdnesses so settled and overburdened with habit that a return to the basic building blocks becomes necessary. (It's true that, for Peirce, habit is in the nature of all things, and always on the increase, but it is always habit shot through with chance and infinitely revisable. It is habit raised to the level of meaningfulness and reasonableness, in the best sense of these words.) It is precisely because self and other, subject and object, interior and exterior, are so settled — and at the same time so shot through with dissatisfaction — that one must go back to firstness (and then secondness) with an eye for unsettling them. This enables seeing that things are not what we think they are, but rather, that they are a flow that overflows the boundaries in which we have contained them all along. Once this flow is *observed* in experience and *lived* in action, it can be *realized* as "complete experience."

Observation is therefore the first step of a disciplined program for learning what the bodymind can do. But this observation — if it successfully notices the process-relational nature of all things, including self and world, subjects and objects — becomes a movement *with* what is observed. There is no halting the process at firstness or secondness. Insofar as attending to what is before us is a choice, a movement on our part, we can say that conscious firstness *is* secondness. Similarly, conscious secondness — intentional, reflexive responsiveness to that which moves us to response — *is* thirdness, or realization. And conscious thirdness is completion in the moment, which impregnates the next moment with its novel possibilities. As always and ever *moving,* we (bodyminds) enter into relations with other bodyminds — entities or processes characterized both by mentality and physicality — which are all moving in their own ways, and which are ultimately never quite "their own."

Even if one follows an object-oriented metaphysics here and opts for thinking of these as entities that ultimately *withdraw* or *withhold* something from all relationality, that withdrawn *essence,* in a process-relational view, is always a withdrawing-*to*: it is never simply a withdrawing-*into*, that is, a withdrawing into something stable, steady, and predetermined called "oneself." What the withdrawal withdraws to is the source of the flow that gives rise to it, which is the destination for the dark flow of the universe, and which is always — if we follow Deleuze and Whitehead — becoming different from itself. It is, in a word, elusive. The stream moves as we speak, as Heraclitus suggested and as Derrida, in his wordsmithy ways, demonstrated. (Derrida demonstrated it only for words, but we can take the next step, with Nāgārjuna, to the deconstruction of experience itself.)[34]

Toward a logo-ethico-aesthetics of existence

If there is process both at the heart of every "eventity" and folded into, and unfolding through, the capacities that are actualized in every moment, then we are at the core of the crystallization of every moment in our experience. But, then, who we?

We are those who attend, act upon, and realize. To the extent that something — anything — is capable of noting, responding to, and realizing something, of subjectivating in relation to objectified facts so as to create a new realization, a living effect that is added to the universe — to that extent it is a real agent. (And to the extent that our agency is intimate only to ourselves, we are *secret* agents. We become public through recognition by others, but our own experience always retains its secrecy. Not only that — it always dissolves from us when we attempt to still and to grasp it. Its secrecy retains its own secrecy.)

Agency is an *event* in the sense that its realization eventuates, at which point it is turned into grist for the mill for future events. But if there is continuity from one event to the next — which there is for anything that works to maintain some stability of identity over time — then it is a real entity that can be said not only to act, but note and to realize. This is the Peircian contribution to how we understand agential things. The simultaneous "folding into" and "forking out of" that *sense* of our own agency is what makes us up, and in the unfolding of triads — of noting, acting, and realizing — there is continual flowering. (It is a

34 On the parallels between Derridean deconstruction and Nagarjuna's Madhyamika philosophy, see Harold Coward and Toby Foshay, eds., *Derrida and Negative Theology* (Albany: SUNY Press, 1992); Robert Magliola, *Derrida on the Mend* (West Lafayette: Purdue University Press, 1984); and Cai Zong-qi, "Derrida and Madhyamika Buddhism: From Linguistic Deconstruction to Criticism of Onto-Theologies," *International Philosophical Quarterly* 33, no. 2 (1993): 183–95.

rhizomatic flowering, always on the move. But its aroma is real, knowable, tastable, for the moment that it lingers.)

Another Peircean triad that plays a particularly acute role in the moments of decision by which entities (or "eventities") like us become, is the triad referred to by Peirce under the deceptively technical label of "normative sciences." Unlike phenomenology, which for Peirce inquires into *phenomena as they appear* (that is, in their firstness), and metaphysics, which inquires into *reality as it really and ultimately is* (in its thirdness), the normative sciences examine phenomena in their secondness — that is, in the ways they act upon us and we in turn act upon them. It is with these that we find our opening to act and affect the world, to respond to it creatively, and to renegotiate and reframe our own and others' potentialities for future action.

The three normative sciences, for Peirce, are aesthetics, ethics, and logic.[35] As entities capable of acting both upon others and upon ourselves, we are, for Peirce, called upon to cultivate habits by which we can manifest the ethically good, the logically true, and the aesthetically beautiful — or at least to decide upon how we would define our own "good, true, and beautiful," to be tested out in action within our lives. Insofar as they are mat-

---

35 The division of the normative sciences into aesthetics, ethics, and logic came relatively late in the development of Peirce's thought and is found in its most complete form in his writings and lectures from 1902 onward. See especially the fifth of his Harvard Lectures on Pragmatism, "The Three Normative Sciences," in *The Essential Peirce: Selected Philosophical Writings,* Vol. 2 (1893–1913), ed. Peirce Edition Project, 196–207 (Bloomington: Indiana University Press, 1998); and "An Outline Classification of the Sciences" in the same volume, 256–62. See also Beverley Kent, *Charles S. Peirce: Logic and the Classification of the Sciences* (Montreal: McGill–Queen's University Press, 1987); Bent Sørensen and Torkild Leo Thellefsen, "The Normative Sciences, the Sign Universe, Self-Control and Relationality — According to Peirce," *Cosmos and History* 6, no. 1 (2010): 142–52; Martin Lefebvre, "Peirce's Esthetics: A Taste for Signs in Art," *Transactions of the Charles S. Peirce Society* 43, no. 2 (2007): 319–44; Carl M. Smith, "The Aesthetics of Charles S. Peirce," *Journal of Aesthetics and Art Criticism* 31, no. 1 (1972): 21–29; Herman Parret, ed., *Peirce and Value Theory* (Amsterdam: John Benjamins, 1994); Aaron Massecar, *Ethical Habits: A Peircean Perspective* (New York: Lexington Books, 2016).

ters of cultivation, the normative sciences are as much science as art. They are akin to Michel Foucault's "techniques of the self" or "arts of existence"[36] — arts by which we cultivate habits that allow us to appreciate and manifest the beautiful or admirable (aesthetics), the just and virtuous in our relationships with others (ethics), and the truthful in our understanding of the world (logic).

A "logo-ethico-aesthetics" is in this sense not mere study, but always an appreciation (being aesthetic), an action (that is ethical), and a commitment to learning alongside others into the indefinite future (which is logic, as conceived broadly by Peirce). With his focus on the cultivation of habits, Peirce strove in his ethics, in Aaron Massecar's words, "not to advocate for one ideal over another, but to ensure that the ideals that one is *already* striving for are actually worthy of admiration."[37] Aesthetics, here, involves the capacity to appreciate the admirable; ethics, the capacity to pursue it through action; and logic, the pursuit of it through thought.

It is through the cultivation of new habits of mind and body that we can modify our behavior in coordination with our beliefs, so as to test whether those beliefs ought to be accepted or rejected. Aesthetic habits concern firstness, the "quality of feeling" of a phenomenon, and so an important supplement to aesthetics will be the cultivation of "habits of feeling" that allow us to appreciate the "admirable."[38] Ethical habits concern secondness, or reaction and relation, such that ethics relate to "the deliberate formation of habits of *action* consistent with the

---

36 See Michel Foucault, *The Hermeneutics of the Subject: Lectures at the Collège de France 1981–1982*, ed. Frederic Gros (New York: Picador, 2005); Luther H. Martin, Huck Gutman, and Patrick Hutton, eds., *Technologies of the Self: A Seminar with Michel Foucault* (Amherst: University of Massacusetts Press, 1988).

37 Aaron Massecar, *Ethical Habits*, 139.

38 See Charles S. Peirce, *Collected Papers of Charles Sanders Peirce*, eds. Charles Hartshorne and Paul Weiss (Bloomington: Indiana University Press, 1958), 5.129 and 8.256; and Parret, "Peircean Fragments on the Aesthetic Experience," 181ff.

ethical ideal" and with the "deliberately adopted aim."[39] Logical habits concern thirdness, or mediated representation, pattern, and law. The goal of logic is to discover the "habits of inference that lead to knowledge, including positive knowledge" (supposing there is a reality to a given phenomenon), and "to such semblance of knowledge as phenomena permit (supposing there is no perfect reality)."[40] While logic is about truth and falsity, and ethics is about "wise and foolish conduct," aesthetics is about "attractive and repulsive ideas" and more generally about "expressiveness."[41] Let us examine each of these further in light of process-relational thinking.

Aesthetics. An aesthetic of firstness, for Peirce, was not merely about our appreciation and evaluation of things that appear to us, such as art or physical appearance. It is also about our comportment toward those appearances: about the ways we *allow* things to appear to us and the ways we cultivate the appearance of things *to us.* This aesthetic of appearances concerns perceiving and cultivating something like the beauty in things. "Beauty" is a risky term here, since it is culturally variable. Peirce found it inadequate, preferring the Greek terms *kalos* and *agamai,* since they accommodated the unbeautiful within their scope, and Peirce acknowledged that aesthetic goodness is hardly encompassable within our perception of what is pleasant or not.[42]

Like Peirce, Whitehead prioritized aesthetics as an essential and primordial facet of all experience, more fundamental than either ethics or logic, and from which the latter two are at least in some measure derived. For Whitehead, the production of beauty was in fact the *telos* of the universe. In *Adventures of Ideas,* where it figures as one of five qualities of a civilized

---

39 This phrasing is Beverley Kent's, from *Charles S. Peirce,* 165, 133.

40 Ibid., 170.

41 Peirce, *Collected Papers,* 5.551; "The Three Normative Sciences," in *The Essential Peirce,* vol. 2, 203.

42 Kent, *Charles S. Peirce,* 154–55. Similarly, Whitehead spoke of the value of Discord for the development of Beauty (terms that he capitalized in *Adventures of Ideas,* 252ff.).

society, Whitehead defined beauty initially as "the mutual adaptation of the several factors in an occasion of experience,"[43] but then qualified and complicated this by discussing "major" versus "minor" beauty (the former produces *intensity* through novel contrasts, while the latter merely exhibits harmony among factors), and by insisting on the importance of dissonance or discord in prompting "adventure."

In his theory of aesthetics, Whitehead distinguished the more conventional form of perception "in the mode of presentational immediacy," with its vivid, focused sense percepts, from "perception in the mode of causal efficacy," which perceives through feeling-tones disclosing the wholeness, interrelatedness, and background texture surrounding events in time. Causal efficacy, Catherine Keller writes, "is the underworld of actuality: the past energetically decomposing as the very ground of the present's composition."[44] The two modes combine into the hybrid form of perception Whitehead called "symbolic reference," which he thought was able to render the focal percepts of the first mode as poetic evocations of the flow of time, with its "perishability" and "tragic beauty."[45] Steve Odin compares Whitehead's "poetics of evanescence" with the use of images found in Romantic poetry (which Whitehead often quoted) and in Japanese aesthetics. In his last book, *Modes of Thought,* for instance, Whitehead quotes Percy Bysshe Shelley's poem "Hellas":

World on worlds are rolling ever
From creation to decay,
Like Bubbles in a river,

---

43 Whitehead, *Adventures of Ideas,* 252.

44 Catherine Keller, "Psychocosmetics and the Underworld Connection," in *Archetypal Process: Self and Divine in Whitehead, Jung, and Hillman,* ed. David R. Griffin (Northwestern University Press, 1989), 141.

45 Whitehead's most extended treatment of aesthetic perception comes in *Symbolism: Its Meaning and Effect* (New York: Fordham Unviersity Press, 1927/1985). Steve Odin's *Tragic Beauty in Whitehead and Japanese Aesthetics* (New York: Lexington Books, 2016) provides a detailed exegesis of the later Whitehead's axiological "process aesthetics" with its focus on "beauty as perishability."

Sparkling, bursting, borne away.[46]

Aside from being an effective evocation of Whitehead's entire ontology, a quote like this demonstrates the kind of "tragic beauty" that is the culminating note of Whitehead's 1933 book *Adventures in Ideas*:

> At the heart of the nature of things, there are always the dream of youth and the harvest of tragedy. The Adventure of the Universe starts with the dream and reaps tragic Beauty. [...] The immediate experience of this Final Fact, with its union of Youth and Tragedy, is the sense of Peace. In this way the World receives its persuasion towards such perfections as are possible for its diverse individual occasions.[47]

In Steve Odin's exegesis, this provides a key to Whitehead's "aesthetic of perishing," which resonates with the Buddhist-Lacanian perception of "dark flow" articulated earlier and with Peirce's sense of aesthetics as the capacity for perceiving the arisings of firstness in the world. Odin compares it also to Dōgen Zenji's thirteenth century Zen Buddhist metaphysics of "reality as *genjokoan*," with its emphasis on the "presence of things as they are" in their perishability and impermanence.

Summarizing, we can say that to the extent that all perceptions arise in relational contexts, aesthetic perception as such involves perception of a thing against and in relation to its background — a perception of the wholeness of what appears in the clarity of its appearance, but always framed by the background of its arising and its passing. This also means an awareness of its emergence into being (firstness), into interactivity (secondness), and into meaning (thirdness). In the context of our everyday lives, this suggests expanding our capacity to perceive and appreciate the nature of things — to see them not just as objects,

---

46 Whitehead, *Modes of Thought,* 44. See Odin, *Tragic Beauty in Whitehead and Japanese Aesthetics.*

47 Whitehead, *Adventures of Ideas,* 296.

present-at-hand (*Vorhanden*) or ready-to-hand (*Zuhanden*), but as processual enactments and achievements with a fragile and distinct integrity of their own, set against the background of their disappearance.

Ethics. The tradition of ethical thought associated with process-relational theory is longstanding and rich. The core of such thought commonly rests on a disavowal of the fact-value distinction, wherein values are considered to be separate from the concrete particulars of existence. At the foundation of a Whiteheadian ontology, Brian Henning posits, is the rejection of "independent existence": "every entity," Whitehead wrote, "is only to be understood in terms of the way in which it is interwoven with the rest of the Universe."[48] With his understanding of creativity as the "universal of universals," Whitehead simultaneously affirmed the particular and the universal, the individual "actual occasion" and the solidarity of the whole to which it is responding and contributing. At the same time, it is not the abstract judgment but the concrete, relational act that is central in his account. As Whitehead wrote, "in the case of those actualities whose immediate experience is most completely open to us, namely, human beings," he writes, "the final decision of the immediate subject-superject, constituting the ultimate modification of subjective aim, is the foundation of our experience of responsibility, of approbation or of disapprobation, of self-approval or of self-reproach, of freedom, of emphasis. This element in experience," he continues, "governs the whole tone of human life."[49] Beyond any causally constitutive determinations of any action, in other words, there is always the decisive act by which subjectivation occurs, the act by which subjectivity, responsibility, and effectiveness is constituted. Biologist Charles Birch and theologian John Cobb have influentially advanced the

---

48 Whitehead, "Immortality," quoted in Brian G. Henning, *Ethics of Creativity: Beauty, Morality, and Nature in a Processive Cosmos* (Pittsburgh: University of Pittsburgh, 2005), 29.

49 A.N. Whitehead, *Process and Reality,* ed. David R. Griffin and Donald W. Sherburne, corr. edn. (New York: Free Press, 1978), 47.

argument that Whiteheadian theory advocates the "liberation of life," at all levels at which decisions-making are made, "from the cell to the community" — which Cobb has argued must extend today to that of the planet.[50]

Judith Jones has proposed an ethic based on Whitehead's notions of attention and intensity, wherein agency is reconceived as "the organ of attention to reality."[51] For Whitehead, she writes,

> Each moral event, in its quest for intensity of feeling, stands forth as the locus of our moral being. The moral significance of our existence cannot be relegated to some dim 'other' time, for we pervade all times by virtue of our very immediacy. Any given individual experience bears not only on the cumulative history of our past, but also on the real potentialities of our future.[52]

What endures, in all cases of our action, "is the character of the present achievement, not a self that can disown it or 'make up' for it."[53] Ethical action is therefore not a matter of living up to a standard, but a matter of acting in a way as to yield beauty, a beauty conceived as the "intensity of feeling" arising from the patterns of experience that are possible among the subjectal arisings akin to this one, and those that are conceivable as contributing to the greater beauty of the whole in which we find ourselves.

The ethical imperative, conceived in this way, is also about cultivating ways of responding to others such that we sympathetically recognize *their* positioning in their interactions with

---

50 Charles Birch and John B. Cobb, *The Liberation of Life: From the Cell to the Community* (London: Cambridge University Press, 1981). And see Theodore Walker Jr. and Mihály Tóth, eds., *Whiteheadian Ethics: Abstracts and Papers from the Ethics Section of the Philosophy Group at the 6th International Whitehead Conference at the University of Salzburg, July 2006* (Newcastle: Cambridge Scholars Publishing, 2008).

51 Judith Jones, *Intensity: An Essay in Whiteheadian Ontology* (London: Vanderbilt University Press, 1998), 182.

52 Ibid., 181.

53 Ibid.

us. If ethics is the cultivation of skillful action in response to others, and if self and other are perceived as dynamically interactive forms arising out of patterned relations, then ethics is a matter not of rules and injunctions, but of motivated action amidst encounter. Ethics (a second), for Peirce, builds on aesthetics (a first), just as logic (a third) builds on both. An aesthetic of process-relational ethics is a cultivation of empathic relations, relations amidst subjectal arisings — self-semioses (since the self, as understood by Peirce, is a sign) that we know arise independently of us, yet are in some sense analogous to our own subjectivation. Those encountered become not mere objects for our admiration or judgment, but elusive strangers, whose faces beckon to us even as they decline to reveal themselves fully. Each relation places us at risk that out of it we may emerge no longer ourselves, but other.

Logic. Finally, informed by the aesthetic (in-habited feelings and percepts) and the ethical (in-habited action), logic is also something different from the rule-based form of reasoning that is commonly counterposed against the failings of illogic. It is, for Whitehead and for Peirce, more akin to what we might call *eco*logic, a skillful understanding of relational emergence (appearance), interaction, and generality. An *ethico-aesthetics* of ecologic — an eco-logo-ethico-aesthetics — involves recognizing, and in turn cultivating, the vitality of the systemic connections that sustain a whole, which means a cultivation of skillful understanding that emanates as *praxis,* since it enfolds action and perception within itself.

Each of these three aesthetics I have outlined — of appearances, of relational encounters, and of ecology — is a selective response to a broader array of possibilities that encompass beauty alongside ugliness, good alongside evil, justice alongside injustice, and systemic cohesion alongside disorder and collapse. Being attentive to these options, and acknowledging their viability even as one opts for one of them over another, means recognizing that chaos or injustice, for instance, are not necessarily "bad." In given circumstances one might even decide that it is right to cultivate the beauty and truthfulness of the chaotic, or the dissonance of justice.

Such a logo-ethico-aesthetics, in other words, is not pre-scriptive in advance of a situation. It is a method of movement through situations that recognizes the dependence of thirdness (logic, ecology, pattern) on secondness (ethics, action, actual-ity), and of both on firstness (appearance, aesthetics, qualitative potency).[54] It involves a continual "thickening" or "deepening" of the moment, with its arisings and passings, to receive its "soulful" call to us for action and response in light of their back-ground of flow and transitoriness.

If there is an essential action here — a kind of primal gesture of process-relational awareness — it is a movement that proceeds from (1) careful attending to (2) "widening" and "deepening" to (3) motion or action, which in turn realizes the valuative capaci-ties presented by those widened and deepened contexts. That is, one begins by *attending* to that which is there (whatever it is we are encountering); expands that attention through a simul-taneous *widening* of contextual relevances and a *deepening* of valuative feeling; and responsively *moves* with and in relation to the object or matter at the center of our concern. Through that movement, the contexts and values are "played," as it were, in a kind of echoing or rippling of the resonant harmonies set off by the responsive action. (For an exercise related to this "gesture," see "Widening and deepening practice," Appendix 3, Exercise 5.)

In attending respectfully to what we encounter and open-ing ourselves to the perception of what in it is admirable, we learn to master the art of firstness, or the aesthetic. In valuing

---

54 Peirce's thinking on beauty and ugliness, good and evil, and coherence and incoherence, retained some ambiguity right through to the end of his life. For instance, he wrote: "Man comes to his normal development only through the so-called evil passions, which are evil, only in the sense that they ought to be controlled, and are good as the only possible agency for giving man his full development" (cited in Kent, *Charles S. Peirce*, 155). Evil is, in this sense, "perfection in God's eyes," but while people can move to-ward a God-like vision, they have not at present (if ever) attained that vi-sion.

and contextualizing the significances of the situation, we do the same with the art of thirdness, that of logic. And in acting according to the valuative resonances enabled thereby, we exercise ourselves in ethical secondness. (The order of the categories, as you see, is not linear; they interact at every level and in each direction.) This "triple gesture" involves a willingness to consider the multiple factors at play in a given situation, to weigh them out in terms of the intensities they make available and the opportunities for producing beauty in any resulting synthesis, and to seek always to "go beyond" any given synthesis as one reaches toward a future that remains open and pregnant with further possibility. To act *logically,* in this sense, is to give sustenance to the flowering of an open and dynamic universe.

Praxis. Any such ongoing effort when turned into a logo-ethico-aesthetic praxis, if it is to be effective, ought to become embodied and in a sense "ritualized," so that it can sediment within the "in-habited" bodymind of its practitioner. Doing this requires developing some set of iterative techniques, with ritualized ways of taking account of how one is doing. In his later years, Peirce seemed to be moving toward an elaboration of techniques for this cultivation of habits — an elaboration that Aaron Massecar classifies into nine steps by which aesthetically derived "ideals" are adopted, tested, and embodied as habits aimed toward the growth of what Peirce called "concrete reasonableness."[55] Fortunately, examples of how such practices can be incorporated into one's life are found much more widely than this, scattered as they are across the world's religions and their respective traditions of "self-cultivation," from those of Stoic, Neoplatonic, Daoist, or Confucian philosophers to Christian, Jewish, and Sufi mystics, to those practiced by Neo-Pagans, ritual magicians, and other psychospiritual explorers today. I will not elaborate on these except to say that in almost all of these traditions, a daily regimen has been recognized as particularly helpful.

---

55   Aaron Massecar, "The Fitness of an Ideal: A Peircean Ethics," *Contemporary Pragmatism* 10, no. 2 (2013): 97–119.

A morning practice, for instance, might include the ritualizing of concepts and images guiding one's current practice, embodied in some physical and psychological gestures, movements, and reflective practices that prepare one for the day ahead. An evening practice might include a retrospective overview of the day, its challenges, one's responses to those challenges, and the action-points at which those responses themselves might be tweaked in future iterations. The larger triadic point with these is that the practices are taken on deliberately to cultivate one's capacities for reflective action in the service of desired goals. The goals are not always known in advance; they may be shaped in part by a level of trust, either in the communal institutions that aid one in these practices or in the "images" that guide them (and to which we will turn in a moment).

A logo-ethico-aesthetics built on these understandings situates us as active respondents in the midst of matters of concern, and nudges us toward perceiving these matters as relational in ever widening contexts. At a time when these contexts raise urgent questions about our relations with a thickening and expansive array of others — all of those others implicated in the climate changes and ecological disruptions industrial humanity's actions are producing — such a practice of "integral ecology" (if you will) becomes far more than a mapping of scenarios, a strategy of containment or crisis management. It becomes a cosmopolitical project, an active and ongoing logo-ethico-aesthetic practice whose ends we cannot foresee or forestall.

As we are all caught amidst matters of concern, minding our matters and mattering what we mind, and as our interrelations become ever more conjoined — agonistically, yet always with a promise of reaching new perceptions and understandings — so we grasp toward a cosmopolitics that brings ever more of us together. With the prospect of a radically altered cosmos, the "us" that is called into being is open-ended, never pre-determined, and will ultimately take us beyond any "us" we might imagine.

It is in this sense that Michel Foucault may have been correct when he described the figure of "man" as "a recent invention" that, with a shift in structural relations, might "be erased, like a face drawn in sand at the edge of the sea."[56] The time of the Anthropo(s)cene is a time of recognition that this figure of Man has drawn its imprint upon all the sands surrounding all the seas of the earth. But it is a figure not of humanity, but of a particular constellation — of "man" as written by a certain caste of men, and of capital, and of petrochemicals and other allies — that in denying its dependencies is also denying its ultimate survivability. Sand, salt, and sea will outlast the figures we draw in them, but the figures to come will need to be of a different order than those marking the appearance and imperium of this figure of "man," the Anthropos of the present Scene. All will depend on how we respond to the others with whom we share our predicament.

Process-relational aesthetics, ethics, and (eco-)logics begin not from the ontological task of describing what the universe and the things in it are, but from specifying what matters concern us and how we might come to mind, attend, and respond to them. As subjects of concern, we then raise such questions as "who are *we*?", "who are the others who bring these questions to us?", "how do we meet with them in coming to grips with these concerns?", and "what abstractions — what ontological fabrications and abductive guesses — might help us to do this creatively and satisfyingly, for all those concerned?" This means starting from where we are not merely out of expediency but because we — all of us in this universe — start from there, from the matters of concern in which we find ourselves, which means from our relations. It is there that we can find our commonalities. From such a start we might build a more common world. Let us turn to that task now.

---

56 Michel Foucault, *The Order of Things: An Archaeology of the Human Sciences* (New York: Vintage, 1994), 387.

3

ENGAGING IMAGES: BUILDING COMMON WORLDS

Mundus imaginalis

If objects, as detailed earlier, are nothing but objectifications co-arising alongside subjectifications as parts of events, then the status of *perception* becomes different as well. The third and final part of this book explores the ramifications of that difference in the world of perception, of images, of signs and meanings, and of the ways those images take us with them, inhabiting and possessing us like gods, angels, and demons.

Object-oriented ontologist Graham Harman argues that there are *real* objects — self-sufficient entities that are what they are in and of themselves — and there are *sensual* objects — things that arise between objects, that mediate for them, that do the touching for the real objects that cannot possibly touch. In Harman's dichotomy, perception is a matter of these sensual objects that arise at the interface between real objects.

A process-relational view shares the view that *results* from this, which is that relationality is impossible without sensuality, or in fact without aesthetics. Harman calls aesthetics "first philosophy" because it is what arises whenever an object encounters another — whenever it reaches out beyond itself. As he and Timothy Morton describe it, aesthetics *is* the way objects encounter each other, even if they can never fully exhaust each other. It is the way I encounter the sights and sounds of this autumn morning (which I do today by noting and admiring it, and by adding my own exhalation to it as it adds pleasure to my day). Aesthetics *is* the way fire encounters cotton (which it does by burning it).[1]

As we have seen, Whitehead and Peirce, like others in the process-relational tradition, agree about this firstness or primacy of aesthetics. For Whitehead, "the teleology of the Universe is directed to the production of Beauty."[2] For Peirce, aesthetics precedes ethics, which in turn precedes logic. The object-oriented ontologist and her process-relational cousin agree also in their *insistence on reality.* The difference comes in the objectologists' insistence on something *beyond* the aesthetic — beyond the relational — that both precedes and completely eludes the aesthetic and relational. If that "beyond" is something that belongs to an object, which is never touched in its depths, then here is where the process-relationists part company. The latter consider this a spatialization — a kind of reification, or thingification — of something that is *temporal* because it is in the nature of the *process* of all things.[3]

Process-relational ontology, in other words, rejects this dichotomy of the real and the sensual. It takes the touchings, or prehensions — the sensual perceptions, mediations, sense-makings, interpretations, graspings, prehensions, efforts to move or act upon things as they are grasped — as *fundamentally real* and not as secondary to anything else. There is, in this view, no thing separate from its thinging.

That is not to say that there is no separation *in* the thinging; there is. It is what occurs in the relational act itself: in the movement by which the world is grasped, or prehended, and in the

---

1   Graham Harman, "Aesthetics as First Philosophy: Levinas and the Non-Human," *Naked Punch* 9 (2007): 21–30; Timothy Morton, *Realist Magic: Objects, Ontology, Causality* (Ann Arbor: Open Humanities Press, 2013).

2   A.N. Whitehead, *Adventures of Ideas* (New York: Free Press, 1961), 264.

3   My lengthier critique of the object-oriented position on this is found in Adrian Ivakhiv, "Beatnik Brothers? Between Graham Harman and the Deleuzo-Whiteheadian Axis," *Parrhesia* 19 (2014): 65–78.

movement toward the world that the prehension is *for* (that is, in the subjectivation). And, on the underside of all this, there is separation in the withdrawal of the world *from* that grasp. Insofar as there is continuity across thingings (which there is in the worlds that we deal with every day), that continuity comes from relational coordination — which can be spatial, temporal, or both — across thingings. To *thing,* in this sense, is to respond to things, which is always a matter of perception or creative integration of what is given.

This means that reality itself *is* perceptual; it is prehensive. There is nothing beyond that except the movement toward and away from it. Reality is imagistic. It consists of mediations that arise out of the congealed mediations of previous arisings. It is prehension all the way down, with crucial differences arising in the qualities of each prehension — how they reshape what they (selectively) inherit, how they move with that which they have gathered.

Image is, in this sense, everything. But image is never pure, true, accurate, or complete. It is never a perfect representation of something else, because it is always slipping from what it is imaging. It is always in motion, between what is imaged *from* and where it images *to*. Image, in this definition, is a creative reconfiguration of elements perceived or prehended, a configuration that, once satisfied, is passed on to the world for further refiguration.

This thought of the image as immanent, active, moving, and engaging, is enriched by a certain tradition of thought on the imagination that runs parallel to the tradition of processual realism, a tradition that we can now bring to the aid of the latter.

Traditionally, imagination has been thought of as something like the ability to produce internal images, and as intermediate between sensing and thinking, but prone to fallacious perception of the world. William James defined "imagination" as "the faculty of reproducing copies of originals once felt," but added that this can be both "reproductive" and "productive," where "elements from different originals are recombined so as to make new wholes."[4] The German idealists, including Kant, referred to a productive and "transcendental" imagination that, in forming images, was a precondition for all knowledge of the world.

A series of twentieth-century philosophers and psycho-analysts — including Ernst Cassirer, Paul Ricoeur, Gaston Ba-chelard, Gilbert Durand, and Cornelius Castoriadis — have pursued this idea of a productive and dynamic *imaginaire* which underpins human interpretive and symbolic activities.[5] Some have drawn on the writings of French historian of religion Henry Corbin, whose idea of *l'imaginal,* or the *mundus imagi-nalis,* was intended as a revival of Islamic Sufi and Neoplatonic conceptions of the "intermediary world" between the sensible world of material forms and the ideal or intelligible world of Platonic or spiritual forms.[6] This idea of the imagination as an active, creative capacity that mediates between human percep-tion and an ontologically real *beyond*-human world has long found a home within the tradition of esoteric and hermetic thought, a tradition historians have traced back to the late Hel-lenistic world, but which emerged more fully in the Renaissance and early modernity (in figures like Marsilio Ficino, Pico della

---

4   William James, *The Principles of Psychology,* vol. II (New York: Henry Holt & Company, 1902), 44.

5   Ernst Cassirer, *Philosophy of Symbolic Forms,* 3 vols. (New Haven: Yale Uni-versity Press, 1965); Cornelius Castoriadis, *World in Fragments: Writings on Politics, Society, Psychoanalysis, and the Imagination,* ed. David Ames Cur-tis (Stanford University Press, 1997); Gilbert Durand, *The Anthropological Structures of the Imaginary,* trans. Margaret Sankey and Judith Hatten (Bris-bane: Boombana, 1999); Richard Kearney, *Poetics of Imagining: Modern to Post-Modern* (New York: Fordham University Press, 1998).

6   Corbin drew on medieval Islamic thinkers such as Suhrawardi (1154–91) and Mullā Sadrā Shirazi (1571–1640). See Henri Corbin, "Mundus Imagi-nalis, or, the Imaginary and the Imaginal," *Spring* (1972): 1–19; Henri Cor-bin, "Towards a Chart of the Imaginal," *Spiritual Body and Celestial Earth: From Mazdean Iran to Shi'ite Iran,* 2nd edn. (Princeton University Press, 1977), xv–xix; Laura Marks, "Real Images Flow: Mullā Sadrā Meets Film-Philosophy," *Film-Philosophy* 20 (2016): 24–46; Christopher Vitale, "The Metaphysics of Refraction in Sufi Philosophy: Ibn Arabi, Suhrawardi, and Mulla Sadra Shirazi," *Networkologies,* May 17, 2012, http://networkologies. wordpress.com/2012/05/17/the-metaphysics-of-refraction-in-sufi-philoso-phy-ibn-arabi-suhrawadri-and-mulla-sadra-shirazi/.

Mirandola, Paracelsus, and Jacob Boehme), to be picked up later by Romantics (such as Blake, Coleridge, and others) and occult and New Age metaphysicians of the last few centuries.[7] Others, suspicious of any notion of a "higher reality," nevertheless speak of an intersubjectively shared, intermediate world of symbolic forms and cultural meanings, variously described as an "imagosphere," "iconosphere," or "semiosphere."[8]

A key point here is that the image is not merely visual; it is perceptual, polysensorial, and affectively primed. An image is itself — it is *an* image, *the* image — but it is always also part of a relational network by which images and meanings, material objects and interpreting subjects, intersect, and from which their *acts* of imaging originate, deviate, and to which they remain always tethered. Imaging, or image-making, is subjective, intersubjective (or collective), and infrasubjective (unconscious or preconscious) all at once. There is no such thing, really, as *the* imagination, or *one's* imagination. There is imaging.

In the post-Freudian context of psychological theorizing, the notion of the "imaginal" has been most thoroughly rendered by archetypal psychologist James Hillman. Following Corbin and

---

7   See Antoine Faivre, *Western Esotericism: A Concise History,* trans. Christine Rhone (Albany: SUNY Press, 2010); Wouter Hanegraaff, *Esotericism and the Academy: Rejected Knowledge in Western Culture* (Cambridge: Cambridge University Press, 2013); Ioan P. Couliano, *Eros and Magic in the Renaissance* (Chciago: University of Chicago Press, 1987). On the creative imagination more generally, see Richard Kearney, *The Wake of Imagination: Toward a Postmodern Culture* (New York: Routledge, 1988); Eva Brann, *The World of Imagination: Sum and Substance,* 25th anniv. edn. (Lanham: Rowman & Littlefield, 2017); Gillian Robinson and John Rundell, eds., *Rethinking Imagination: Culture and Creativity* (New York: Routledge, 1994); Joshua Ramey, *The Hermetic Deleuze: Philosophy as Spiritual Ordeal* (Durham: Duke University Press, 2012).

8   Corin Braga, "'Imagination', 'Imaginaire', 'Imaginal': Three Concepts for Defining Creative Fantasy," *Journal for the Study of Religions and Ideologies* 16 (2007): 59–68; Jesper Hoffmeyer, *Signs of Meaning in the Universe* (Bloomington: Indiana University Press, 1996); Juri Lotman, "On the Semiosphere," *Sign Systems Studies* 33, no. 1 (2005): 205–29; Chiara Bottici, *Imaginal Politics: Images Between Imagination and the Imaginary* (New York: Columbia University Press, 2014).

Carl Jung, the foundational datum for Hillman's archetypalism is the image conceived not as a representation of something else but as irreducible and autochthonous, "psyche itself in its imaginative visibility."[9] The source of images, for Hillman, is "the self-generative activity of the soul itself," with "soul" being a term for the "*tertium* between the perspectives of body (matter, nature, empirics) and of mind (spirit, logic, idea)." Soul, in Hillman's definition, is "the perspective *between* others and from which others may be viewed," "a perspective rather than a substance, a viewpoint toward things rather than a thing itself."[10] This makes it a close relation to the mental-perceptual mediating dynamic between subjectivation and objectivation, or Shinzen Young's "flow," that is at the heart of reality conceived as relational process.

The image, in Hillman's account, is not only what is seen but also the *way* of its seeing, and *soul* is the way of seeing that "deepens" events into experiences.[11] It is, in this sense, a way of perceiving that allows the fruition of secondness (action) into thirdness (realization). Archetypal or mythic images are not images that "ground" or "compensate" for some lack or deficiency, as in other forms of psychoanalysis. Rather, they enable and open up: they are "images of intelligibility" that disclose "the plot of things, the way in which the world appears and we are in its images."[12]

Humans, in this account, are not mere viewers of images; we *dwell* in (and as) images, and in so doing we make the world. The human is "a sense-enjoying, image-making creature," an animal "in an ecological field that affords imagistic intelligibility." Our task is not merely to see and respond to things, but to see "the face of the Gods in things." This requires an active imagination and an "aesthetic culture," and it calls for a "polytheistic psychol-

---

9   James Hillman, *Archetypal Psychology: A Brief Account* (Dallas: Spring, 1983), 6.

10 Ibid., 5, 16.

11 Ibid., 16.

12 James Hillman, "On Mythic Certitude," *Sphinx: A Journal for Archetypal Psychology and the Arts* 3 (1990): 224–43, at 230.

ogy" appropriate to a pluralistic universe — the kind of universe proposed, among others, by Whitehead and James.[13]

The method of archetypal psychology is a "giving over to the images and cultivating them for their sake."[14] Images, according to Hillman, make a "moral claim" upon their subjects, and the appropriate response to this claim is metaphorical, poetic, and imaginative, a method of "sticking to the image" so that the image can "release and refine further imagining."[15] This releasing is a releasing *into the image,* which, since it is a moving image, always means *into a world that takes one somewhere else.* In and through that movement one becomes other. Where a more conservative Jungian interpretation (and Hillman was a close, if somewhat iconoclastic, follower of Jung's) might consider archetypal images to be those things that keep us tethered to an underlying substrate of foundational meanings, the reading I am proposing is one that keeps us tethered only to the ongoing creative becoming of the universe. In selecting which images to enact, we become the aesthetic, ethical, and (eco-)logical enactors of the worlds we create, alongside the others we create them with.

This notion of cultivating images *for the sake* of the images themselves is not the kind of thing one hears from a semioticist like Peirce, for whom semiosis is ultimately moving in the direction of greater reasonableness. For Hillman, by contrast, the movement often seems to be away from reasonableness toward something more mysterious and unfathomable. Yet the movement, for both, is in the direction of *realization.* And to the extent that Peirce's reason remains grounded in ethics and, ulti-

13 James Hillman, "Back to Beyond: On Cosmology," in *Archetypal Process: Self and Divine in Whitehead, Jung, and Hillman,* eds. David Ray Griffin, 213–31 (Evanston: Northwestern University Press, 1989), 226. See also James Hillman, *Archetypal Psychology,* 14, 34. For an updated, neo-Jamesian argument espousing a pluralistic universe, see William Connolly, *A World of Becoming* (Durham: Duke University Press, 2010).

14 James Hillman, *Re-Visioning Psychology* (New York: Harper Colophon, 1975), 40.

15 Hillman, "Back to Beyond," 253; Hillman, *Archetypal Psychology,* 9.

mately, in aesthetics, the implication is that reason itself is the fruition of the very possibilities found in ethics and aesthetics. If the image is understood in a process-relational sense *as movement,* or, more precisely, as a particular constellation of possibilities for movement, as a fragment of time that looks simultaneously backward and forward to its past and future virtualities, then every image ought to be seen as a *living and moving* image. Images in this sense contain affective and semiotic capacities, vectors along which we can move if we open up to them.

Iconoclash

And if image is everything (or at least *part* of everything), then we are fated to dwell in a universe of what Bruno Latour calls *iconoclash* — conflict over the nature of the images by which we reflect, refract, and diffract ourselves and our world, and from which we can never extract ourselves except at the expense of self-delusion.

The two extreme reactions to such a world, Latour posits, are *iconoclasm* and *idolatry.*[16] The first denies the power of icons, or images, except as passive intermediaries of other things. (Most commonly, it denies the power of *others'* icons, not recognizing its own denial to be iconic or imagistic in the least.) Iconoclasm takes images to be mere representations, dead photographs, more or less accurate, of something else that may be or may have been alive and whose significance is primary. Dreaming of an "unmediated access to truth," it distinguishes the thing itself from its representation, and assumes the first is of an order of

---

16 Latour's taxonomy of responses to the image is more complex; see "What Is Iconoclash? Or Is There a World Beyond the Image Wars?" in *Iconoclash: Beyond the Image Wars in Science, Religion, and Art,* eds. Bruno Latour and Peter Weibel (Cambridge: MIT Press, 2002). The two extreme positions, with Latour's "iconophilia" mediating between them, are introduced in "How To Be Iconophilic in Art, Science, and Religion?," in *Picturing Science, Producing Art,* eds. Caroline Jones and Peter Galison, 418–40 (New York: Routledge, 1998).

reality and significance that the latter cannot possibly attain.[17] Alternatively, it may deny that even the object of the representation has any reality apart from what people fallaciously ascribe to it. In this harsher version, iconoclasm not only denies the icon any validity outside the realm of humanly created meaning; it also denies such validity to anything else. (Strict social constructivism, if taken as a claim about reality rather than as analytical method, belongs in this category.)

The second reaction, idolatry, takes the images as fully present and final, as only what — and as powerful as — they claim to be, and not as relationally dependent at all. They are "transcendental signifieds," which stand in independent glory apart from the universe of muddy entanglements that define the rest of us.

Instead of these two opposed positions, Latour advocates *iconophilia,* which he calls "respect not for the image itself but for the movement of the image," for "the movement, the passage, the transition from one form of image to another."[18] Images, by this definition, are always in motion. They are the responsiveness that objectifies in subjectivating, the vehicles for the mutually co-constitutive subject-objectifications that make up reality in any and every moment.

Adam Miller takes Latour's writings on religion as the basis for theological speculations that approximate what I am getting at here. Miller writes, "Every object is a kind of icon that bears rather than reflects the mobile presence of the other objects that constitute it." In contrast to iconoclasm and idolatry, iconophilia is the approach that "patiently solicits" the icon. It "stay[s] with objects and suffer[s] the grace of their work, the grace of both their making-available and their packing-away."[19] Iconophilia is much like the "critical idolatry" advocated by W.J.T. Mitchell, which "does not dream of destroying" idols, but "recognizes

---

17 Latour, "How to be Iconophilic," 421.

18 Ibid.

19 Adam S. Miller, *Speculative Grace: Bruno Latour and Object-Oriented Theory* (New York: Fordham University Press, 2013), 131.

every act of disfiguration or defacement as itself an act of creative destruction for which we must take responsibility." It is a "playing" and "sounding" of idols, by which they are made to "speak and resonate."[20]

For the iconophile, icons or images are the vehicles that carry us and the world across the spaces that render the immanent transcendent, and the transcendent immanent. They are the gods, the angels and *daimones,* the deities with whom we are co-dependent. "If the gods exist in Latour's pluriverse," Miller writes, "they are not pure, unconditioned, or exceptional. They are not free from the necessity of translation, negotiation, and compromise. Nor are they free from a need for techniques, instruments, technologies, calculations, and metrologies. The gods too, like every other object, must receive the resistant availability of the proliferating multitude as the gift that it is."[21]

If image is everything, and if image is always impure — never a mere representation, but also never a totality in and of itself — then we find ourselves in a universe that is once again polytheistic and pagan: a universe in which images are as gods that possess those who are imaged, but who never do so fully and whose possessions must always be negotiated. The question is always *how* to subject ourselves to them, how to venerate the gods, comply with them, transgress against them, defile them, and negotiate our relations with them.

Without us, no gods; without the gods, no us. The gods here may well be Whitehead's "eternal objects," which are eternal only insofar as they are not dependent on time, as they can arise anywhere when the conditions are ripe for their appearance. They are dependent, rather, on us, for without our active participation they have no reality. Without us, they remain only as "pure potentials."[22] In and through us they are worlded.

---

20 W.J.T. Mitchell, *What Do Pictures Want? The Lives and Loves of Images* (Chicago: University of Chicago Press, 2005), 26–27.

21 Miller, *Speculative Grace,* 43.

22 Whitehead, *Process and Reality,* 22.

What I am suggesting here is that a certain paganism — an iconophilic and pluralistic practice of engagement with deities, or something akin to deities — can help us think through the place of the image in perception and sensibility. Paganism serves as something like the ancient and original ground of imagistic consciousness, the ocean in which we semiotic beings swim.

In my book *Ecologies of the Moving Image,* I argued that the moving image is central to how moderns make sense of the world. If the modern world, as Martin Heidegger claimed, was the "age of the world picture," then it makes sense to think of the twentieth and twenty-first century worlds as the "age of the world *motion* picture."[23] (That it has become a *digital* age, in part, is relevant, but let us leave that for later.) And, of course, the oral and textual traditions of literacy that mark much of human history have hardly gone away. But if we take prehension — the creative act of taking account — as the paradigmatic act, then it is precisely acts of imaging, of moving semiotically from what is given to its uptake, via whatever organs or vehicles of perception and cognition may be available, that make up the universe. How we image the world, and how we take up those images in our acts *of imaging,* is both how we add to the world and how we constitute ourselves in the process. There is no safe space into which we can retreat without being defiled and transformed by our acts of imaging.

A pagan world

Adding a word like "pagan" to our vocabulary at this point is not intended to confuse. It is intended to acknowledge an original confusion, an original hybridity — between self and other, image and imaged, within which we always find (and lose) ourselves. The term *paganus* emerged historically, in the late Roman empire, as part of an effort of purification whereby the

---

23 See also Adrian Ivakhiv, "The Age of the World Motion Picture: Cosmic Visions in the Post-Earthrise Era," in *The Changing World Religion Map*, vol. 1, ed. Stan Brunn, 129–44 (London: Springer, 2015).

complex meta- and trans-human politics of appeasement and local obeisance, a politics of negotiated relations and genuflections, translations and syncretisms, idols and propitiatory rites, was subsumed within the universal calculus of a monotheistic verticality.[24] Here was the self, sinful and needing of correction, agent-like within clear limits. There was the one true God, ultimate agent and arbiter.

Christianity almost inevitably failed at this purification. From the Catholic veneration of saints, angels, and the Holy Theotokos herself to the spirit-filled graces and possession-like movements of Pentacostalism, the world's complex enchantments have continued to churn up from the imagistic production engine of reality. Here is where Charles Taylor's thesis on the "immanent frame" — a thesis that poses modernity as a kind of purification of transcendent realities — needs to be examined (which we will do presently).

In an account of the political theology of ancient Greece, historical anthropologist Marcel Detienne claims that "over three-quarters of the world is naturally polytheistic." "Consider," he writes, "the eight hundred myriad deities in Japan, the countless metamorphoses of the deities of Hinduism, the thousands of genies and powers of Black Africa. Likewise, the forests and mountain ranges of Oceania, the Indian subcontinent, and South America are teeming with pantheons with great clusters of deities."[25] These, like the gods and goddesses of ancient Rome or of West Africa, with their descendant mixtures in the Afro-Caribbean religions of Vodoun, Santeria, Candomble, and others, are characterized by fluidity and flexibility, with multi-

---

24 See Owen Davies, *Paganism: A Very Short Introduction* (New York: Oxford University Press, 2011); Ramsay McMullen, *Christianity and Paganism in the Fourth to Eighth Centuries* (New Haven: Yale University Press, 1999); Ken Dowden, *European Paganism: The Realities of Cult from Antiquity to the Middle Ages* (London: Routledge, 2000); A.D. Lee, *Pagans and Christians in Late Antiquity: A Sourcebook,* 2nd edn. (London: Routledge, 2016).

25 Marcel Detienne, "The Gods of Politics in Early Greek Cities," in *Political Theologies: Public Religions in a Post-Secular World,* eds. Hent de Vries and Lawrence Sullivan, 91–101 (New York: Fordham University Press, 2006), 95.

ple names and personalities blurring into others and fulfilling overlapping functions as one moves from one place to another. The "field of polytheisms," in Detienne's account, "constitutes a vast continent," one in which gods are not only everywhere, but are "plural, constituted by the intersection of a variety of attributes."[26]

The figure of paganism has played a curious role in the intellectual history of the modern world, bobbing up and down at various times against the horizon of philosophical thought. It thoroughly infused the humanism and artistic flourishing of the Renaissance, just as it helped power the Enlightenment project with hopes of a revitalization of the worldliness of Classical thought.[27] More recently, pagan thoughts have figured heavily in the ruminations of philosophers from Nietzsche and Heidegger to Lyotard, Serres, and Sloterdijk. To deepen our understanding of the implications of the "pagan" perspective I am proposing and to better establish its polytheistic iconophilism — this open engagement with the middle-ground of images and icons and of how they take and carry us, and we them, in turn — will require engagement with some alternative perspectives.

Specifically, in the forthcoming pages I will engage, critically but I hope productively, with two alternatives to my proposed iconophilism: Canadian social philosopher Charles Taylor's analysis of modernity and secularism, and Slovenian cultural theorist Slavoj Žižek's critique of all manner of "holist" or totalizing metaphysics (which echoes similar critiques by Graham Harman and Timothy Morton). The first of these laments (albeit ambivalently) the loss of an enchanted world, while the second celebrates it, but both agree on a kind of alignment between left-wing politics and Christianity (in name if not in substance). To negotiate the differences between an iconophilic process-relationalism and these alternative perspectives, I will draw upon

---

26 Detienne, "The Gods of Politics," 95.

27 See, e.g., Jean Seznec, *The Survival of the Pagan Gods: The Mythological Tradition and Its Place in Renaissance Humanism and Art* (New York: Harper, 1953), and Peter Gay, *The Enlightenment: An Interpretation — The Rise of Modern Paganism* (New York: A.A. Knopf, 1967).

the work of allies: in particular, political philosopher William Connolly's "immanent naturalism" and Bruno Latour's and Isabelle Stengers's writings on cosmopolitics.

In the process, I hope to build a case for an iconophilic and imagistic process-relationism that is neither secular nor postsecular, but that can mediate between the world-building efforts of theists and secularists alike. In a world where the play of images, deities, religiosities, and the ghosts of multiple life-ways are all in undiplomatic flux, such an approach can help us navigate the rapids.

The immanent frame

According to a well established narrative, most closely identified with sociologist Max Weber, technological modernity has disenchanted our world and created rifts between humans and nature, spirit and matter, body and soul, sacred and secular. Many modern thinkers celebrated this disenchantment as a liberation from the shackles of faith and superstition. Others accepted it as the price to pay for the benefits of modernity. For thinkers like Condillac, Marx, and Comte, an enchanted world may have had its comforts, but we are past it now and there is no going back. Enlightenment requires a clearer, more sober understanding of ourselves and our world.

A second, more critical tradition lamented this disenchantment and preferred ways of reversing or revaluing that which was lost in the process. Representatives of this critical tradition range across the political spectrum: from pessimist Romantics, religious fundamentalists, and conservative traditionalists — whose ranks include the likes of Carl Jung, Rene Guenon, Ananda Coomaraswamy, Ernst Jünger, Martin Heidegger, and Alain de Benoist — to socialists and neo-Marxists like Max Horkheimer, Theodore Adorno, Ernst Bloch, and Michael Löwy. Some, like medieval historian Lynn White, Jr. and cultural historian Morris Berman, have suggested a quasi-religious solution to what is essentially a problem of the disappearance of religion. Variations on such a "re-enchantment" are popular among ecological thinkers.

There is a third tradition that rejects the disenchantment/re-enchantment frame altogether, seeing it as a modern construct that misses the complexity underlying terms like enchantment, wonder, and even the sacred — qualities that have not disappeared at all, but have simply shifted from some places (temples and religious experiences) to others (technological gadgets, Hollywood stars, bodies, sexual conquests, ostentatious displays of wealth, nature, the world itself).[28] Here we find the views of those who see the universe as open, emergent, and in a state of ceaseless becoming, a world in which enchantment, wonder, or spirit are immanent rather than transcendent: philosophers and scientists like Gilles Deleuze, Félix Guattari, Bruno Latour, Donna Haraway, Stuart Kaufmann, Ilya Prigogine, William Connolly, and Catherine Keller.[29] It is from them that I take my impetus in teasing out the fault-lines of the secular and the religious.

In recent thinking about the sacred and the secular, the second, critical view has found an influential champion in Cana-

28 Jane Bennett, *The Enchantment of Modern Life: Attachments Crossings, Ethics* (Princeton: Princeton University Press, 2001); Birgit Meyer and Peter Pels, *Magic and Modernity: Interfaces of Revelation and Concealment* (Stanford: Stanford University Press, 2003); Alex Owen, *The Place of Enchantment: British Occultism and the Culture of the Modern* (Chicago: University of Chicago Press, 2004); Randall Styers, *Making Magic: Religion, Magic, and Science in the Modern World* (Oxford: Oxford University Press, 2004); Christopher Partridge, *The Re-Enchantment of the West*, vols. 1 and 2 (London: Continuum, 2005–6); Steve Pile, *Real Cities: Modernity, Space, and the Phantasmagorias of City Life* (London: Sage, 2005); Joshua Landy and Michael Saler, *The Re-Enchantment of the World: Secular Magic in a Rational Age* (Stanford: Stanford University Press, 2009); Jason Josephson-Storm, *The Myth of Disenchantment: Magic, Modernity, and the Birth of the Human Sciences* (Chicago: University of Chicago Press, 2017).

29 E.g., Stuart Kauffman, *Reinventing the Sacred: A New View of Science, Reason, and Religion* (New York: Basic, 2008); William Connolly, *Why I Am Not a Secularist* (Minneapolis: University of Minnesota Press, 2000); Catherine Keller and Mary-Jane Rubenstein, eds., *Entangled Worlds: Religion, Science, and New Materialisms* (New York: Fordham University Press, 2017); and many books already cited.

dian social philosopher Charles Taylor. Taylor's celebrated 2007 tome *A Secular Age* presented an exhaustive analysis of the "malaises of modernity," including a wide-ranging account of the constitution of modern secular subjectivity and of the "conditions of belief" that shape it. Inspired in part by Heidegger's hermeneutic phenomenology and by Foucault's analysis of the discursive and pre-discursive shifts shaping people's orientations in the world, Taylor posited a categorical opposition between "transcendence" and "immanence," an opposition he aligned closely with religious belief and "unbelief."

Taylor's argument, in a nutshell, was that modernity has achieved a "great disembedding" that has produced a "buffered" modern self — a kind of self-as-object, which is as disconnected from other selves as it is from the world at large. This bounded object-self has become disengaged from the larger world in at least three significant ways. First, in the "enchanted" and "embedded" world of pre-modernity, religious life had been "inseparably linked with social life,"[30] with sociality embedded in a cosmos "populated by spirits, demons, and moral forces."[31] For moderns, this embeddedness has been sundered. Second, "the primary agency of important religious action" had always been "the social group as a whole, or some more specialized agency recognized as acting for the group," such that people "related to God as a society."[32] Today, the primary agent is the individual. And, third, "Divinity's benign purposes" were "defined in terms of ordinary human flourishing";[33] that, too, for Taylor, is gone.

According to Taylor, this triple embedding within "social order, cosmos, and human good"[34] was disrupted not in one fell swoop, but over the course of several historical shifts. The emergence of "Axial" religions and philosophies in the middle of the first millennium BCE — including the teachings of Plato and

---

30 Charles Taylor, *A Secular Age* (Cambridge: Harvard University Press, 2007), 147.
31 Ibid., 26.
32 Ibid., 148.
33 Ibid., 150.
34 Ibid., 151.

Aristotle, the Buddha, Confucius, Lao Tzu, and Jesus — enabled a transcendence of the human condition that, significantly, was *individual*. For instance, elements within Christianity individualized the understanding of religion through their focus on repentance, the monastic vocation, the facing of Judgment Day rather than seeing death as part of the round of life, and so on. But these eventually developed into "post-Axial compromises" wherein individual salvation could be sought, but always within a moral landscape shaped by socially shared understandings of virtue and wickedness.

It was not until much later that a fully non-religious alternative became available as a counter-force to religious faith. This alternative was "exclusive humanism," which first developed as an intellectual alternative to Christianity. Exclusive humanism was "an achievement" that required "training, or inculcated insight, and frequently much work on ourselves"[35] — work that included articulating and internalizing a notion of benevolence as internally rooted (either in reason or in a natural propensity to sympathy, or in a synthesis of the two), of disengaged reason and individual agency (accompanied by many forms and practices of "interiorization"), and of secular public space. For those who followed this shift, the "porous self" was replaced by a "buffered" self, "for whom it comes to seem axiomatic that all thought, feeling and purpose, all the features we normally can ascribe to agents, must be in minds, which are distinct from the 'outer' world."[36] And the social and cosmic embeddedness of the person was replaced by out-and-out individualism. Gradually, there emerged the possibility of a self that is both "ontologically prior to and independent of its surroundings."[37]

Once this stage was set, a variety of religious and non-religious options began to spread along the continuum between traditional religion and "exclusive humanism," with belief itself

---

35 Ibid., 255.

36 Ibid., 539.

37 David Gordon, "The Place of the Sacred in the Absence of God (a review of Charles Taylor, *A Secular Age*)," *Journal of the History of Ideas* 69, no. 4 (2008): 661.

becoming an individual option. Taylor calls this proliferation of options a "nova effect," which contributed to the spreading of a background "malaise" of meaninglessness. This "malaise of modernity" was characterized by a sense of the *fragility* by which meaning and over-arching significance can be attained, a flatness experienced, for instance, in the lack of ways to solemnize the crucial moments of passage in our lives, and an "emptiness of the ordinary." The inevitable yearning for "something more" created "cultural cross pressures."

Finally, as a response to this malaise, there was a flourishing of "expressive individualism" rooted in Romanticism but democratized by the cultural revolutions of the 1960s. In the end, the previously reliable, if not natural, links between spirituality, society, and a felt experience of order within which we humans were embedded, was gone. We live, today, in an "immanent frame" in which "the buffered identity of the disciplined individual moves in a constructed social space, where instrumental rationality is a key value, and time is pervasively secular," and all of this is understood as "natural."[38] This immanent frame, which for Taylor has become hegemonic, *allows* for an openness to "something beyond," but does not demand nor necessarily encourage it.

Taylor's ambivalence toward this immanent frame is palpable. He tries to view it positively, but also seems to fear its implications, saying that if one opts against transcendence, "one can indeed live in a world which seems to proclaim everywhere the absence of God. It is a universe whose outer limits touch nothing but absolute darkness; a universe with its corresponding human world in which we can really experience Godlessness." This means "the sense of an absence; [...] the sense that all order, all meaning comes from us. We encounter no echo outside." The implication is that something novel has appeared in the world: "A race of humans has arisen which has managed to experience its world entirely as immanent." "In some respects," he acknowl-

---

38 Taylor, *A Secular Age*, 542.

edges, "we may judge this achievement as a victory for darkness, but it is a remarkable achievement nonetheless."[39]

More than one way to be porous

The scope of Taylor's argument is audacious, and his method is rich and engaging. In probing into the framework of tacit assumptions by which people make sense of the world — its embodied intentionalities, discursive frames and practices, communal bonds and conditions of belief — Taylor pushes far beyond the behavioral, mechanistic, and rational choice assumptions that characterize too much of modern psychological theory. His may be, as Wendy Brown calls it, "the first erudite phenomenology of secularism."[40]

But critics have pointed out that Taylor's critique is both too ethnocentric and too monological. It is, on the one hand, too focused on the experience of a small subset of humanity — those who personally experience the loss of what sociologists of religion have called a "sacred canopy." The majority have remained either strongly committed to religion or do not abide by the particular parsing of the "transcendent" and the "immanent" that Taylor insists on. As Cassidy writes, even Augustine had taught "that God is neither to be found outside of nor beyond us, but is rather to be found in the depths of interiority, even 'closer to me than I am to myself'."[41] For other Christians, God is to be found in the face of "the other," the neighbor and stranger, and not at all somewhere beyond humanity. At the same time, counter to Taylor's assumption that God brings "fullness" while the im-

---

39 Ibid., 376.

40 Wendy Brown, "Idealism, Materialism, Secularism?" *The Immanent Frame,* October 22, 2007, https://tif.ssrc.org/2007/10/22/idealism-materialism-secularism/.

41 Eoin G. Cassidy, "'Transcending Human Flourishing': Is There a Need for Subtler Language?" in *The Taylor Effect: Responding to a Secular Age,* eds. Ian Leask et al., 26–38 (Newcastle Upon Tyne: Cambridge Scholars Publishing, 2010), 31.

SHADOWING THE ANTHROPOCENE

manent frame remains "empty," there are Christian mystics for whom God precisely offers an "emptying" rather than a "filling."

More significantly, Taylor relies on an overly internal understanding of the North Atlantic "West," as if there has been no rest of the world against which the West both defined itself historically and depended on for its self-constitution. As a heterogeneous group of scholars and historians have been persuasively arguing for decades now — Edward Said, Aimé Césaire, Frantz Fanon, Gayatri Spivak, Walter Mignolo, Enrique Dussel, Talal Asad, Chandra Mohanty, Tomoko Masuzawa, Dipesh Chakrabarty, Arturo Escobar, Gloria Anzaldua, Timothy Fitzgerald, Boaventura de Sousa Santos, Akeel Bilgrami, and others — the last five centuries of western history are inconceivable without reference to the expansion of imperialist and masculinist European economies to other continents, the "discovery" and colonization of the Americas, the Trans-Atlantic slave trade, and encounters (direct or indirect) with the "otherness" of China, India, the Ottoman Muslim world, Orthodox Christianity, and the West's internal other, Judaism.[42] Then there is the persistence of a dynamic natural world that has interacted with human society in complex and mysterious ways: through plagues, diseases, and natural disasters, and through intermeshing political-ecological dynamics such as the rise of an international merchant class, the enclosure of common lands, intensification of private property relations, rural to urban migrations, and the production of new "natures" around the world.

---

42 E.g., Edward Said, *Orientalism* (New York: Pantheon, 1978); Arturo Escobar, *Encountering Development: The Making and Unmaking of the Third World* (Princeton: Princeton University Press, 1995); Peter Van der Veer, *Imperial Encounters: Religion and Modernity in India and Britain* (Princeton: Princeton University Press, 2001); Walter Mignolo, *Local Histories/Global Designs: Coloniality, Subaltern Knowledges, and Border Thinking* (Princeton: Princeton University Press, 2000); Talal Asad, *Formations of the Secular: Islam, Christianity, Modernity* (Stanford: Stanford University Press, 2003); Tomoko Masuzawa, *The Invention of World Religions: Or, How European Universalism Was Preserved in the Language of Pluralism* (Chicago: University of Chicago Press, 2005); Enrique Dussel, *Ethics of Liberation: In the Age of Globalization and Exclusion* (Durham: Duke University Press, 2013).

Once these are all added to the picture, it becomes clear that various forms of otherness — cultural and ecological difference — have perpetually bubbled to the surface, to be encountered as background and as foreground, and to be made sense of both ideologically and practically. These have given rise to new projections or imaginaries of transcendence, from classical to Enlightenment and evolutionist notions of "the savage" and "the barbarian" to Rousseuian ideals of the "noble savage," and for reaction formations in which efforts to gain cultural superiority were made through the vertical projection of identity towards a distant God and affirmed through hierarchic ideologies, technologies of discipline and control, and the like. Discourses of "religion," "barbarism," "civilization," and "primitivity" arose in the midst of such encounters.

In light of these complexities, Taylor's account appears to rely on an ahistorical discourse of transcendence-versus-immanence that is unable to account for the ways in which transcendence itself has been relational and historically mutable. His analysis is premised on a duality according to which "believers" hold to a faith in a "fullness" that is "beyond human life" and beyond the living world itself, while "unbelievers" believe in other things — in nature, the power of art and sensual beauty, human generosity and kindness, and so on — but fall short of the transcendence Taylor seeks. For Taylor, as David Gordon observes, "the sacred is historically invariant, *always* and *only* God," a divinity that transcends not only the human world but the natural world as well.[43]

A more relational view would have to acknowledge that any historical change in fundamental background assumptions — which is what Taylor is aiming to diagnose — "means a transformation in the sorts of entities that can show up": such as gods or a single transcendent God, a lawfully defined Nature, the sovereign Nation, the Economy, a Humanity that is the single source of meaning, and so on and so forth.[44] If each of

---

43 Gordon, "The Place of the Sacred," 670.
44 Ibid., 669.

these discursive objects is a product of history alongside other products, then Taylor's dichotomy of an exclusively *human* immanence and an exclusively *divine* transcendence comes to look fragile indeed.

This suggests that there may be many other ways of being "porous" than the one that Taylor privileges. Why, for instance, would it not be possible to conceive of a world *inclusive of humans* but *not exclusively human* that is itself meaningful, value-filled, and agential in its nature?[45] As Gordon puts it, "To conceive of oneself as a purely material being of flesh and bone is to understand oneself as more porous to one's surroundings, not less so, since one is metaphysically of the same substance as the world." Naturalism, he suggests, "has its own humility."[46] And the range of variations between religiosities and naturalisms comes to seem much richer when they are not assigned some point on a historical timeline — from pre-Durkheimian to Durkheimian to post-Durkheimian, as Taylor calls them.[47] If religion is not exclusively about transcending "the world," then the embedded cosmos that ostensibly made up the pre-modern world might not be entirely played out. And if we have not all fallen from grace, we may not need to choose between climbing back or lamenting the loss.

All that said, there is something to Taylor's frame that speaks to a recognizable division among people today. It makes sense to claim that something like secularism — in combination with capitalism, modernization, liberalism (or neoliberalism), developmentalism, and other factors — has tended to corrode and dissolve the bonds that have kept "traditional culture" alive today, whether among indigenous or peasant communities or reli-

---

45 This is Akeel Bilgrami's argument in *Secularism, Identity, and Enchantment* (Cambridge: Harvard University Press, 2014), particularly in the chapter "The Political Possibilities of the Long Romantic Period."

46 Gordon, "The Place of the Sacred," 667.

47 For examples of other variations on the spectrum of hybrids between religion and naturalism, see Bron R. Taylor, *Dark Green Religion: Nature Spirituality and the Planetary Future* (Berkeley: University of California Press, 2009).

giously unified regional, national, or transnational cultures. The term "traditional" is loose at best, and it is exceedingly difficult to qualitatively compare the different forms of such "traditional culture." Cultures have always been multiple, disunified, stratified, and complex. Cultural encounters and clashes have always resulted in divergent outcomes, ranging from peaceful or contentious assimilation of one group by another to various forms of mutual acommodation, co-existence, or syncretic mixing. Positing a singular culture of "global, liberal, secular modernity" is hazardous at best, and opposing it to any and all other cultural variants is an even more outrageous overgeneralization.

Yet, just as it is possible to situate people and communities on a scale divided between those who benefit most from the conditions of Anthropocenic capitalism (the A/Cene) and those who are almost entirely victims of it, so it is also possible to situate people somewhere on a spectrum between those who are fully assimilated into a globalizing "liberal, secular, modernity" and those who have almost entirely resisted such assimilation. Most of the world falls somewhere in between, with options for leaning one way or another (as Taylor skillfully points out). In this sense, Taylor's argument, if not taken as a historical one, succeeds in addressing a profound divergence in the world today, one that helps explain a variety of significant global developments — from "9-11" and the "wars" on "terror" to the rise of religiously fundamentalist, ethnically exclusivist, anti-globalist, and anti-immigrant movements in many countries.

"Secularism," "liberalism," "tradition," "faith," "globalism," "fundamentalism," "development": all these terms carry potent punch today, even as they are notoriously slippery in their definitions. Religious traditions have certainly not gone away, as secularization theorists had long predicted. The question has become not *when* they will finally go away, but whether the world is becoming *post*-secular in any recognizable way, or whether it is merely continuing in a kind of see-saw dance between faith and secularity, multiple modernities, and other forms of identity-making and contesting on scales ranging from the local and

infra-local to the national and transnational.[48] If a shift "beyond
the Anthropo(S)cene" is to take hold among a significant pro-
portion of humanity, it will have to do so across these divides
between the educated, urban, liberal, secular "moderns" and the
rest — which may mean a majority — of humanity.

Jamesian maneuvers

In the debates that followed the publication of Taylor's book, a
third position took shape that attempted to navigate between
the religious "transcenders" or "traditionalists" and the areli-
gious secularists or "exclusive humanists." This position, rep-
resented in the writings of David Gordon, William Connolly,
Patrick Lee Miller, Lars Tonder, Elizabeth Hurd, Akeel Bilgrami,
and others, in one way or another attempted to bring together a
sense of "enchantment" with a "worldly orientation to religion
and politics."[49] This tradition is key to negotiating the "post-sec-
ularizing" terrain of global culture.

Perhaps the most detailed and persistent elaboration of such
a third position is that undertaken by political theorist William Connolly. In a series of books including *Why I Am Not A
Secularist, Neuropolitics, Pluralism, Capitalism and Christianity
American Style, A World of Becoming,* and *Facing the Planetary,*
Connolly has presented a sustained defense of what he calls
"immanent naturalism," a view that sees the universe as open,
creative, and pluralistic, and that advocates a "reverence for the
protean diversity of being."[50] With an eye toward the practical,

---

48 E.g., Michael Rectenwald, Rochelle Almeida, and George Levine, eds.,
Global Secularisms in a Post-Secular Age (Boston: de Gruyter, 2015); Philip
Gorski et al., eds., *The Post-Secular in Question: Religion in Contemporary
Society* (New York: New York University Press, 2012).

49 Lars Tonder, "Spinoza's Immanence," *The Immanent Frame,* December 5,
2007, http://blogs.ssrc.org/tif/2007/12/05/spinozas-immanence/.

50 William Connolly, *Neuropolitics: Thinking, Culture, Speed* (Minneapolis: University of Minnesota Press, 2002); William Connolly, *Pluralism*
(Durham: Duke University Press, 2005); William Connolly, *Capitalism
and Christianity, American Style* (Durham: Duke University Press, 2008);
William Connolly, *A World of Becoming* (Durham: Duke University Press,

I will compare the kinds of spiritual practices suggested in the writings, respectively, of Charles Taylor and William Connolly. To facilitate this comparison, I will focus particularly on their respective use of a shared resource, the ideas of pragmatist philosopher and student of religion William James, and on the thread of the imagination and the "imaginal."

As mentioned, Taylor's *A Secular Age* is highly attuned to the background assumptions and pre-discursive orientations shaping our understandings of the sacred, but his analysis is overly constrained by the elite internal dialogues of the North Atlantic "West." If, following Corbin and others, we think of the middle-ground between explicit thinking and tacit background assumptions and orientations as an "imaginal" field or "imagosphere," then Taylor's understanding is constrained by the Eurocentric model he assumes for our history. The constitutive "others" that have shaped that history — internal and external, cultural and natural others — might well seem unimaginable from within that frame.

In his analysis of modernity's "immanent frame," Taylor invokes William James in his description of the "open space where you can feel the winds pulling you, now to belief, now to unbelief."[51] To stand in this "open space," he writes, "is to be at the mid-point of the cross-pressures that define our culture."[52] He singles out two particular forms or "leanings" within this "open space": that of the ex-believer who feels "the imminent loss of a world of beauty, meaning, warmth as well as of the perspective of a self-transformation beyond the everyday,"[53] and that of the believer who remains "haunted by a sense that the universe might after all be as meaningless as the most reductive materialism describes."[54] "Confidence," for the latter, "must

---

2010); William Connolly, *Facing the Planetary: Entangled Humanism and the Politics of Swarming* (Durham: Duke University Press, 2017); Connolly, *Why I Am Not a Secularist*.

51 Taylor, *A Secular Age*, 549.

52 Ibid., 592.

53 Ibid.

54 Ibid., 593.

always remain anticipatory. Parallel to the continuing regret of ex-believers is this sense that the struggle for belief is never definitively won."[55]

Where Taylor's Jamesian "open space" remains epistemological, caught between the two views that ostensibly frame our culture, William Connolly's use of James is ontological, making a claim about the universe itself as being pluralistic and, on some level, undecideable. For Connolly, James is "a pluralist in two senses: in the image of the universe that he embraces," which is pluralistic through and through, "and in his appreciation that others might legitimately adopt other images of it."[56] In Connolly's take on James, the universe itself is considered "open" and capable of bringing in unexpected novelty. Translated into Taylor's terms, this is a recognition of a transcendence that, instead of being relegated to an outside (whether to a transcendent deity or a supernatural realm), is built into the immanent structure of the cosmos itself.

The upshot for practice is significant. When Taylor comes, in his final chapter, "Conversions," to discuss spiritual practice, it is to the "experience" of transcendence, "(re)conversion," and "fullness," in which "one feels oneself to be breaking out of a narrower frame into a broader field, which makes sense of things in a different way."[57] Taylor urges us to resist the temptation to psychologize this as individual "experience." Rather, it is a breakthrough to a transcendence which "corresponds to reality" outside of the "immanent frame."[58] He refers to various mystics and saints, but focuses particularly on three modern figures — Ivan Illich, Charles Peguy, and Gerard Manley Hopkins — who in different ways grapple with "the inescapable tension between the ultimate order of the Parousia, which is in gestation today" and "the established order of civilization as we live it," and who

---

55   Ibid.
56   William Connolly, "Deep Pluralism," in *William E. Connolly: Democracy, Pluralism and Political Theory*, eds. Samuel A. Chambers and Terrell Carver, 85–104 (New York: Routledge, 2008), 85.
57   Taylor, *A Secular Age*, 768.
58   Ibid.

find "their own way" within this tension. The choice of the three, interestingly, reflects the persistent influence on Taylor of Martin Heidegger: Illich is as much a critic, if not more so, of instrumental technological rationality as was Heidegger; Peguy, building on Bergson, is said to "anticipate" Heidegger's "famous analysis of the three ekstaseis"; and Hopkins is a Christian version of the kind of poet Heidegger came to celebrate in his later writings. What we see, then, is an expansive interpretation of spiritual practice, including social critique and poetry, held together only by the fact that each of them is a Christian.

Taylor does refer on numerous occasions to Buddhist or other forms of religion, occasionally suggesting, for instance, that "what may have to be challenged here is the very distinction nature/supernature itself,"[59] but he fails to follow up on these suggestions. In the book's final two pages he gestures, hesitantly, to the potential virtues of "paganism" or "polytheism" in a brief critique of two weaknesses found in Christianity and the "axial religions" — Christianity's "repression and marginalization" of embodiment and its tendency "to homogenize." But he internalizes these critiques by claiming that "Christianity, as the faith of the Incarnate God, is denying *something essential to itself* as long as it remains wedded to forms which excarnate."[60] This potential opening onto something *transcendent to Christianity* is thus deflected into itself.[61] Meanwhile, the thinkers who show a more radical openness to embodiment, pluralism, and the blurring of the nature/supernature dichotomy are mostly brushed aside as marginal voices of an "immanent revolt" that, for all its revolting, remains always "immanent."

William Connolly has long championed an "immanent revolt" that redefines transcendence in ways consistent with the process-relational thinking of this book. Connolly consistently calls for a Spinozist "ethic of cultivation," a philosophy "of ethics not as *obedience* to the command of a personal God or a categori-

---

59 Ibid., 732.
60 Ibid., 771, emphasis added.
61 Ibid., 772.

cal imperative, but as cultivation by tactical means of *hilaritus,* a love of life that infuses the body/brain/culture network in which we live."[62] For him, the kind of "deep pluralism nourished by a generous ethic of engagement" that he calls for "requires micropolitical work on the subliminal register,"[63] work that includes the kinds of things he variously refers to as "relational arts," "arts of the self," "spiritual exercises," "ethical artistry," and "corporeal practices." Such activities "work on interceded layers of relational being. They help to organize those complex mixtures of word, image, habit, feeling, touch, smell, concept, and judgment that give texture to cultural life." It is in these "interceded layers" that the "dense, often intense, relation between mystical/subliminal states and doctrinal representation and interpretation" is "effectuated": not only "by gods, genes, traumatic experiences, and neurotransmitters such as dopamine, norepinephrine, serotonin, and acetylcholine," but also "by ritual, tactics, arts, and exercises variously practiced by members of religions of the Book, Buddhists, Freudians, and Nietzschians."[64]

This list may bring to mind many of the techniques of spiritual exploration found in today's spiritual marketplace — the sundry healing practices, meditation and visualization techniques, image and symbol systems from runes to Tarot cards to *I Ching* to "centering prayer" and "Sufi dancing" and spiritual journaling and "power place" pilgrimage, all intended to bring about change in the consciousness of the technique-accumulating seekers. Neither Taylor nor Connolly would uncritically endorse all (if any) of these methods. Taylor would undoubtedly find them too instrumental, too invested in the "self" that does the seeking, self-exploring, and self-enhancing, with little necessary reference to a transcendent domain. Connolly, on the other hand, deploys language (such as "arts of the self") that suggests some complicity with this individualist frame. But his

---

62 William Connolly, "Europe: A Minor Tradition," in *Powers of the Secular Modern: Talal Asad and His Interlocutors,* eds. Charles Hirschkind and David Scott, 75–92 (Stanford: Stanford University Press, 2006), 84.

63 Connolly, *Neuropolitics,* 129.

64 Ibid., 132.

voluminous writings on politics conveys the clear message that selfhood is *not* a bounded and unchanging container, but is always in process, dynamically related to others and to a world on which it is intimately dependent. His ethos of pluralization specifically encourages an engagement with one's critics and interlocutors, and his "quasi-pagan faith" of immanent naturalism is one that, he claims, cultivates a sensibility of care and "love of this world."[65]

Connolly here is proposing an alternative model of the relationship between reason, values, and practice both to those, such as Taylor, who assume a predetermined view of value or transcendent meaning, and to those (like Kant, Habermas, and Rawls) who privilege reason at the expense of affective and prerational processes. His "arts of the self" include practices that "corporealize" culture and reshape both "thinking and sensibility in profound ways."[66] Culture, in this understanding, is embodied "in repetitive practices that help to constitute the dispositions, sensibilities, and ethos through which meaning is lived, intellectual beliefs are settled, and relations between constituencies are negotiated."[67] Ritual, in turn, is "a medium through which embodied habits, dispositions, sensibilities, and capacities of performance are *composed and consolidated.*"[68] All of this is entirely consistent with the Peircean and Whiteheadian views espoused in this book, which aim to change the ways we relate to ourselves and the world through the cultivation of habits of perception, action, and realization.

In all of this, Connolly is no less an urban intellectual than Taylor, if not more so. To say, as Connolly does, that he is "not a secular*ist*" is certainly not the same as saying that he is not *secular*. The Latin word *saeculum,* at any rate, refers to the shared world of the present: the age, time, generation, world, lifetime, or breed of those who belong to a given world. Connolly es-

---

65 On his "quasi-pagan" faith, see ibid., 124. The phrase "love of this world" comes up frequently in Connolly's recent writings.

66 Ibid., 84.

67 Connolly, *Pluralism,* 56.

68 Ibid., 57, emphasis in original.

pouses a certain faith and seeks out practices to render that faith as real as any; in this, he is not *separating* the *saeculum* from the eternal or transcendent, but is *expanding* it to invite in possibilities that others may be leaving out. He mentions churches and other religious organizations in his list of allies for building an "eco-egalitarian resonance machine" to counter the "evangelical-capitalist resonance machine" that has ascended to power in the United States of late.

But Connolly's option of philosophical exploration remains the option of an individual who is quite capable of standing apart from any community because his grounding in the world of modern, secular *culture* is solid. To effectively engage with cultural worlds whose relationship to secular liberalism is much more conflicted may require the capacity to move even further across the divide between the secular world of intellectuals and reasoned arguments, and the worlds of what we might call *other rationalities* — those that are culturally still somewhat intact, but whose cardinal reference points bear little resemblance to those of liberal political dialogue, democratic pluralism, and respectful debate.

For this we require an ontological politics that understands that humans already live in different worlds, different *kosmoi,* and that any effort to bridge them will always be precarious, with neither guarantees nor shared foundations on which to build such bridges.

Ontological politics

In her multivolume work *Cosmopolitiques* (1996–97) and publications that followed it, Belgian philosopher of science Isabelle Stengers forwarded a "cosmopolitical proposal" that, unlike most forms of cosmopolitan*ism,* does not presume the existence or even the possibility of a "good common world," an ecumenically peaceable cosmopolis. It assumes, instead, that such a peaceable common world would always have to be cobbled together by whatever means of negotiation are available. Her proposal, furthermore, is intended to "slow down the construction of this common world, to create a space for hesitation regarding what it means to say 'good.'"[69] The "cosmos" of her cosmopolitics "refers to the unknown constituted by [the] multiple, divergent worlds and to the articulations of which they could eventually be capable."[70] Such a cosmopolitics cannot pre-assume what will count as "common" — whether, for instance, it may be "nature" along with "human nature," the laws and discoveries of science, sovereign nations, "cultural differences," or (on the other hand) gods, souls, ancestors, spirits, demons, or anything else that could be brought to the negotiating table.

Stengers's call has been echoed and amplified by an array of theorists, of whom Bruno Latour has been the most influential. If Latour's decades-long work studying the relations between science, technology, society, and modernity has had a dominant refrain, it is that we can no longer rely on the singular foundation of a "nature" that speaks to us through the unified voice of science — a "nature," as John Law puts it, that is the "unique author of a single account" propping up a "reality that is independent, prior, singular, and definite."[71]

Instead, we must learn to live amidst a multiplicity of ways of knowing, ways of living, and ways of building worlds, a multiplicity in which the very *foundations* of *our* world may not even be recognized by others. One of these foundations for the "moderns" (which means for us, if we align with that world) is the one that sees "culture" and "nature" as radically opposed terms. For Latour, this dichotomy presumes two interlinked things: first, a "multiculturalism" for which *culture* is taken to differentiate us, one group from another, in ways that could be evaluated based on commonly accepted standards of human rights or goods; but, second, a "mononaturalism" that takes *nature* to be simply *there,* singular, lawful, and invariable. Science, in turn, is the

---

69 Isabelle Stengers, "The Cosmopolitical Proposal," in *Making Things Public,* eds. Bruno Latour and Peter Weibel, 994–1003 (Cambridge: MIT Press, 2005), 994.

70 Ibid., 994.

71 John Law, *After Method: Mess in Social Science Research* (New York: Routledge, 2004), 123.

social force that has been delegated with the power to reveal nature for us and to speak on its behalf.[72]

Latour rejects this division: nature, he argues, does not provide a bedrock of reality against which our activities can be measured, because each culture is always already enacted and embedded within a particular set of ecology-making processes. Each is always already no less than a "nature-culture." And all such natures-cultures are both similar and different. They are similar

> in that they simultaneously construct humans, divinities and nonhumans. None of them inhabits a world of signs or symbols arbitrarily imposed on an external Nature known to us [westerners] alone. [...] All of them sort out what will bear signs and what will not. If there is one thing we all do, it is surely that we construct both our human collectives and the nonhumans that surround them. In constituting their collectives, some mobilize ancestors, lions, fixed stars, and the co-agulated blood of sacrifice; in constructing ours, we mobilize genetics, zoology, cosmology and hæmatology.[73]

The key is that there is no privileged vantage point for sorting through these semiotically disconnected worlds. Coordinating some common understanding across the gaps requires not imposing one's own categories, but working toward some form of "translation" and "diplomacy," a process in which "everything takes effort, continuing effort."[74]

How, if there are no pre-given grounds for adjudication, might we navigate between dramatically different interpretations of the world and the human place within it? Latour suggests beginning with a different set of questions than the usual ones. Rather than asking "who is right and who is wrong?" or,

---

72 Bruno Latour, *Politics of Nature: How to Bring the Sciences into Democracy,* trans. Catherine Porter (Cambridge: Harvard University Press, 2004).

73 Bruno Latour, *We Have Never Been Modern,* trans. Catherine Porter (Cambridge: Harvard University Press, 1993), 106.

74 Law, *After Method,* 131–32.

more typically, "why do they persist in believing their wrong ideas?" he proposes such questions as: "What sort of people are they?" (People, after all, are products of formations in which personhood, subjecthood, of one kind or another, is recognized.) "What are the entities under which they assemble?" To what do they ascribe their assembly as such? "And how do they distribute the agencies making up their cosmos?"[75]

Latour takes as a precondition that we live in perilous times, when scientists evoking a looming climate catastrophe are asked, "Why should we trust you any more than anyone else?" His inquiry is intended to answer this question in the only way that is admissible once the foundations are taken away. The answer is always: *look to what they do.* Look to how they make their world, and how we make ours. Compare on the basis of what is made, and what we might make together — through the mediations we might come up with in the diplomatic project that lies ahead of us all. Science, by this account, is not what it *says* it is; it is how it *works.* Much of Latour's earlier work was devoted to showing precisely how carefully and sophisticatedly scientists enact their practices and how, in doing so (when they succeed), they build worlds that are robust and resilient.

In his 2013 Gifford Lectures, Latour refers to the cosmopolitical project that is ahead of us as an experiment in "demogenesis": an attempt at creating a "people" and a "body politic" out of the many who confront each other in the wake of the Anthropocene. These people might include the human as well as the animate, the organic, the technological, the fantastic, and so many others — all those agents formerly called "objects" alongside those formerly called "subjects." The great challenge for his project is this: How does one conduct diplomacy with things that do not speak, at least not in a language known to

---

75 Bruno Latour, "The Puzzling Face of a Secular Gaia," *The Gifford Lectures: Facing Gaia: A New Enquiry Into Natural Religion,* https://www.giffordlectures.org/lectures/facing-gaia-new-enquiry-natural-religion. The lectures have been substantially reworked into the book *Facing Gaia: Eight Lectures on the New Climatic Regime,* trans. Catherine Porter (Cambridge: Polity, 2017).

the moderns? How can we envision a diplomacy — a messy and rambunctious "parliament" — that could translate the languages spoken by all the entities of the shadowy super-entity hesitantly being hailed "Gaia"? (More on her momentarily.)

The take-home point here is that once we abandon the notion of a nature that is fully outside culture, and of a culture that is fully separate from nature, we are left with the fact that all that there has ever been is different kinds of relations made between people (as long as there have been people) and the places, forces, gods, and other beings that are taken to make up the world. Humans have always been thickly entangled within this larger world: we have always been enworlded, enspaced, territorialized, and folded over with so many *other* others. Our relations to places and landscapes have always been morally imbued and ontologically loaded. No "nature" has been pure backdrop, pure "abstract space," in Henri Lefebvre's felicitous phrase — until someone came along to make it so and to enforce such an abstraction onto reality.[76] That abstraction underpins the A/Cene. It is a colonial creation, and it is time for us to decolonize.

If our relationship to the world's other agents has always been variable, it has also always been contractual insofar as those relationalities that "worked" required maintenance over time. The contracts of these natural-cultural collectives take their force from relations that are felt to be morally obligatory and that exceed its participants in time and in space. There is some sort of contract, entity, constellation of divinities, or web of understandings and patterned relationalities that continues beyond the time of our own being here. That is what makes them *non*-Anthropocenic.

At the very least, the cosmopolitical option is one that acknowledges that there are obligations at stake: that we are caught in a world riven with multiple obligations, whether to "the economy" and "infinite growth," or to "the nation," to some "revolution," or to the ancestors and deities, the sacred waters

---

76 Henri Lefebvre, *The Production of Space*, trans. Donald Nicholson-Smith (Oxford: Blackwell, 1991).

of South Dakota, the mountain hollers of Appalachia, or the *Ubuntu* or *Buen Vivir* of any particular natural-cultural collective. (And once we put it that way, is it not evident how few of us are ready to put our lives on the line for "the economy"?) There is some element of choice in these relations, but there is also always some element of *being chosen*: by our places, by our predicaments, by our gods.

The subject and the subjectless

Invoking the spectre of the sacred, of Gaia, of the divine and the ecological, and of the other figures I have stitched into my argumentative fabric (the relational, the pagan, the Buddhist) is bound to raise hackles with those concerned about the disappearance of the human subject. Relational philosophies have frequently been subjected to the criticism that any kind of relational "holism" is anathema to the ethical particularity that is the great gift of modernity, of liberalism, of the Christian West, or of some related historical protagonist.

In the debates over rival forms of speculative realism, object-oriented ontologists have made some variation of this argument (though the fault lines might be drawn a little differently, as when Timothy Morton argues on behalf of an "object-oriented Buddhism"). Where Harman, Morton, and others have defended the object, others have defended the human subject. Slavoj Žižek's arguments are compelling in this regard, and are worth considering here for at least three additional reasons: because his psychoanalytical approach engages with an affective level of the political that other approaches fail to adequately consider; because of certain parallels between his Lacanian model of the psyche and the process-relational view I am proposing; and because of Žižek's resonance in today's anti-capitalist political left.

In a world of manifest injustice, Žižek has come to celebrate a Leninist decisiveness in political action, which he allies with a Pauline Christian love of "the act," and which he sees as ineradicably linked to the possibility of subjectivity. In opposition to these, he has critiqued a long line of theoretical opponents and ideological "ersatzes," from complacent "liberal multicultural-ism" to obsessive ecology, "New Age spiritualism," "neo-pagan-ism," and "Western Buddhism." To all of them he ascribes some version of an "indifference" or "noninvolvement," which alleg-edly comes from their shared ideal of "absorption" in a cosmic "balance of the One-All,"[77] a "balanced circuit of the universe" that, according to Žižek, Pauline Christianity and its political successor, Leninist revolutionism, throw off the rails. In particu-lar, Žižek claims that "Western Buddhism" has established itself as "the hegemonic ideology of global capitalism."

To understand his critique, we must start by understand-ing his own presuppositions. In tracing his "creative synthe-sis of German idealism and Lacanian psychoanalysis," Adrian Johnston's analysis in *Žižek's Ontology* helps us immensely with this. (About Johnston's book, Žižek himself has said that "While reading it, I often had the uncanny feeling of being confronted by a line of argumentation which fits better than my own texts what I am struggling to formulate — as if he is the original and I am a copy."[78]) Johnston articulates Žižek's ontology as a form of "transcendental materialism" according to which "Cogito-like subjectivity ontogenetically emerges out of an originally corpo-real condition as its anterior ground," but "once generated, this sort of subjectivity thereafter remains irreducible to its mate-rial sources."[79] In other words, autonomy or subjectivity "imma-nently emerges" as an "excess or surplus" from out of a plurality of corporeal-material, pre-subjective existence. That founda-tion — which is "asubjective, heteronomous" and "libidinal-ma-terial" — includes conditions that make it possible for subjective autonomy to emerge. But once it has emerged, it "cannot be re-inscribed back" within that "ontological register out of which it

---

77 Slavoj Žižek, "Human Rights and Its Discontents," Olin Auditorium, Bard College, November 15, 1999, http://www.lacan.com/zizek-human.htm.

78 Žižek, quoted on back cover of Adrian Johnston, *Žižek's Ontology: A Tran-scendental Materialist Theory of Subjectivity* (Evanston: Northwestern Uni-versity Press, 2008).

79 Ibid., xxiv.

grew." For better or worse, the genie of subjectivity, one might say, cannot be put back into the bottle.[80]

All of this is to say that, for Žižek, we are not *born* as subjects, with anything like the "freedom" to act, but we *become* subjects and thereafter act within a socio-linguistic system that recognizes our subjectivity. From the moment we have done that, there is no going back. We are left, instead, with an irreparable "gap, a non-dialecticizable parallax split" that haunts our being and, at the same time, makes some measure of freedom possible. This freedom is both precious and, in an important sense, anti-systemic. It is eccentric. "Being free," Johnston writes, "is a transitory event arising at exceptional moments when the historical, psychical, and biological run of things breaks down."[81] The genesis of subjectivity, then, is material, but its essence is non-material, yet more than epiphenomenal.

A process-relationalist might ask in response to this: what can be more Deleuzian than this account of networked systems, productive organic-machinic assemblages out of which arise the capacity to act and, from one moment to another, to perpetually *become*? And what can be more Whiteheadian than the gap that opens up in the event of every moment that makes up the (processual) universe? But where Žižek and Lacan seem to limit the experience of subjectivity to the human, and Johnston to "exceptional moments" of humanity, Whitehead and Deleuze would extend it to all things — which in each of their systems are always events rather than object-things.

Moreover, what can be more Buddhist than the recognition that the "gap" that opens up in each moment, between each thought or mental impulse, can be penetrated through meditative practice precisely to free us from the fantasy images and objects and "things" we think are real, so as to make it possible to experience the fluidity of life with some measure of liberated equanimity?

---

80 Ibid., 271.
81 Ibid., 286–87.

Let us explore this latter point of apparent convergence. Buddhism (for the most part) and Lacanianism both posit an emptiness at the center of the human subject, which that subject perpetually strives to fill. Lacan sees the psyche as built on an inassimilable gap between the bodily-material substrate on which subjectivity is built and the subject itself. Buddhism sees the self as a relational construct with no essence, whose underlying reality is a flux of dependently-originative causal forces. Both traditions aim to help us face the emptiness or gap that is at our core, so that we can live with it rather than deflecting it into illusory and ultimately unsupportable fantasy-constructs — such as those of the ego (the subject, the "I") and the objects that will ostensibly satisfy its desires, or various collective identity projects (ethnic, national, or other kinds) with their ideological props and scapegoats. And both posit that only by facing this gap directly can some kind of amelioration (salvation, or genuine love) be possible.

Žižek admits this commonality. In *Less Than Nothing,* he writes, "The only other school of thought that fully accepts the inexistence of the big Other is Buddhism." Considering Buddhist ethics, he continues:

Does not Buddhism lead us to "traverse the fantasy": overcoming the illusions on which our desires are based and confronting the void beneath each object of desire? Furthermore, psychoanalysis shares with Buddhism the insistence that there is no Self as a substantive agent of psychic life: [...] the Self is the fetishized illusion of a substantial core of subjectivity where, in reality, there is nothing. This is why, for Buddhism, the point is not to discover one's "true Self"; but to accept that there is no such thing, that the "Self" as such is an illusion, an imposture. [...] Crucial to Buddhism is the reflexive change from the object to the thinker himself: first, we isolate the thing that bothers us, the cause of our suffering; then we change not the object but ourselves, the way we relate to (what appears to us as) the cause of our suffering [...]. This shift involves great pain [... it is] the violent experience of losing the ground under one's feet, of being deprived of the most familiar stage of one's being.[82]

But in the end, for Žižek, Buddhists "do not repair the damage; rather, [they] gain the insight into the illusory nature of that which appears to need repair."[83] The difference between Buddhism and psychoanalysis, he claims, is that

> for Buddhism, after Enlightenment (or "traversing the fantasy"), the Wheel no longer turns, the subject de-subjectivizes itself and finds peace; for psychoanalysis, on the other hand, the wheel continues to turn, and this continued turning-of-the-wheel is the drive.[84]

The death drive, according to Freud, "is the tension which persists and insists beyond and against the nirvana principle." Žižek calls Buddhists' "nirvana principle" the "highest and most radical expression" of the "pleasure principle," which psychoanalysis (according to Žižek) militates against. "Even if the object of desire is illusory," he continues, "there is a real in this illusion: the object of desire in its positive content is vain, *but not the place it occupies, the place of the Real*; which is why there is more truth in the unconditional fidelity to one's desire than in the resigned insight into the vanity of one's striving."[85]

This last passage is revealing: instead of recognizing "the vanity of one's striving" and opting for inner peace, Žižek seeks an "unconditional fidelity to one's desire." That desire, for him, arises out of the tensions in the (Freudian) drives, generating the subject and making us human. Ironically, this "unconditional fidelity to one's desire" sounds not so different from what some forms of Vajrayana Buddhism aspire to. In Vajrayana, what the practitioner aims for is not *extinction* in the blissful passivity

---

82 Slavoj Žižek, *Less Than Nothing: Hegel and the Shadow of Dialectical Materialism* (London: Verso, 2013), 129–30.

83 Ibid., 130.

84 Ibid., 131.

85 Ibid., 132–33, emphasis added.

of nirvana, but the following of desire in order to unite with the deities that are its emanations — which, since those deities are themselves "empty," means a union with Desire itself. Žižek dispenses with Vajrayana by caricaturing it as one of the most "ridiculously ritualized" religious forms, humorously comparing its invention of the prayer wheel with television's canned laughter.

But the difference can be specified more precisely. In Žižek's understanding, it is the empty *subject* that we need to retain. For Mahayana Buddhism (at least), it is *emptiness itself,* which is taken to be something like an open cognizance that is empty of all reifications, all stillings of the flow, yet which is irrepressible in its nature. (I'm drawing more on the Tibetan tradition of Dzogchen here than on other forms, but the general point holds for other strands of Mahayana Buddhist thought.) The difference, then, is this: what counts for Žižek is the subject *at the point of his or her individual production*; for Buddhists, it is *subjectless* subjectivity, or subjectivity at the point of its disappearance, its self-emptying.

Understanding this distinction requires asking not only what subjectivity is, but also what the nature of reality is. If reality is inert substance, mute matter, or mere existence without subjectivation, and if the human subject is the one thing that *transcends* mere matter, then there is nothing more significant than human subjectivity at the point of its origin. Žižek would in this case be quite right about what needs to be protected, defended, and cultivated: human subjectivity in its preciousness, and the individual human subject above all. The only alternative would be passivity (of the sort that Žižek ends up ascribing to Buddhism). But if reality — not just human but *all* reality — is the ongoing production of subjectless subjectivity, or subjectivation-objectivation, then subjectless subjectivity is always already *active,* not merely passive, and it is not something that belongs to anyone.

In this sense, Buddhist prayer wheels are not exactly identical to sitcom laugh tracks, but they operate on the same principle. Both acknowledge that the world is a*lways already in affective-semiotic motion,* and that we, moving beings, are affected on a preconscious level by the in-motionness at work around us. With its mantras, prayer wheels, and other habit-making practices, Mahayana Buddhism attempts to shift that motion into a movement toward liberation. Sitcom laugh tracks, by contrast, attempt to shift that motion into pleasurable distraction. The goals are entirely different. If Žižek dislikes both equally, it is because he values willful subjectivity — the kind that speaks "I" into the void of its own creation — at the expense of the affective but subjectless subjectivity that a more processual ontology would ascribe to both humans and to the world.

Concluding his foray into Buddhism in *Less Than Nothing*, Žižek refers to a paradox, whose formal structure is that of the "double vacuum" of a Higgs Boson field. This double vacuum "appears in the guise of the irreducible gap between ethics (understood as the care of the self, as striving towards authentic being) and morality (understood as the care for others, responding to their call)." For Žižek, "the authenticity of the Self is taken to the extreme in Buddhist meditation, whose goal is precisely to enable the subject to overcome (or, rather, suspend) its Self and enter the vacuum of nirvana."[86] To this, a Buddhist might say: yes, perhaps this is part of Buddhism (though neither "overcoming" nor "suspension" sound quite right in a Buddhist context). But it is certainly not the whole of it, at least not in the Mahayana tradition where care for others — or for the liberation of others — is equally, if not supremely, important.

Žižek acknowledges that Buddhism has oscillated between a "minimal" and a "maximal" goal: the first, related more to Theravada Buddhism, is a "spiritual shift" that occurs "within," while the second, Mahayana's, is the more radical goal of liberating *everything* from suffering. But he concludes by pointing to the "irreducible gap between subjective authenticity and moral goodness (in the sense of social responsibility): the difficult thing to accept is that one can be totally authentic in overcoming one's false Self and yet still commit horrible crimes — and vice versa, of course: one can be a caring subject, morally committed to the

---

86 Ibid., 134.

full, while existing in an inauthentic world of illusion with regard to oneself." The "two vacuums," he writes, "never coincide: in order to be fully engaged ethico-politically, it is necessary to exit the 'inner peace' of one's subjective authenticity."[87]

In the end, Žižek's critique is not so much a critique of Buddhism's philosophical core as it is a critique of one of the tropes by which that philosophical core has so often been adumbrated: the trope of inner peace and happiness — the cessation of suffering and attainment of bliss through the elimination of ignorance. In its contrast, he poses the Judaeo-Christian ethic of external, traumatic "encounter," of "the Fall" into the world, and into love. The virtue of his critique of Buddhism is in the value he places on suffering and on choice. Subjectivity is only possible because of our condition of separation, the very gap that underlies our suffering. Eliminating that gap, he argues, should not be the point of a spiritual or philosophical practice. What should be is recognizing that the gap is one we share with all manner of gapped, broken, suffering (because groundless yet ground-seeking) beings.

Analogously, a philosophy that values the arising of subjectivity out of the drives (or wherever subjectivity comes from) without recognizing the fundamental entanglement of those drives with everything else that lives, that moves, that suffers, that dies, is a philosophy that privileges *will* without offering a means for deciding how that will should act. Here is where Žižek's ontology privileges freedom over solidarity — which, ironically, aligns him with political liberals and even libertarians. That is precisely why Žižek needs his Marxism: it provides him with an ethical foundation for action, and a goal wider than freedom itself: that of human solidarity. To the extent that it offers an understanding of our relations with *all* beings who suffer, Buddhism may be more inclusive in this respect. It provides a wider vision for justice and solidarity than Marxism, even at its humanistic best, has ever provided. But to the extent that both seek not inner peace but subjectless subjectivity, both are reach-

---

87 Ibid., 135.

ing out to the "beyond" at which genuine action becomes possible.

Totality, or original hybridity?

Žižek's account of paganism and ecology take a similar tack. He sees both as embracing a cosmic-organic totality, which acts as an imposition on human fallibility and subjective freedom. To critique ecology, he latches onto the idea that ecology, or nature, serves as a kind of Big Other, which with its pattern of regular rhythms and homeostatic balances provides a reassurance that papers the gap that would otherwise tell us that we, and reality, are riven, torn open and fundamentally meaningless, lacking ultimately in any comforting balance and harmony.[88]

Here one could reply with a technical disagreement: the science of ecology has long abandoned the notion of homeostatic balance as a universal baseline for all ecological processes. Instead, it mixes cybernetic metaphors of homeostasis with others taken from the competitive individualism of Darwinian biology, the nonlinear stochastics and "chaotics" of complex systems theories, and the pragmatics of adaptive management.[89] But it is not scientists that Žižek is most concerned with. In his argument's favor, there have certainly been environmentalists who have pursued their cause as if its attainment would provide a "wholeness" and "plenitude" that they (delusorily) imagine will

---

88   For Žižek's ecological writings, see "Nature Does Not Exist," in Slavoj Žižek, *Looking Awry: An Introduction to Jacques Lacan Through Popular Culture* (Cambridge: MIT Press, 1991); Slavoj Žižek, "Of Cells and Selves," in *The Žižek Reader,* eds. Elizabeth Wright and Edmond Wright, 302–20 (Oxford: Blackwell, 1999); Slavoj Žižek, "Nature and Its Discontents," *SubStance* 37, no. 3 (2008): 37–72; Slavoj Žižek, "Censorship Today: Violence, or Ecology as a New Opium for the Masses," *Lacan.com* 18 (2008): 42–43; and Slavoj Žižek, "Unbehagen in der Natur," in *In Defense of Lost Causes,* 420–61 (London: Verso, 2009).

89   E.g., Donald Worster, *Nature's Economy: A History of Ecological Ideas,* 2nd eds. (New York: Cambridge University Press, 1994); Kevin deLaplante, Bryson Brown, and Kent A. Peacock, eds., *Philosophy of Ecology* (Amsterdam: Elsevier, 2011).

close the Lacanian gap for them. A warning against totality — a reminder that we live in an open and fundamentally unknowable and uncontrollable universe — may in this sense be warranted.

All the same, environmental advocacy harbors a long history of writers and activists explicitly aiming to break open the comforting illusions of bourgeois social reality: asking their readers, for instance, to confront the mysteries of the universe rather than merely assume that we are comfortably ensconced in a transcendent social or moral-religious realm locating us humans well "above" and outside of nature. Environmental historians have often pointed to the history of human projections onto nature: as cosmic harmony, as goddess and mother, as "red in tooth and claw," as cybernetic computer, and so on.[90] The more informed response to this history of ideas is neither to fixate on one episode of it — such as the Disney "Lion King" mythology of nature as cosmic harmony, as Žižek sometimes does — nor to reject them all as "social constructions." Rather, the nuanced response is to ask how and why these ideas have reflected and affected their social and ecological contexts and what that means for us today.

As for paganism, Žižek's generalizations again get the better of him. Of course paganism, like any religious system, can be used to excuse the grossest violations of others' rights. (Christianity has itself been no stranger to such abuses.) But paganism in its practice rarely presented the kind of fully systematized cosmic harmony Žižek is suggesting. The world of Greek and Roman religion presented a barely coherent landscape of energies, relations, and divine forces. The polytheism of the ancient Greeks, writes Robert Parker, was "indescribable": "Gods overflowed like clothes from an over-filled drawer which no one felt obliged to tidy."[91] It can more reasonably be argued that polythe-

---

90 See my summary of these in Adrian Ivakhiv, "Nature," in *The Oxford Handbook of the Study of Religion,* eds. Michael Stausberg and Steven Engler, 415–29 (Oxford University Press, 2016).

91 Robert Parker, *Polytheism and Society at Athens* (Oxford University Press, 2005), 387.

istic systems are precisely *not* systems of monological "totality," but that they represent something closer to an "originary hybridity": a production of forces, variously anthropomorphized or not, at the many interfaces between humans and the extra-human world, whose plurality has always been syncretic and endlessly negotiable.

If pagan religion seems to be about a maintenance of systemic relations and mutual obligations between humans and their deities, then, the forms these relations take are neither universal nor unchanging. The generic principle of sacrifice, for instance, so seemingly widespread in those cultures labeled "pagan," can best be thought of as a principle of mutual obligation, a systemicity of a sort characterized by a flowing back-and-forth of relational bonds and expectations. In a messianic Christian context, this back-and-forth systematicity does not disappear, but only becomes centralized and sublimated into the figure of the dying-and-resurrecting messiah (and that only where Marian and saintly cults have not predominated). Monotheistic religion has certainly had its bouts of "totality" and "purification." Secular modernity may have attempted to slough off this sacrificial economy, but in the process merely enabled the other main narrative function of Christian eschatology: its messianic linearity, which became the myth of progress and Enlightenment (later supplemented by the Marxian myth of revolutionary salvation).

Paganisms today (where they are named as such) remain minority persuasions. While they sometimes aim to reconstruct ancient faiths, at least as often they follow the contours of a post-secular persuasion marked by the recognition that the human is not transcendent of nature, but is an intimate part of an open and emergent natural world.[92]

By way of contrast with Žižek's analysis, Jean-François Lyotard has written of a paganism of the borderlands, a place, as

---

92 See, e.g., Graham Harvey, *Contemporary Paganisms: Religions of the Earth from Druids and Witches to Heathens and Ecofeminists*, 2nd edn. (New York University Press, 2011). *The Pomegranate: International Journal of Pagan Studies* presents the best scholarship on the topic.

Martin Jay describes it, "of endless negotiation between peoples, all in a kind of exile, a porous boundary through which different intensities clashed without resolution."[93] Lyotard called his paganism "godless," "without Olympus and without pantheon, without *prudentia,* without fear, without grace, without debt and *hopeless.*"[94] This paganism is "a name" for "the denomination of a situation in which one judges without criteria."[95] As Daniel Smith puts it, Lyotard's paganism reflects the "groundlessness" according to which humans "are constantly having to match wits with the fate that has been given them" by a "shifting plurality of gods who are themselves subject to persuasion and metamorphosis."[96]

To a modern eye, which means to one for whom belief in God is a private matter, the history of God in a western context includes his removal from the world to a place outside it, where he can safely remain as creator, but eclipsed by the processes that maintain that world. By contrast, to see the world as filled with gods — to epistemologically repaganize it — is to break down this barrier between deity and world, flooding it with the possibility of minor interventions everywhere. Paganism in this sense refers to the modes of being and practice — imaginal, ar-

---

93 Martin Jay, "Modern and Postmodern Paganism: Peter Gay and Jean-François Lyotard," in *Cultural Semantics: Keywords of Our Time,* 181–96 (Amherst: University of Massachusetts Press, 1998), 192.

94 Jean-François Lyotard, "Lessons in Paganism," in *The Lyotard Reader,* ed. A. Benjamin, 122–54 (Oxford: Blackwell, 1991), 123; Jean-François Lyotard, "The Grip (*Mainmise*)," in *Political Writings,* trans. Bill Readings and Kevin Paul Geiman, 148–58 (Minneapolis: University of Minnesota Press, 1993), 156.

95 Jean-François Lyotard, *Just Gaming* (Minneapolis: University of Minnesota Press, 1985), 16; and see Martin Jay, "Modern and Postmodern Paganism." Lyotard was to later revise his stance and shift to an ethical position of "obligation." In *Peregrinations: Law, Form, Event* (New York: Columbia Unviersity Press, 1988), he admitted that "the polymorphic paganism of exploring and exploiting the whole range of intensive forms could easily be swept away into lawful permissiveness, including violence and terror" (15).

96 Among the more helpful and provocative accounts of what a contemporary polytheism might look like is Jordan Paper's *The Deities Are Many: A Polytheistic Theology* (Albany: SUNY Press, 2005).

tistic, religious, philosophical, and scientific — that somehow, of their own accord, bleed out of the everyday relationalities and dependencies between people and earth. To use Bruno Latour's terminology, such a post-secular paganism would reflect the "polynaturalism" of a world that has "never been modern," never having been purified into a single cosmic governmentality. Rather, it is always already contaminated by an original hybridity, where image and icon, god and person, community and shadow are and have always been interpenetrated in multiple ways.

Image, archive, cloud: on the ecology of images

All this talk of images makes it difficult to avoid the acknowledgment that we live today in a world of images run amok. Or at least in a sea of images whose thickness and generativity is beyond anything the Earth has seen before. What, if any, is the qualitative distinction between *those* images and the ones that might (or do) serve as our gods?

Consider the following six trajectories.

1. More and more people are being born today, and more and more of them live out a full life. About one in ten people who have ever lived are alive today. (The estimates range from 6.5% to over 12% depending on the weight given to various demographic factors.) With birth rates exceeding death rates, that percentage is increasing.[97]
2. More and more of these people are growing up with recording technologies — image and sound recording tools that preserve something of the present for the future. It is likely that over one-third of humanity now owns digital cameras.

---

97 Jonathan Good, "Crunching the Numbers: How Many People Have Ever Lived?" *1000memories*, May 9, 2011, http://blog.1000memories.com/75-number-of-people-who-have-ever-lived/; Clara Curtin, "Fact or Fiction? Booming Population Growth Among the Living, According to One Rumor, Outpaces the Dead," *Scientific American*, March 1, 2007, http://www.scientificamerican.com/article/fact-or-fiction-living-out-number-dead/.

Facebook users upload over 350 million photos per day to the site, which already includes some 300 billion, more than 15,000 times larger than the Library of Congress. Every two minutes we snap as many photos as the whole of humanity took in the 1800s; and one in ten photos we have were taken in the past twelve months.[98] YouTube and its siblings provide an ever-expanding archive of cinematic material uploaded, downloaded, re-edited, cross-referenced, spoofed, and endlessly commented upon. While some of these images are added to our archive by individuals for their individual and collective consumption and narrative construction, others are added by state or private organizations with an eye for monitoring, surveilling, managing, predicting, marketing, or prognosticating.

3. As images recording the present are preserved, they become past. At the same time, what is past becomes archived and opened to the present. Film reels, photographic imagery, and other productions are being added to the archive of what is digitally viewable, storable, sharable, and remixable. Technologies of retrieval — from digitization software and sampling technologies to historical, archaeological, detective, and forensics tools of various kinds — enable an ever deeper digging into and unlocking of the past. The "datability" of the past — of the earth as fossil repository and echo chamber — adds to the archive of images, sounds, signs, and documents that can be dredged up and set into motion.

With image and sound technologies, the past is now divisible into the era of reproducible images and the era that preceded it: BP (Before the Photograph) and AF (Anno Foto-

---

98 Cooper Smith, "Facebook Users Are Uploading 350 Million Photos Each Day," *Business Insider,* September 18, 2013, http://www.businessinsider.com/facebook-350-million-photos-each-day-2013–9; Jonathan Good, "How Many Photos Have Ever Been Taken?" *1000memories,* September 15, 2011, http://blog.1000memories.com/94-number-of-photos-ever-taken-digital-and-analog-in-shoebox; Salman Aslam, "Facebook by the Number: Stats, Demographics & Fun Facts," January 1, 2018, https://www.omnicoreagency.com/facebook-statistics.

grafici, the Year of Our Lord Photograph). One day we may count backwards to the year 1825, which will be the new Year Zero, when the first permanent photograph was produced by Joseph Nicéphore Niépce in Chalon-sur-Saône, France. Sound technologies came later, and touch and smell reproduction remain in their infancy. But even these demarcations in time are malleable. Recreations of the past, stillings of moments intended for preservation as teaching tools, sacred objects, memory emblems, political symbols, personal mementos — these have been with us at least since the cave walls were painted at Lascaux and Chauvet.

4. Interactive media, from Google Glass (whatever happened to it?) to multiuser video games to increasingly lifelike virtual worlds, render data space more immersive, more embodied, and at the same time more fluid. Even if many of the audio and visual recordings on YouTube and Vimeo are moments found in the "real world" — found objects in a discoverable reality — the default mode of cinematic imaging is no longer the mimetic representation and photo-indexical recording of reality. Rather, it is once again, as it was in its beginning (125 years ago or so), a matter of animation, the graphic manipulation of images. The growing archive of images and sounds becomes a database available for manipulation for a multitude of purposes — aesthetic, economic, political, or religious.

5. Then there is the storage of all of that. Every piece of data is material, and every object that stores, reads, produces, reproduces, manages, recombines, and even deletes data is also material. These entities are premised on an infrastructure by which materials like copper, lead, silver, tin, chromium, barium, silicon, mercury, beryllium, arsenic, and a variety of petrochemicals and otherwise hazardous compounds, are mined, smelted, refined, manufactured, transported, and disposed of, by oil rig, airplane, land and sea cable, human hand and lung, and so on — with handling and exposure extend-

ed all along the way.[99] E-waste has been the fastest growing waste stream for years.[100] Digital storage capacity overtook analog storage capacity in 2002, and within five years of that date, 94% of storage was already digital. As of 2011, humanity stored some 300 exabytes of information — that is, 300 followed by 18 zeroes.[101] Data disks, however, degrade and must be replaced; and with the emergence of new formats, there is a need for format conversion and migration, which means new storage replacing old storage. But old formats do not go away; they remain as relic and waste, a material ghost whose materiality never dissipates.

6. Finally, there is the cloud. Cloud computing is the frontier of the personal computing industry and, in a certain sense, marks its end — the end of the personal and the triumph of the nodal. By definition, the Internet is a distributed system: it links billions of devices into a network of networks that share data, images, and documents across the world. The infrastructure it requires is immense. In theory, cloud computing replaces local storage and software with storage and management of files in distant data centers or "server farms." In practice, it often supplements the former with the latter as a means of adding security to data files, which instead of being saved in one place — on a home computer or hard drive — may be saved in several places to ensure ready

---

99 Sy Taffel, "Escaping Attention: Digitla Media Hardware, Materiality and Ecological Cost," *Culture Machine* 13 (2012): 1–28; Leslie Byster and Ted Smith, "The Electronics Production Lifecycle, from Toxics to Sustainability: Getting off the Toxic Treadmill," in *Challenging the Chip: Labour Rights and Environmental Justice in the Global Electronics Industry*, eds. Ted Smith, David Sonnenfeld, and David Naguib Pellow, 205–14 (Philadelphia: Temple University Press, 2006); *Electronics Take-Back Coalition*, Facts and Figures on E-Waste and Recycling, http://www.electronicstakeback.com/wp=content/uploads/Facts_and_Figures_on-EWaste_and_Recycling.pdf.

100 Byster and Smith, "The Electronics Production Lifecycle," 210.

101 Lucas Mearian, "Scientists Calculate Total Data Stored to Date: 295+ Exabytes," *ComputerWorld*, February 14, 2011, http://www.computerworld.com/s/article/9209158/Scientists_calculate_total_data_stored_to_date_295_exabytes.

access by home computer, smart phone, tablet, and an array of wireless devices. Cloud computing contributes to the perception that digital media "dematerialize" our relations with the earth, but any image or data requires materiality for its existence. As Maxwell and Miller put it, "The metaphor of a natural, ephemeral cloud belies the dirty reality of coal-fired energy that feeds most data centers around the world."[102]

Debates over the sustainability of cloud computing revolve around the possibility of its shifting from fossil fuels to renewable energy sources, and toward a smart grid that accounts for how much data one is using, through what operations, and so on. To date, data centers' energy usage pales in comparison with that of transportation technologies (about 2% to about 25%), which shows, as Google's Urs Hölzle has argued, that it takes less energy to ship electrons than atoms. But even as data storage moves to the cloud, 15% of global residential energy is spent on powering domestic digital technology. Even so, a smart-grid style accounting of the cloud would limit its "rematerialization" to the arithmetical and statistical. Inherent in the expanding archive of digital information, images, texts, audio and video recordings, is a slipperiness where data objects cannot be pinned down. They are not exactly here, where I am accessing them, nor there, on a server somewhere in Wyoming or Illinois or Central Australia; they are in between, mobile, in the rush of semiosis. As the amount of data each of us produces increases, and as more of it gets stored in multiple data servers, available upon request in the ever more ubiquitous datasphere, so does the need for data security measures that also require secure storage and accessibility.

As the archive of images and sounds continues to grow, and as it "dematerializes" — that is, as it is globalized into a cloud

---

102 Richard Maxwell and Toby Miller, "Greening Starts with Ourselves," *New York Times*, September 24, 2012, http://www.nytimes.com/roomfordebate/2012/09/23/informations-environmental-cost/greening-starts-with-ourselves.

that is fuzzy in its spatial parameters, but is as thoroughly material as anything — boundaries distinguishing the personal from the public are deterritorialized into a multitude of spaces, traces, databanks, strata, and flows. Access to these spaces and databanks — and, more importantly, the capacity for management and manipulation of the data they hold — becomes the prize among a competing array of local and global players. With this de- and re-territorialization, the struggle to re-establish a democratic commons takes on new forms.

Ultimately, such struggle is part and parcel of every de- and re-territorialization the planet has seen. Image technologies bear witness to this history. As Nadia Bozak delineates in *The Cinematic Footprint*, cinema, like photography, has always been ecologically embedded. It depends on a powerful combination of at least two forms of solar energy: the capture of reflected solar light, and the indirect products of that energy that have been stored and compounded over millennia in the form of fossil fuels.[103] As Henri Bergson might have put it, cinematic images are a form of captured, organized, and released light-heat-energy-movement. In this, they take what is common to all of us — all living substances — and reorganize it in the crafting of meaningful worlds. To make cinema is to craft worlds from worlds, and in doing so, to bear an obligation to the light, heat, and energy used in their making.

All life on this planet is the product of one or another permutation of the interaction between energy originating from the sun (light and heat) and the surface of the Earth that it strikes. Everything we know is an evolved permutation of that endlessly differentiating process. Modern image technologies, analog or digital, are products of a certain political ecology: they arose alongside the industrialization of material production, an unleashing of productive capacities that had been stored on or beneath the surface of this planet for millennia. The digitalization of the image (still or moving, or some combination of the two) is

---

103 Nadia Bozak, *The Cinematic Footprint: Lights, Camera, Natural Resources* (New Brunswick: Rutgers University Press, 2012).

not of a matter of *post*-industrialization, but merely of the digital, post-Fordist globalization of that same political ecology. It is the latest phase of the development of the bio-socio-technical apparatus that has undergirded industrialization. Image technologies are part and parcel of a world that has become faster, more mobile and fluid, and more diversely integrated — economically, politically, and culturally — even as its tensions have become intensified and globalized.

Time of the image

If we live in a world whose outer circumference has become thickened with the production of millions of images, it is important to realize that these images are not merely visual: they are bits or "moments" of "world," which are produced, reproduced, and sent reeling into an ocean already thick with recombinant imagery. And these moments of world are not *individual* images so much as they are *affective currents*.

Take music videos. This form packs in, often with utmost intensity, the animate mobility of the audiovisual image: the affective spectacle of a particular set of motions, speeds, sounds, glimpses, gazes, sensations, feelings; the cutting together of one thing into another, sutured by rhythm and song, to create some sense of a narrative arc, or at least of movement or tension between the kinds of structuring oppositions that make narrative possible; and the semiotic openness by which what would normally stand on its own — a song or musical piece — becomes overlaid by and adjoined to other things entirely. One might argue that music videos *reduce* the interpretive openness of a piece of music by locking it into a series of visual and narrative reference points. But every such reduction is also a transformation that creates new possibilities for interpretation. The images of a music video, propelled by its music, are intended to stay with viewers, and because most music videos are under five minutes in length, those images are carefully chosen, with little digression from their basic sense. Their external reference points may be focused, more than anything else, on the production of the artist's persona, such that the viewer might be expected to say something like "This is the best thing she's done yet!"—where she may be Lady Gaga, Beyoncé, Rihanna, Adele, or Katy Perry. But this artist's persona is always implicated in broader cultural relations, within which fan responses find their meanings and chart their affective paths through the world. At their most effective, music videos elicit a deeply affective charge, a *frisson* or wave intended to carry a viewer somewhere, both over the satisfactory burst of duration that constitutes the video itself and well beyond it afterward.

Much the same could be said of any video that goes viral on the Internet. This is the same whether they are "found" or "spontaneous" videos—random shots of life that happened to be caught on camera—or carefully planned and orchestrated works of budding video auteurs. In the first category, one finds, for instance, the video shot by a Chinese security camera showing a two-year-old girl being hit and run over by a truck, followed by several passersby ignoring her—a video that elicited a round of anguished soul-searching, blame seeking, and recriminations among Chinese citizens. The clip itself was short, no longer than the original film reels of the Lumière brothers, and just as silent, but it became a live and mobile moment, a moving episode, an event that captured and transmitted an intensity of feeling for its viewers.

Also in this category one might include the images from the undersea "Spillcam" that brought the Deepwater Horizon oil spill seeping eerily into thousands of viewers' bedrooms in the summer of 2010, or the many YouTube videos of the massed movement of starling murmurations (as the formations are called), or of cute or bizarre animal encounters—brief cinematic outtakes from a trans-human world that delights viewers irrespective of any extinction crisis we might collectively be responsible for.

Taken collectively, cinematic imagery in the digital age presents a universe whose outer circumference is always expanding. That circumference is not bounded; it is open, with new works being added like thoughts and exhalations of a cinematic humanity. And within that circumference, the dots that connect it are no longer singular, bounded units so much as they are fluid bursts — more like bacteria that share genetic information across boundaries, or rhizomes that connect with others in ever-widening webs, than like sedentary organisms that take root and bear fruit in a single plot of soil. The moving images shared on YouTube and other social media mix with the reports of cable television and other forms of reportage to provide a staged running commentary about the world that, in turn, builds and binds our world. By the minute, they are adding new vectors of transmission on which future worlds might be borne if only the creative advance — the reach toward a new intensity of beauty, relationality, and meaning — was there.

Whether this situation strikes us as fortunate or not, it is here where experimentation can occur for carving out spaces in which the A/Cene could be challenged.

Of gods and the eyes of the world

Filmmaker Werner Herzog has argued that while "destruction of the environment" is an "enormous danger," "the lack of adequate imagery is a danger of the same magnitude." "If we do not develop adequate images," he warns, "we will die out like dinosaurs."[104]

If we define images as broadly as a pansemiotic, process-relational ontology suggests, then Herzog's claim is both trivial and comprehensive. It is trivial in that we will die out, after all, like dinosaurs, and perhaps much quicker than they did. It is comprehensive in that it is precisely our capacity to develop adequate images that will define the future of our worlds. If moving images are not just things that we see, but ways of seeing that draw us in and take us places, and if we ourselves are made of such drawings-in and takings-places, then the play of such drawings, takings, goings, movings, and becomings constitutes

104 Cited in Werner Herzog, Roger Ebert, and Gene Walsh, *Images at the Horizon: A Workshop with Werner Herzog* (Chicago: Facets Multimedia, 1979), 21.

the universe. And then it is fitting to consider our most powerful moving images as the "gods" that carry us across the gaps of a folded, bumpy, fraught, and turbulent universe.

Countenancing gods may seem retrograde and contrary to the democratic and humanistic goals many of us harbor. But gods have more to do with democracy's origins than is evident at first blush. The earliest examples of democratic public assembly including those in ancient Athens, the Hellenistic city-states, and republican Rome, did not separate the political from the religious, artistic, scientific, legal, or other domains. The Greek political world, as Nancy Evans puts it, "was governed by civic rites." Every Greek city "relied on countless religious practices in every aspect of its daily functioning. Citizens stood not only in political and social relationship to each other but also in religious and cultic relationship to each other, to their children and ancestors, and to the city's gods."[105]

Assuming the category of gods to be not yet exhausted is something that a post-secular world may need to do. In any case, we should define that category liberally, to include spirits, angels, prophets, saints, ancestors, descendants, culture heroes, tricksters, and many other non-human or para-human agencies — "meta-personal" powers, as Marshall Sahlins calls them, to which people defer, which they attend and honor, with which they maintain relational compacts, and which they are generally loath to give up.[106] They may or may not be human constructs, but they are always also more than that, and it is that "more than" that largely defines them. Gods in this sense can be male or female, neither or both, human-like or utterly other than hu-

---

105 Nancy Evans, *Civic Rites: Democracy and Religion in Ancient Athens* (Berkeley: University of California Press, 2010), 5.

106 I prefer "para-human" to "metahuman," the term Sahlins employs in his important recent piece on "The Original Political Society," *Hau: Journal of Ethnographic Theory* 7, no. 2 (2017). "Para-" suggests something similar but different, "beside" or "near" to the human. "Meta-" suggests something "later," "beyond," or of a different order to the human. Each has its virtues, but I prefer to leave the ontological ordering ambiguous. That said, "meta-personal" works well. And see Paper's *The Deities Are Many* for a well argued case on behalf of a theology of such meta-persons.

man, and they can be something discovered along the way, not pre-existing history but elaborated alongside it in the historical unfoldment of a people, a *demos*.

But to the extent that there exists "a people" — and it is always risky to define such a group — that people will have its gods. And when there are multiple and overlapping configurations of such *demoi* — organized in families, clans, moieties, batallions, neighborhoods, cities, tribes, nations, gangs, political parties, sports teams, secret societies, and other formations — they will be engaged with multiple and overlapping configurations of divinities, spirits, or ancestral and other powers.

We can see such configurations in ancient Greece, Rome, and Egypt, and endless variations of them in indigenous and tribal societies. They are among us today as well, in the bumpy and multifaceted religious landscapes of East and South Asia, Africa, and South America, and in Catholic and Orthodox christianities to the extent that that monotheistic faith has allowed its polymorphous impulses to thrive. To a visitor unprepared for it (as I was on a recent visit), the presence of altars, shrines, and temples across the urban and rural landscapes of a country like contemporary Taiwan is overwhelming and somewhat perplexing. (One expects it more in India, Bali, or Thailand.)

It is not necessary to argue that every form of social organization is a religion and that its symbols are deities; or that religion is exclusively social in a Durkheimian sense. But it is worth considering that to the extent that social forms maintain allegiance, it is through mediators that act something like gods — that sometimes are explicitly that, but more often are something a little godlike, a little humanlike, and more than a little mysterious.

Continuing this speculative exercise, we might say that gods have always been the ones who see us and in whose presence we justify our existence. As Diana Eck writes in her study of the divine image in India, the "single most common and significant element" of religious practice in India is *darśan,* or *darśana,* the "seeing" of the divine image which is simultaneously a meeting of gazes, a seeing and being seen through the mediator of the divine image.[107]

Accounting for such divinities has been one of the many goals of Bruno Latour's ambitious *Modes of Existence* project, a collaborative and international scholarly-*cum*-artistic endeavor that aimed to develop a language that could help bring diplomacy to the gapped and fractured worlds of a "multinatural" humanity. In his monograph initiating the project, Latour divided up the powers of the godlike into "beings of presence" and "beings of metamorphosis." The first are recognizably religious, forces which initiate conversion or salvation in us, but who are not subject to transaction, while the second are psychologically dynamic and centrifugal in their effects. This distinction may betray Latour's own Christian assumption that some forces ("divinities," which "bear psyches"[108]) take us *out* of ourselves, to some unspecified *elsewhere,* while others ("gods") bring us *back* to ourselves, to the fundamental *with*ness of being with others, here, now, not in chronological time but in eternal, *kairotic* time.[109] (Latour may share a Christian bias with Charles Taylor, but he insists precisely on the kind of God who is closer to us than we ourselves, not the kind seemingly preferred by Taylor, who is transcendent of ourselves and of nature.) In times when we may need to be brought back to a new and different sense of ourselves, our community, and our Earth, this distinction between beings of metamorphosis and beings of presence may not hold up very well: they all take us out of ourselves and into ourselves, for the movement "out" is the movement that shapes the next subject in the sequence.

In any case, together these beings would mediate the relationship between psyche, earth, and cosmos, where the bounded, modern, liberal "subject" is rendered open and permeable to the passages of elemental winds and divine circulations. What

---

107 Diana L. Eck, *Darśan: Seeing the Divine Image in India,* 3rd edn. (New York: Columbia University Press, 1998), 1.

108 Bruno Latour, *An Inquiry into Modes of Existence: An Anthropology of the Moderns* (Cambridge: Harvard University Press, 2013), 309.

109 Ibid., chs. 7 and 11.

would such beings *see* if they were to look at us? What, for that matter, does the world see when it looks back at us? (This may or may not be the same question.)

The first thing to say in response, of course, is that in the planetary context there most certainly is no "us" yet. Humanity as a collective agent does not yet exist; and whether it ever will is an open question. In our global world, there is no single people, no *demos*. The *demos* of a reassembled democracy remains to be constituted. Nor, then, is there any unified compact of earth, sky, gods, and mortals, as Martin Heidegger famously called for. But it is apposite to ask whether it is possible for a *demos* to emerge without the appropriate gods — gods who would look back at that people and offer it an opportunity to cultivate the capacity to see themselves as they appear in eternity's eyes. That eternity, of course, is the same one that will bury that *demos*, along with the Anthropos that masquerades as one today.

Paul Klee's 1920 ink, chalk, and watercolor drawing "Angelus Novus" (pictured as the frontispiece of this book) presents a suggestive model here. As related earlier, Walter Benjamin took it to represent the "angel of history," with his face "turned toward the past" and seeing "one single catastrophe" piling "wreckage upon wreckage" at his feet. "The angel would like to stay, awaken the dead, and make whole what has been smashed." Benjamin's reading was his own, a wartime reading of a relatively unknown (at the time) artwork from a previous wartime. We could equally choose to see the angel as facing not the wreckage of the past, but us as we view the wreckage of the present building up around us, or the wreckage of a future we might, in some measure, avert.

Of the fifty or so paintings of angels produced by the Swiss-born Klee, most of them in his last few years of life, this early one remains the one that most directly faces us, the viewer. It gazes less *at* us than *into* us. This gaze that discomforts us — what does it see, in the Era of the Human?

Film still from *Austerlitz,* dir. Sergei Loznitsa, Germany, 2016. Courtesy of the director.

In Sergei Loznitsa's remarkable 2016 film *Austerlitz,* the eye of the camera plays the role of such an unseen angel.[110] What it sees is visitors to the Sachsenhausen and Dachau concentration camps — Holocaust tourists, in effect. Loznitsa sets up his camera in front of the crowds to give us several-minute long blocks of time watching the visitors arrive and move through the camps, with tour guides, listening devices, or without. Loznitsa's ethical challenge here is: how to show us the ~~Event~~ of the death camps today, three-quarters of a century after they were used for the machinery of mass slaughter? How to lead us into it, without providing the decades of narrative that have become customary to it, but which have lost their potency? His answer is: by not showing us that machinery at all, but instead, by showing *us* — today's viewers and visitors — and letting us lead ourselves into it.

"We" are, of course, not we, for as long as we maintain the distance afforded by the viewer's irony — we, viewers, on this side of the screen; they, the tourists, on the other. But that distance, which is what gives us the sense that we are superior to them, cannot be maintained indefinitely, and this is our viewerly

---

110 *Austerlitz,* dir. Sergei Loznitsa, Germany, 2016.

challenge. If it — the world, the dead, the death camp victims, the Angel of History, Time itself — could look back at us, this is what it would see today: these faces of curious, T-shirted, camera-toting onlookers and selfie-takers. The materiality of a tourist mass making its way across the viewscape of death. Looking, snapping photos, eating, looking, moving, chatting, listening (to a hand-held device), looking some more. Advertising a bodyscape of T-shirt logos, brands, and slogans that identify us as incorporated into the symbolic order of our society.

Are not the death camp victims, and the death camps themselves, the ancestral deities to whom the visitors pay their respects, haltingly, haphazardly, not quite knowing how? Can they, can we, learn to do that better? The film, in its open-endedness, suggests that perhaps we can.

What I am trying to suggest is that there is a need for divinities, for angels, or for ancestors and descendants to serve as the eyes and faces by which we see ourselves. Those gods and descendants exist, circulating spectrally at the peripheries of our worlds. Sometimes they are more human than ourselves. What does not yet exist is the People that can account for its own collective action on this earth. If and when such a People comes into being — the "new earth" and the "people to come" that Deleuze and Guattari heralded, in their final co-authored volume[111] — will it look anything like us? And will it not include a range of intermediate beings, angelic or godlike ones that help us deal with the more elusive tricksters on which our planetary future inescapably rests?

Skin of the living

One of the names of the deities being invoked into presence today is that of Gaia. First named by novelist William Golding to denote his neighbor's, James Lovelock's, theory of a quasi-

---

111 Gilles Deleuze and Félix Guattari, *What Is Philosophy?*, trans. Hugh Tomlinson and Graham Burchell (New York: Columbia University Press, 1994), 109.

unified system of planetary biogeochemical processes, Gaia's icons have proliferated into numerous scientific, popular, and para-religious forms.

Bruce Clarke describes the scientific majority view on Lovelock's hypothesized Gaia as denoting "an Earth system with a panoply of open and closed loops, circular feedbacks interconnecting biotic and abiotic systems into an elastic but coherent consortium."[112] He qualifies this "consortium" as "heterogeneous," "disunified," and "metabiotic" — meaning that it is emergent from "the systemic coupling of living operations with the abiotic dynamics of their cosmic, solar, and Earthly elements."[113] As far as the science goes (and it's been shown to be a fruitful theory, if hardly accepted so far by anything approaching a consensus), so far, so good.

Isabelle Stengers tweaks this Gaia in the direction of something a little different — not a Gaia that is the Earth-sized goddess of New Age and pagan religiosity (which she is well aware of), but a Gaia that is "the name of an unprecedented or forgotten form of transcendence: a transcendence deprived of the noble qualities that would allow it to be invoked as an arbiter, guarantor, or resource." This Gaia is "a ticklish assemblage of forces that are indifferent to our reasons and our projects."[114]

This indifferent but ticklish assemblage responds, unfeelingly, to our activities. And yet she is one whose responses we need to figure into *our* calculations — which is something that, to be effective, will need to be done *feelingly*. How, then, to do that?

The short answer is: experimentally, through trial and error. Ideas are not enough, and nor are images. As Jane Bennett writes in *Vibrant Matter,* "We need not only to invent or reinvoke concepts like conatus, actant, assemblage, small agency, operator, disruption, and the like" — I would add Gaia, gods,

---

112 Bruce Clarke, "Rethinking Gaia: Stengers, Latour, Margulis," *Theory, Culture & Society* 34, no. 4 (2017): 3–26, at 17.

113 Ibid., 18, 22; and see Michael Ruse's *The Gaia Hypothesis: Science on a Pagan Planet* (Chicago: University of Chicago Press, 2013).

114 Isabelle Stengers, *In Catastrophic Times: Resisting the Coming Barbarism,* trans. A. Goffey (Ann Arbor: Open Humanities Press, 2015), 47.

the posthuman, cosmopolitics, the parliament of things, and all the rest. We need also "to devise new procedures, technologies, and regimes of perception that enable us to consult nonhumans more closely, or to listen and respond more carefully to their outbreaks, objections, testimonies, and propositions."[115]

The first step, in any case, is to retrain our perception so that we could learn to hear those outbreaks, objections, testimonies, and propositions. Bennett suggests one "everyday tactic" by which to begin doing that, a method that she associates with Charles Darwin's practice of allow himself to "anthropomorphize, to relax into resemblances discerned across ontological divides." As examples she offers: "you (mis)take the wind outside at night for your father's wheezy breathing in the next room; you get up too fast and see stars; a plastic topographical map reminds you of the veins on the back of your hand; the rhythm of the cicadas reminds you of the wailing of an infant; the falling stone seems to express a conative desire to persevere."[116]

There is a playfulness and gentleness here, a relaxing into the folds of a larger, livelier world, that seems at odds with any injunction to pay heed to the stern-faced gods of some new dispensation. Bennett reminds us that there is pleasure to be gained in a re-entry into the world of the living. There is tenderness to be found in the folds of a world of overlapping bodies, once the shadow of the Anthropos dissipates into the leafy textures of a half-lit, half-shadowy world with its soft embraces. That is where, amidst the wind outside and the rhythms of the cicadas, we might come to hear the outbreaks, testimonies, and other propositions of our suitors.

In a piece on the cosmology of Whitehead, James Hillman addresses this question of the intelligibility of the world and how to regain it. All things, he argues, "are inherently intelligible"; their intelligibility is "given with the shapes or physiognomy of the world which is afforded directly to our sensate im-

---

115 Jane Bennett, *Vibrant Matter: A Political Ecology of Things* (Durham: Duke University Press, 2010), 108.
116 Ibid., 120.

aginations, to us as animals." Why, then, "do we feel lost, behind a dark glass, disoriented?" Hillman asserts that it is our Lockean theory of perception that has removed "the emotional face of things."[117] Hillman is referring here to John Locke's carving up of nature into its mathematically measurable "primary qualities" and the "secondary qualities" that are byproducts of perception — a "bifurcation of nature" that Whitehead spent his last twenty-five years attempting to overcome.

Theories of how things went wrong inevitably mislead, but the point for Hillman, and by extension for Whitehead, is that it is a matter of perception to correct this: "Seeing the face of the Gods in things means noticing qualities as primary and speaking in a richly qualified language. Adjectives before nouns." For Hillman, it is in paying attention to the sensually perceptible *qualities* of the world that we can recover an "aesthetic cosmology" in which human beings would be "resituated" within "a world ensouled."[118]

Sacrifice zones, Chernobyl, and the post-human

The place of the gods, from which they would gaze down upon us, has in the past been the scene of sacrifice. The only details to be determined might typically be: what is to be sacrificed, how, when, and to whom?

Two linked but differently inflected histories of modern sacrifice could be instructive here. The first national parks were created in part with the intent to "save" nonhuman Nature from us, to honor and protect it as a relic of an earlier time. These places, in effect, sacrificed the instrumental or commodity value of these lands for their perceived intrinsic, ecological, or even spiritual values. That America's first national parks were sacrificed at the altar of the nation — as part of America's effort to be-

---

117 James Hillman, "Back to Beyond: On Cosmology," in *Archetypal Process: Self and Divine in Whitehead, Jung, and Hillman,* ed. David Ray Griffin, 213–32 (Evanston: Northwestern University Press, 1989), 225–26.
118 Ibid.

come a respectable nation among other nations, one that lacked cathedrals but made up for it in "nature's cathedrals" — is simply reflective of the fact that the nation itself was the prime deity of the young American becoming-nation. (And that its indigenous inhabitants and their worlds were also sacrificed was an unstated precondition.)

At a global level, UNESCO's world heritage sites and biosphere reserves have in turn sacrificed instrumental uses for the sake, and at the altar, of a more global concept of heritage, patrimony, legacy, ancestrality, and by implication, futurity — the future of a world and an Earth imagined to be held in common by all humanity living and to come. Insofar as it preserves the nonhuman world from the hands of those who would destroy it (and often its effects are more complicated), this first form of sacrifice could be thought of as a form of self-sacrifice.

The second form of sacrifice is less gratifying to ponder, and its victims are still among us all around. In 1972, the US National Academy of Sciences recommended that the Four Corners Area of the US Southwest, primarily populated by Native American tribes and subjected to decades of uranium and other forms of mining, be designated a "National Sacrifice Area." Industrial technologies have since produced hundreds of scars on the landscape and imposed sacrifice on many communities, who have been forced to relocate or simply left to suffer the consequences.

In a time of climate crisis, much of the world is becoming an ecological sacrifice zone. And in times of Anthropocenic crisis, one might suggest that a summons, a call to prayer, is being issued by these zones of sacrifice, and by the victims of sacrifice — calling upon us to sacrifice of *ourselves* at the altar of a larger Earth community whose membership is not yet known and whose contours not yet shaped.

The Chernobyl Zone offers a suggestive model here. When reactor number four of the Chernobyl nuclear power plant in northern Ukraine exploded on the night of April 26, 1986, it launched a series of events that was to dramatically affect the lives of hundreds of thousands of Soviet citizens, along with a

Rooftop view of the post-human city of Pripyat, abandoned in 1986. Chernobyl Exclusion Zone. Photo by the author, 2016.

vast geography of living organisms and ecological relations. The accident qualifies as an Event, or hyper-event — an event that triggered chain reactions, which in turn rearranged agential relations operating on multiple spatial and temporal scales.

A few of the ways it did this are evident to anyone who has studied the details.[119] More than any other single event, the Chernobyl catastrophe and its aftermath — including a near-total state-wide news blackout about the extent of the event for a full eighteen days — served to sunder the emotional commitments that held together the Soviet Union. It not only tolled a final death-knell to the "sputnik religion" that had guided many Soviet scientists' commitments to the state-celebrated marriage of technology and socialism,[120] but it also unleashed popular forces

---

119 I've detailed these more fully in Adrian Ivakhiv, "Chernobyl, Risk, and the Inter-Zone of the Anthropocene," in *The Routledge Companion to Risk and Media*, eds. Bishnupriya Ghosh and Bhaskar Sarkar (New York: Routledge, forthcoming).

120 I take the term "sputnik religion" from Joachim Radkau, *The Age of Ecology* (Cambridge: Polity, 2014), 214. And see Eva Maurer et al., eds., *Soviet Space Culture: Cosmic Enthusiasm in Socialist Societies* (London: Palgrave Macmillan, 2011), and Sonia D. Schmid, *Producing Power: The Pre-Chernobyl History of the Soviet Nuclear Industry* (Cambridge: MIT Press, 2015).

that had begun to boil during the economic stagnation of the late Brezhnev, Andropov, Chernenko, and Gorbachev eras. The environmental movements that resulted paved the way, in turn, for the emergence of republican independence movements, until the Union could no longer hold together. For Ukraine, in turn, Chernobyl's legacy provided a set of narrative resources — both about Ukraine's historical victimhood and about its long-denied sovereignty — that served as powerful impetus for that country's herky-jerk dance away from its "elder brother" Russia and toward "Europeanization," both in the overwhelming initial vote for independence in 1991 and in the partial if not entirely successful revolutions of 2004 and 2014.

On a more global scale, the accident, which unleashed the largest release of radioactive contamination in human history, helped propel humanity into a "global risk culture," as Ulrich Beck designated it, characterized by deep uncertainty, instability, and disparity in social groups' capacities to avoid or absorb risk.[121] Like similar events, the accident remains a harbinger of a more global ecological collapse that remains ever virtual, hovering on the horizon, yet which is manifested in countless data points connecting the impacts of industrial activities — the production of pollutants, toxins, and hazardous wastes affecting terrestrial and aquatic ecosystems, climate systems, and social systems, and together resulting in a sense of the future's precarity and uncertainty. The full impact of the Chernobyl accident remains hotly debated, with competing reports claiming wildly varying tolls of excess cancers and related fatalities.[122]

---

121 Ulrich Beck, *The Risk Society* (London: Sage, 1992).

122 E.g., see International Atomic Energy Agency, Division of Public Information, *Chernobyl's Legacy: Health, Environmental and Socio-economic Impacts and Recommendations to the Governments of Belarus, the Russian Federation and Ukraine,* 2nd rev. edn. (Vienna: IAEA, 2006); Alexey Yablokov, Iryna Labunska, and Ivan Blokov, eds., *The Chernobyl Catastrophe: Consequences on Human Health* (Amsterdam: Greenpeace, 2006); Alexandra Dawe et al., *Nuclear Scars: The Lasting Legacies of Chernobyl and Fukushima* (Amsterdam: Greenpeace International, 2016); Pamela Abbott, Claire Wallace, and Matthias Beck, "Chernobyl: Living with Risk and Uncertainty," *Health, Risk and Society* 8, no. 2 (2006): 105–21.

But it is what transpired in the Zone of Exclusion, or Zone of Alienation (*Zona Vidchuzhennya*), that is most evocative of the Event's otherness. Depopulated of its human residents after the accident, the area known as the 30-kilometer Zone (while not exactly 30 km in diameter, it totals approximately 1000 square miles within the territory of Ukraine) includes the former city of Pripyat, a handful of smaller towns (including Chernobyl), and over a hundred now empty villages.

Over the years, several hundred of the resettled villagers, generally elderly, have elected to come back and effectively squat on their land. Others have come to loot: for home appliances, carpets, metals, cultural-historical artifacts, jewelry, and anything else of potential value on any market.

Still others have come to "stalk" the Zone. The latter term is taken from Andrei Tarkovsky's 1979 film *Stalker* and the science-fiction novel, *A Roadside Picnic,* on which it was based, about an anomalous Zone (created, in the novel, by extraterrestrial debris) that is cordoned off behind an army-patrolled border, with travel into it prohibited.[123] Those who do lead unsanctioned tours into the Zone are called "stalkers." As an apparently un-inhabitable Zone, the Chernobyl Zone has attracted hundreds, and perhaps a few thousand, such stalkers over the years. The Zone invites curiosity and even a kind of utopian aspiration. It has more recently become a zone of "dark" or "doom tourism," with some 15,000 to 20,000 visitors a year touring it since tours were legalized in 2011. Then there are the gamers — avid enthusiasts of the S.T.A.L.K.E.R. video games (*S.T.A.L.K.E.R.: Shadow of Chernobyl, Call of Pripyat,* and *Clear Sky*), in which players "battle zombies, mutant animals, and other improbable foes in a hyper-sensationalized contaminated 'zone of alienation.'" "Imagine Chernobyl's absolute worst possible effects," Sarah Phillips

---

123 See my account of the film in Adrian Ivakhiv, *Ecologies of the Moving Image: Cinema, Affect, Nature* (Waterloo: Wilfrid Laurier University Press, 2013), 13–22.

writes, "multiply by ten, add steroids, bring on the Kalashniko-vs, and you have S.T.A.L.K.E.R."[124]

Finally, there is the tremendous ecological bounce-back that has transpired in the exclusion zone ever since most of the humans left it. As Mary Mycio wrote in *Wormwood Forest: A Natural History of Chernobyl,* the Chernobyl zone has become "a vast and beautiful wilderness of forests and wetlands that are gradually consuming the remains of towns and villages" and "teeming with moose, deer, wild boars and some 250 species of birds," with wolves seen in broad daylight, wild Przewalski horses reintroduced and thriving, and even endangered lynx making a comeback.[125]

The Zone has thus become a zone of presence and absence: the presence of forces unleashed by industrial calamity; the absence of the very causes of those forces — the human and industrial activities that precipitated them, except as ruins, memories, and odd remainders and bizarre outliers. Most interesting is that the abandoned city of Pripyat, once a Soviet "model nuclear city," has now become the model *post*-human city, featuring as a stand-in for the post-apocalypse, or for the simple idea of the disappearance of humanity, in numerous media projects including National Geographic's *Aftermath: Population Zero,* History Channel's *Life After People,* and the book that inspired both of these, Alan Weisman's *The World Without Us,* and in fictionalized dramatizations like the post-nuclear horror flicks *Chernobyl Diaries* and the *Return of the Living Dead* series.[126]

---

124 Sarah D. Phillips, "Chernobyl Forever," *Somatosphere,* April 25, 2011, http://somatosphere.net/2011/04/chernobyl-forever.html. See also Sarah D. Phillips, "Chernobyl's Sixth Sense: The Symbolism of an Ever-Present Awareness," *Anthropology and Humanism* 29, no. 2 (2004): 159–85; and Sarah D. Phillips and Sarah Ostaszewski, "An Illustrated Guide to the Post-Catastrophic Future," *Anthropology of East Europe Review* 30, no. 1 (2012): 127–40.

125 Mary Mycio, *Wormwood Forest: A Natural History of Chernobyl* (Washington: Joseph Henry Press, 2005).

126 Alan Weisman, *The World Without Us* (New York: St. Martin's Press, 2007); *Aftermath: The World After Humans* (National Geographic/Cream Productions, Canada, 2008); *Life After People* (dir. David De Vries, History Chan-

The trope of post-humanity situates the Event of Chernobyl into the narrative of the Anthropocene and what would follow it. There are four main variations of this narrative, which date it back, respectively, to the agricultural revolution,[127] the demographic collapse in the Americas following the Columbian encounter,[128] the Industrial Revolution, and to the so-called "great acceleration" of the mid-20th century, with its atom bombs, petrochemicals, fertilizers, and other novel substances disseminating rapidly into the Earth's biosphere, hydrosphere, and lithosphere.[129] Of these, Chernobyl most obviously fits the fourth variation, its release of radioactive isotopes being the single largest in history. Michael Marder writes in *Chernobyl Herbarium* that "Chernobyl's 30-km radius is an advanced laboratory, at the leading edge of what is going on with the entire planet. In a consummation of the alienation or self-alienation that has unfortunately proved to be constitutive of the human, the whole world is on its way to becoming Chernobyl or a gulag." "Entire regions of the world," Marder continues, "are converted into no-go areas, whether as a consequence of wars or environmental devastation. The effects of climate change leave no place unaffected."[130]

Chernobyl in this sense qualifies as part of a growing list of ecological sacrifice zones, sites of "negative ecological heritage" that mark the places where the sacrifice that is algorithmically

---

nel, USA, 2008); *Chernobyl Diaries* (dir. Bradley Parker, USA, 2012), *Pripyat* (dir. Nikolaus Geyrhalter, Czech Republic, 1999); *Return of the Living Dead: Necropolis* (dir. Ellory Elkayem, USA, 2005); *Return of the Living Dead: Rave to the Grave* (dir. Ellory Elkayem, USA, 2005).

127 William F. Ruddiman, "The Anthropogenic Greenhouse Era Began Thousands of Years Ago," *Climatic Change* 61, no. 3 (2003): 261–93.

128 Simon L. Lewis and Mark A. Maslin, "Defining the Anthropocene," *Nature* 519 (March 12, 2015): 170–80.

129 Paul Crutzen and Eugene Stoermer, "The Anthropocene," *Global Change Newsletter* 41 (2000): 17–18; Jan Zalasiewicz et al., "When Did the Anthropocene Begin? A Mid-20th Century Boundary Level is Stratigraphically Optimal," *Quaternary International* 383 (2015): 196–203.

130 Michael Marder, *Chernobyl Herbarium: Fragments of an Exploded Consciousness* (Ann Arbor: Open Humanities Press, 2016), 54.

factored into global risk society takes its specific toll on distinct human and nonhuman populations. This makes it also the scene of a kind of global future heritage, a *virtual* heritage insofar as it represents both the much anticipated eco-apocalypse and the return of "nature" implied in the geological model, according to which the Anthropocene will be followed by an era in which humans are no longer central at all. (And another layer after that, and another.)

In this, we can argue that the Zone may not be the 30-km Exclusion Zone at all. Rather, it is the other way around: *the Zone is us,* industrially equipped human collectives transforming the surface of the Earth on a scale that is geological. The Zone, at its maximum extent, may also be the Holocene, the safety zone shaped around human activities over the last 12,000 years, which in fact provided the conditions for everything we know as civilization, and which today may be on its way out.

Chernobyl, in its multiple visualizations — as an error registering the nuclear and technological sublime; as the limit case of a bipolar military-industrial modernity; as a cipher of contested narratives, including those that would yoke it to an emergent new-old national sovereignty (that of Ukraine); as an emptied yet ambiguous and alluring terrain; and as a signpost on the accelerometer of the Anthropocene — scrambles the reference points that preceded it and renders them anomalous. It is both an anomaly and a new set of references that marks *us* as anomalous. It is a hyper-event and an ~~Event~~, which serves to remind us that we might begin to mark limits around ourselves — in the same way that the Onkalo deep geological nuclear repository in Finland has been conceived as needing a circle cast round it, "to create a boundary between the world of humans and the realm of all that exceeds us."[131] Or at least to begin enclosing and excising the System to which we have been sacrificing, the AnthropoCapitalist Moloch — so as to create sacrificial spaces in

---

131 Friends of the Pleistocene, "Containing Uncertainty," *FOPnews,* February 24, 2010, https://fopnews.wordpress.com/2010/02/24/containing-uncertainity-design-for-infinite-quarantine/.

which the Earth and its intermediaries, its intercessors, may appear to us of their own accord, in their own time, if and when they choose to do so.

In this sense, the key is not sacrifice so much as it is vulnerability (*vulnus* meaning wound, thus, woundability). It is by recognizing our mutual vulnerability, as humans and nonhumans sharing today's interstitial spaces, that our Zones of Sacrifice can become emblems of the temporal interstitiality in which we might together negotiate a common world. In these interstitial spaces we might begin to hear new divinities calling us to the Agoras of a new *Demoikracy*—an *oikos* consisting of many *demoi,* each ruling itself and gathering in unspecified *maidans* where a new post-global commons might be conceived and assembled. Its assembly would scramble the contours of our own worlds, with their nation-states and property relations, and produce new ones around very different forms of neighborliness, eco-regional assemblage, and biotically complex "transnations" consisting of agents known and as yet unknown to us.

There is today neither a humanity nor any other "we" capable of taking this on by ourselves. The new *demoi* must be cobbled together from diverse ensembles of moving parts, all of them living, dynamic, and elusive in their agency and in their commitments, and many of them not at all human.

Cultivating anthropocenic mindfulness, in this context (let us finally decapitate the "A" of the anthropos), means cultivating the capacity to wait watchfully, with eyes and hearts open to the ethico-political dynamics of the webs that bind us. Our material, social, and perceptual ecologies are the sites of multiple projects, formations, and legacies, both oppressive and liberatory. Through them we might hear the calls of rival ancestries, descendancies, and image-bearing divinities. It is our task to open to those who might carry us through the mutual vulnerabilities of the work of creating a habitable Earth that is not ours to own, but is ours to honor.

POSTLUDE

The long revolution

This book has argued for a realism that acknowledges the ultimate unsustainability of current human systems of living on this planet. Some, of course, are more sustainable than others, and there is even a reasonable chance that we, or some version of us anthropomorphs, will make it through the current sustainability bottleneck. But in the end we will all get buried.

Is this realism a form of cosmic pessimism? I don't think so.

C.S. Peirce's whole philosophical work was an extended argument for an expanded concept of reason. Reason, for Peirce, was rooted in human nature and in nature itself; it is a development of the very process of making meaning that is the essence of all living things (and, Peirce would say, all things living or not). Reason grows out of intuitive common sense — the hunches that Peirce labeled "abduction," which supplement and ground the better-known processes of induction and deduction. As logical reasoning, it is rooted, furthermore, in aesthetics and ethics — the capacity to cultivate habits of perception and relation commensurate with the habits of reason that beckon to us through our efforts to know the universe. And reason develops through dialogue and increasingly refined communication into something that is shared across a community of reasoning beings.

Peirce of course is not a Cartesian. He does not believe in a division between mind and matter, soul and body, reason and passion. This brings him closer in spirit to those — Buddhists, Daoists and neo-Confucians, Sufis and Catholic integral ecologists (like Pope Francis), and others — for whom reason is subordinate to the heart, that organ of perception by which we feel the solidarity of those whose sentience (like ours) appears and disappears on a sea of interdependent relationality.

The following quote from Peirce is the kind of thing that gives me hope:

> Inanimate things do not err at all; and the lower animals very little. Instinct is all but unerring; but reason in all vitally important matters is a treacherous guide. This tendency to error, when you put it under the microscope of reflection, is seen to consist of fortuitous variations of our actions in time. But it is apt to escape our attention that *on such fortuitous variation our intellect is nourished and grows.* For without such fortuitous variation, habit-taking would be impossible; and intellect consists in a plasticity of habit.[1]

In other words, reason alone is risky, and it is often better to go with our instinct. But it is *because* we can err that we can learn, and because learning is *possible,* learning will ultimately occur, however long it may take.

Other process-relational philosophers have conjured up other driving forces to the cosmic process — something that would account for a built-in "upward" trend in the universe. For the

---

1   Charles S. Peirce, *Collected Papers of Charles Sanders Peirce,* eds. Charles Hartshorne and Paul Weiss (Bloomington: Indiana University Press, 1958), 6.86, emphasis added. Peirce sometimes claimed a preference for instinct over reason, especially when it came to moral questions, and he referred to this as his "sentimental conservatism." For a nuanced account of what this consisted of, see Richard Atkins, *Peirce and the Conduct of Life: Sentiment and Instinct in Ethics and Religion* (Cambridge University Press, 2016). See also Lara Trout, *The Politics of Survival: Peirce, Affectivity, and Social Criticism* (New York: Fordham University Press, 2013).

Whitehead of *Process and Reality,* it was a dipolar God who acts as a "poet of the world" and "fellow sufferer": a God who "spurs" the universe forward in his "primordial nature" by acting as a divine "lure" for the envisagement of all aesthetic value possibilities, and who in his "consequent nature" saves and enjoys every vestige of every heartfelt struggle. In Whitehead's next major book, however, he dropped the deity and replaced it with a nontheistic "Eros of the Universe" which serves as "the living urge towards all possibilities," and with "the Unity of Adventure," or "an Adventure in the Universe as One," which "embraces all particular occasions" and "claims" the "goodness" of the realization of their possibilities. "In this Supreme Adventure," he wrote, "the Reality which the Adventure transmutes into its Unity of Appearance, requires the real occasions of the advancing world each claiming its due share of attention. This Appearance, thus enjoyed, is the final Beauty with which the Universe achieves its justification."[2]

There are more down to earth variations of "realistic optimism" to choose from. Novelist and cultural historian Raymond Williams referred to the faith that things are moving, however chaotically (or dialectically), towards a better human future, as the "long revolution." Williams was a socialist, and the optimism of his particular formulation may not ring as true today as it did for him sixty years ago. It is interesting, however, that Williams wasn't just intending this as a description of change; he was also aiming to cultivate an attitude toward that change. "In naming the great process of change the long revolution," he wrote, "I am trying *to learn assent to it,* an adequate assent of mind and spirit. I find increasingly that the values and meanings I need are all in this process of change."[3]

If, as this book has tried to suggest, and as Peirce, Whitehead, and many new ontologists and speculative realists have argued,

---

2   A.N. Whitehead, *Adventures of Ideas* (New York: Free Press, 1961), 295; and see pages 253, 296, xvii.

3   Raymond Williams, *The Long Revolution* (Orchard Park: Broadview Press, 1961/2001), 13.

the social and the natural are not opposed to each other but are integrally, if complexly, intertwined, then there is something beyond *socialism* that would be a good description of Peirce's long-term optimism. A socialist in this understanding is a believer in the eventual triumph of an ever better, more just and more sustainable *social* world. A naturalist, by the same token, would be a believer in the eventual triumph of an ever more beautifully evolved *natural* world. (The Darwin of *The Origin of Species* is one of our better representatives of the latter view.) Peirce would instead be something like a *cosmist* (and there was a tradition of Russian thought by that name which envisioned things rather similarly), or a *cosmopolist,* a believer that the cosmos itself is evolving toward something better, more complete, or more fully harmonized. In that evolution, sociality and reason play important, and increasing, roles, but never in separation from nature.

Such an "even longer revolution" may take many deep, dark turns along the way. Contrary to what our human pride suggests, it may shed civilizations, even worlds (not to mention species like our own), in the process. Peirce seemed to believe that those, too, will be redeemed in the end — that, to paraphrase Russian philosopher Mikhail Bakhtin, they, too, will have their homecoming festivals. That is a leap of faith that might be difficult for those without experience conforming to it. But there are forms of logo-ethico-aesthetic practice (such as those outlined in Part Two of this book) that aim explicitly to engender such experience.

With his insistence that habits are to be cultivated, Peirce belongs to the class of *believers in the practice of cosmopolism,* or the practice of William Connolly's "immanent naturalism" — that is, the cultivation of a better, more reasonable, more ethically satisfying, and more beautiful universe *by the universe itself,* which fortunately includes us within it. Just as the ontological constructivism of Whitehead, Stengers, and Latour is broader and more capacious than social constructionism, so this cosmopolism is more capacious than socialism as heretofore understood. In the end, its vision is very much a social vision, but its sociality is extended, deepened, and redefined by the deepest withdrawals of dark matter we can imagine. It is a faith in what is unencompassable by faith itself. It is a realism that believes in a reality that supersedes and outwits all our ideas about it — believes in it not only intellectually, but emotionally and spiritually. And it believes in its goodness, "assents" to it "in mind and spirit," as Williams would have it.

Will such a faith help us respond to the refugee emergencies that are and will be arising all around us as climatic and ecological crises continue to deepen? The refugees are not only our fellow humans — Syrians, Iraqis, Somalis, Bangladeshis, Haitians, Maldivians, and others. They are also Gaia's vast proletariat of threatened nonhumans, whose abodes are being demolished, destroyed, and abandoned in the wake of the growing emergency. To deal with them adequately, we will need all the resources we can muster. One of those is the faith in responsiveness itself, "agapistic" responsiveness, as Peirce would call it. Because that is what grows the universe into the new folds that are worth growing into.

Of times and beyond time

In a literal sense, a revolution is nothing spectacular: it is an Event, but viewed in the context of time, it is mere turbulence. It may be a reclaiming, an overturning, an upheaving of things that needed to be upheaved. But in the solar time of planetary circling (or the growth rings of trees), a revolution is just a measurement of one.

So it is worth pondering three kinds of time in which we find ourselves in this time of the AnthropoCapitalocene.

First, there is chronological time, the time of Chronos, which is the time that dates, that punctuates, that traces causes and orders them into their sequence. This time finds us constantly pursued by our own demise: one moment replaced by another, all of them subjected to the indifferent measure of a universal timekeeper. The Anthropocene, measured thus, is a matter for scientists to probe and debate. Its significance is that we will be measured to our fate as a layer among layers, a fate to be determined by Saturn, who oversees this time. We will be subject to the exhaustion that comes to all things in their own time. That is the sobering realization at the heart of our realism, which recognizes the mundane fatedness of itself alongside that of all things: the fatedness *to pass* (while passing *on* something, nevertheless). An era, a revolution, a turning, to be followed by the next, and the next.

A different kind of time is that of Aion, who is the god that takes the measure of *our* time and installs it within the sacred time of eternity. This is the time of our destiny, our world-historical significance, but it is a time that cannot be known in advance unless we are willing to give the game away at the outset. The Anthropocene, rightly considered as a minor block of time in earth history, is nevertheless an achievement, whose ultimate significance we can only guess at. If Chronos measures the time of "one thing after another," the time of determining but blind secondness, Aion is the time of qualitative thirdness, the time of significance that may or may not be determined in advance.

But before and between them, there is the time of Kairos. Kairotic time is the time of possibility, a time we can only intuit when we engage with the timeliness of the moment. What action can we take right now? What action is appropriate to this moment? This is the time of firstness, in which we must forget ourselves in order to hear the call of the *kairoi,* the gods who beckon us toward a new creative advance.[4]

While acknowledging the times of Chronos and of Aion, it is the time of Kairos that I have favored in my negotiation with our time(s). Without the Kairotic, any process-relational ontology risks becoming the predigested stew of "one occurrence after another," one thing turning into another, as the universe churns forward in the turning of its wheels. Alternative to chronological forward motion, there is the cyclical time of organisms, seasons, lives (births and deaths) and, yes, revolutions. Aionic

---

4   I am grateful to Michel Weber and Matthew Segall for provoking my thinking on these three temporalities, even if my interpretation differs from each of theirs.

time is Zodiacal time, the movement of the wheels across the qualitatively rich, archetypally anchored heavens. It is the time of gods, but precisely those whose time is eternal. It is the time of Whitehead's "eternal objects." Kairotic time, by contrast, is discontinuous and ruptured: it is the time that always remains open. Kairotic time is premised on the leap of faith in a future that is neither determined nor determinable. It is the time of now.

We will, of course, be buried. Dorion Sagan manages a note of sober optimism in his evocation of the Cyanocene, the era he playfully (if darkly) envisions as following the Anthropocene. "We should worry," he urges, "but not despair." This is because the "rock record shows that after each mass extinction, the organismically interweaving biosphere has regrown to form more species, cell types, metabolic skills, areas settled, networked intelligences, and complex sensory skills than before. Maybe this time, instead of hurting it," Sagan suggests, "we can help it continue its multispecies energy-transducing recycling ways for billions of years more."[5]

We have options. *We* do not even have ourselves, a viable "we," yet, but it is an option for us to work toward one, a workable *demos* of some sort or other. We are poised at a bifurcation point, if we opt to take ourselves that way. And we certainly have many *others,* companions and secret agents, to work with, to work for, and to work alongside.

And no matter how beautifully, if fleetingly, we succeed, and how miserably we fail (for fail we must), there are many good planets in the universe besides ours. They will get their try as well. And their own homecoming festivals.

But there is no better time for action than now.

---

5 Dorion Sagan, "Coda: Beautiful monsters: Terra in the Cyanocene," in *Arts of Living on a Damaged Planet: Ghosts and Monsters of the Anthropocene,* eds. Anna L. Tsing, Heather Anne Swanson, Elaine Gan, and Nils Bubandt, M169–74 (Minneapolis: University of Minnesota Press, 2017), M174.

APPENDIX 1

Contemporary Process-Relational Thought: A Primer

The term "process-relational" has been most closely associated with the later metaphysical writings of Alfred North Whitehead, and Whitehead's influence on contemporary process-relational thought is undeniable. The influences of others, however, including Henri Bergson, C.S. Peirce, William James, and Gilles Deleuze, are also evident in current writing. All (though less frequently Deleuze) are sometimes included in the broader category of "process philosophers," but this term alone does not adequately capture the centrality of *relations* in process-relational ontology. Similarly, the term "relationalism," frequently understood to be opposed to various kinds of atomism, individualism, and "essentialism," and more recently to object-oriented ontology, fails to adequately emphasize the *processual* nature of any and all relations. My use of the term "process-relational" is thus intended to highlight the temporal dynamism, emergent relational systematicity, and inherently creative openness of a living universe composed of interactive events characterized by some measure of perception, responsiveness, subjectivity, or "mind."

Seen this way, process-relational philosophy overlaps in key respects with other classifications, including "panpsychism" (see especially David Skrbina's volumes on the topic), "new materialism" (a larger and more amorphous category, which says less about what it *is* than how it is *new*), "constructive postmodernism" (a category proposed and developed by David Ray Griffin, but which has not been taken up widely outside the Whiteheadian community), some forms of semiotic theory in the tradition of Peirce, several forms of post-Deleuzian thought (including the "assemblage theory" of Manuel DeLanda and the ever evolving work of Levi Bryant), and various network- and systems-based approaches, including developmental systems theory and other ecological approaches in the life sciences, and the post-actor-network "method assemblage" of John Law, Annemarie Mol, and others.

More generally, process-relational themes can be found scattered across a wide historical swath, and this background is relevant to the resurgence of the tradition today. In the ancient world, such themes are clearly found in some of the Greek and Hellenistic schools (most obviously in the thought of Heraclitus, fragmentary as it has come down to us, but also in Stoicism and Neo-Platonism) and in various ancient Chinese and Indian schools of thought, especially Daoism, Buddhism, and neo-Confucianism in their many stripes (sometimes the latter have been lumped together as "Asian field theories," though the category is rather elusive). The historical thread can then be pursued to medieval Islamic thought (Suhrawardi, Mulla Sadra), the early modern thought of Bruno, Spinoza, Leibniz, and others, Romanticism in its many variations (as in Schelling, for instance), the Japanese Kyoto school of Nishida, Nishitani, and others, the American Transcendentalists and pragmatists (James and Dewey especially, alongside Peirce), and even to some key aspects of such central modern figures as Hegel, Marx, Nietzsche, and perhaps Heidegger.

Beyond the purely philosophical realm, process-relational thinking has flourished in the arts, as in the work of Coleridge, Blake, and Goethe, and it is highly resonant with many indigenous philosophies around the world, which have typically been more pragmatic "knowledge-practice complexes" than "pure" philosophies. It is clearly linked also with the mystical and spiritual writings of historical figures from Plotinus and Shankara to

Jelaluddin Rumi, Jakob Boehme, and more recently Sri Aurobindo Ghose, Pierre Teilhard de Chardin, and Ken Wilber (most
of them philosophers in their own right). A simple iteration of
a process-relational ontology can be found, for instance, in Af-
rican-American science-fiction writer Octavia Butler's "Earth-
seed" tenet, which opens her futuristic-dystopian novel *Parable
of the Sower*[1]:

> All that you touch
> You Change.

> All that you Change
> Changes you.

> The only lasting truth
> Is Change.

> God
> Is Change.

Analogous statements can be found in oral and written litera-
tures from around the world.

While there is great diversity and divergence between these
many strands of thought, focusing on their commonalities
has the benefit of clarifying important differences over and
against other philosophical positions. It has been argued (for
instance, by David Ray Griffin, Freya Mathews, and Christian
de Quincey) that process-relational thought provides an alternative to two forms of thought that have long dominated western philosophy: *materialism,* which views matter as fundamental and human consciousness or perception as a by-product or
"epiphenomenon" arising out of material relations, and *idealism,* which takes perception, consciousness, thought, spirit, or
some other non-material force as fundamental and material
relations as secondary, if not illusory. A range of interactive and

---

1   Octavia Butler, *Parable of the Sower* (New York: Warner Books, 1993), 3.

dialectical philosophies have been proposed to mediate between the material and the ideal, but many of these presume the underpinning of a relatively static binary structure of one kind or another, such as matter versus spirit, idea, or mind, or, alternatively, a conception of opposites (such as the Chinese *Yin* and *Yang*), in which homeostatic balance rather than evolutionary change is considered the baseline norm. Process-relational thought, by contrast, focuses on the dynamism by which things are perpetually moving forward, interacting, and creating new conditions in the world. (Arguably, the traditional Chinese conception is process-relational even if it favors balance or a "middle way.") Most especially, process-relational thought rejects the Cartesian idea that there are *minds,* or things that think, and *bodies,* or matter that only acts according to strict causal laws. Rather, the two are considered one and the same, or two aspects of an interactive and dynamically evolving reality. In this sense, process-relational views are clearly related to panpsychism (and to "pan-experientialism," a term applied commonly to Whiteheadian metaphysics), that is, to philosophies that understand "mind" or "mental experience" to be not the possession of specific objects or subjects, but part of the relational expression or manifestation of all things.

At the core of process-relational thought, then, is a focus on the world-making creativity of things: on how things *become* rather than what they are, on their emergence (which may be structured) rather than on their structure alone. According to this understanding, the world is dynamic and always in process. As Søren Brier puts it, describing the ontology of C.S. Peirce, reality is a spontaneously dynamic "hyper-complexity of living feeling with the tendency to form habits."[2] That is to say that reality is emergent, evolutionary, and creative — a view that, not coincidentally, finds much resonance within twentieth-century developments in physics and biology including quantum mechanics, ecology, chaos and complexity theories, and develop-

---

2   Søren Brier, *Cybersemiotics: Why Information Is Not Enough* (Toronto: University of Toronto Press, 2008), 204.

mental systems theory. This resonance is especially visible in the speculative writings of theoretical physicists and biologists such as David Bohm, Ilya Prigogine, Brian Goodwin, Stuart Kauffman, Lee Smolin, and John Dupré. (See David Bohm, *Wholeness and the Implicate Order* [London: Routlege, 1980]; Ilya Prigogine, *From Being to Becoming: Time and Complexity in the Physical Sciences* [New York: W. H. Freeman & Company, 1981]; Brian Goodwin, *Form and Transformation: Generative and Relational Principles in Biology* [Cambridge: Cambridge University Press, 1996]; Stuart Kauffman, *At Home in the Universe: The Search for Laws of Self-Organization and Complexity* [New York: Oxford University Press, 1995]; Lee Smolin, *Time Reborn: From the Crisis in Physics to the Future of the Universe* [New York: Houghton, Mifflin, Harcourt, 2013]; Daniel J. Nicholson and John Dupré, eds., *Everything Flows: Towards a Processual Philosophy of Biology* [New York: Oxford University Press, 2018].)

Comparatively oriented explications of process thought include Nicholas Rescher's *Process Metaphysics: An Introduction to Process Philosophy* (Albany: SUNY Press, 1996) and *Process Philosophy: A Survey of Basic Issues* (Pittsburgh: University of Pittsburgh Press, 2000); Douglas Browning and William T. Myers's *Philosophers of Process* (New York: Fordham University Press, 1998); and David Ray Griffin's *Founders of Constructive Postmodern Philosophy: Peirce, James, Bergson, Whitehead, and Hartshorne* (Albany: SUNY Press, 1992). David Skrbina's works, as mentioned, present panpsychist philosophy in all its variations; see Skrbina, *Panpsychism in the West*, rev. edn. (Cambridge: MIT Press, 2017), and Skrbina, ed., *Mind That Abides: Panpsychism in the New Millennium* (Amsterdam: John Benjamins, 2009).

The rapidly evolving dialogue between different processual and relational positions is evident in many books of the last two decades. Listed chronologically, these include Catherine Keller and Anne Daniell, *Process and Difference: Between Cosmological and Poststructuralist Postmodernisms* (Albany: SUNY Press, 2002); Guy Debrock, ed., *Process Pragmatism: Essays on a Quiet Philosophical Revolution* (Amsterdam: Rodopi, 2003); Michel Weber, ed. *After Whitehead: Rescher on Process Metaphysics*

(Frankfurt: Ontos, 2004); Anne Fairchild Pomeroy, *Marx and Whitehead: Process, Dialectics, and the Critique of Capitalism* (Albany: SUNY Press, 2004); Janusz Polanowski and Donald W. Sherburne, eds., *Whitehead's Philosophy: Points of Connection* (Albany: SUNY Press, 2004); Keith Robinson, ed., *Deleuze, Whitehead, Bergson: Rhizomatic Connections* (Basingstoke: Palgrave Macmillan, 2008); Steven Shaviro, *Without Criteria: Kant, Whitehead, Deleuze, and Aesthetics* (Cambridge: MIT Press, 2009); William Connolly, *A World of Becoming* (Durham: Duke University Press, 2011); Roland Faber and Andrea Stephenson, *Secrets of Becoming: Negotiating Whitehead, Deleuze, and Butler* (New York: Fordham University Press, 2011); William S. Hamrick and Jan Van der Veken, *Nature and Logos: A Whiteheadian Key to Merleau-Ponty's Fundamental Thought* (Albany: SUNY Press, 2011); Roland Faber and Andrew Goffey, eds., *The Allure of Things: Process and Object in Contemporary Philosophy* (London: Bloomsbury, 2014); Steven Shaviro, *The Universe of Things: On Speculative Realism* (Minneapolis: University of Minnesota Press, 2014); Christopher Vitale, *Networkologies: A Philosophy of Networks for a Hyperconnected Age — A Manifesto* (Washington: Zero Books, 2014); Erin Manning and Brian Massumi, *Thought in the Act: Passages in the Ecology of Experience* (Minneapolis: University of Minnesota Press, 2014); Levi Bryant, *Onto-Cartography: An Ontology of Machines and Media* (Edinburgh: Edinburgh University Press, 2014); Brian G. Henning, William T. Meyers, and Joseph D. John, eds., *Thinking with Whitehead and the American Pragmatists: Experience and Reality* (London: Lexington, 2015); Manuel DeLanda, *Assemblage Theory* (Edinburgh University Press, 2016); and Catherine Keller and Mary-Jane Rubenstein, eds., *Entangled Worlds: Religion, Science, and New Materialisms* (New York: Fordham University Press, 2017).

On Whitehead's process-relational metaphysics more specifically, the best sources are of course his magnum opus *Process and Reality: An Essay in Cosmology,* rev. and corr. by David Ray Griffin and Donald Sherburne (New York: Free Press, 1978), and the more elegant synopsis found in Part Three of *Adventures of Ideas* (New York: Free Press, 1933/1967). His writing from *Sci-*

ence and the Modern World (New York: Macmillan, 1925) onward reflects variations on the processual metaphysics that he took many years developing. C. Robert Mesle's *Process-Relational Philosophy: An Introduction to Alfred North Whitehead* (West Conshohocken: Templeton Foundation Press, 2008), while a simplified introduction to his thought, makes clear why the titular term is appropriate. Other concise and accessible introductions to Whiteheadian metaphysics include Philip Rose's *On Whitehead* (Belmont, California: Wadsworth/Thomson, 2002) and Pierfrancesco Basile's *Whitehead's Metaphysics of Power: Reconstructing Modern Philosophy* (Edinburgh: Edinburgh University Press, 2017). More extended and rigorous treatments include recent works by Leemon McHenry (*The Event Universe: The Revolutionary Metaphysics of Alfred North Whitehead* [Edinburgh: Edinburgh University Press, 2015]), Didier Debaise *(Speculative Empricism: Revisiting Whitehead* [Edinburgh: Edinbugh University Press, 2017]), Steven Shaviro, and others.

David Ray Griffin's longstanding championing of Whiteheadian metaphysics in the "postmodern" context has been notable; see, for instance, his *Whitehead's Radically Different Postmodern Philosophy: An Argument for Its Contemporary Relevance* (Albany: SUNY Press, 2007). On Whitehead's more recent uptake within the loosely "continental" philosophical milieu, see especially Isabelle Stengers's influential treatise *Thinking With Whitehead: A Free and Wild Creation of Concepts,* trans. M. Chase (London: Harvard University Press, 2011); Nicholas Gaskell and A.J. Nocek's anthology *The Lure of Whitehead* (Minneapolis: University of Minnesota Press, 2014); and some of the comparative works listed above. For intriguing applications to physics, psychology, ecology, and neuroscience, see Timothy Eastman and Hank Keeton, eds., *Physics and Whitehead: Quantum, Process, and Experience* (Albany: SUNY Press, 2013); Michel Weber and Anderson Weekes, eds., *Process Approaches to Consciousness in Psychology, Neuroscience, and Philosophy of Mind* (Albany: SUNY Press, 2009); Ralph Pred, *Onflow: Dynamics of Consciousness and Experience* (Cambridge: MIT Press, 2005); neuropsychologist Jason Brown's *Process and the Authentic Life:*

Toward a Psychology of Value (Lancaster: Ontos Verlag, 2005); and Robert Ulanowicz's *A Third Window: Natural Life Beyond Newton and Darwin* (West Conshohocken: Templeton Foundation Press, 2009).

Much of the literature on Charles Sanders Peirce has focused on his significant contributions to logic and to semiotics; his work on metaphysics has often taken a back seat to these, but this has begun to change. Notable contributions include Vincent M. Colapietro's *Peirce's Approach to the Self: A Semiotic Perspective on Human Subjectivity* (Albany: SUNY Press, 1989); Carl R. Hausman's *Charles S. Peirce's Evolutionary Philosophy* (New York: Cambridge University Press, 1993); Sandra Rosenthal's *Charles Peirce's Pragmatic Pluralism* (Albany: SUNY Press, 1994); Kelly A. Parker's *The Continuity of Peirce's Thought* (Nashville: Vanderbilt University Press, 1998); and Leon Niemoczynski's *Charles Sanders Peirce and a Religious Metaphysics of Nature* (New York: Lexington, 2013). Perhaps the clearest general exposition of Peirce's philosophy is Albert Atkin's *Peirce* (New York: Routledge, 2016).

The territory between Whitehead and Peirce has been insightfully traversed by Charles Hartshorne, who studied with the former and edited the latter's manuscripts; see his *Creative Synthesis and Philosophic Method* (LaSalle: Open Court, 1970) and *Creativity in American Philosophy* (Albany: SUNY Press, 1984). Peirce's influence in semiotics, including its many cognate fields (such as biosemiotics, ecosemiotics, and zoosemiotics), is bearing interesting metaphysical fruit as well. Terrence W. Deacon's *Incomplete Nature: How Mind Emerged from Matter* (New York: W.W. Norton, 2012) presents an ambitious synthesis of Peircian semiotics and emergent systems theory. Eduardo Kohn's *How Forests Think: Toward an Anthropology Beyond the Human* (Berkeley: University of California Press, 2013) applies Peircian theory to human-ecological systems in the Amazon. For more general background, see Vinicius Romanini and Eliseo Fernandez, eds., *Peirce and Biosemiotics: A Guess at the Riddle of Life* (Jansas City: Springer, 2014). And Floyd Merrell's writings offer particularly intriguing complements to my own suggestions for Peircian "practices" in Part 2 of this book; see, for instance, his *Change Through Signs of Body, Mind, and Language* (Prospect Heights: Waveland Press, 2000).

Other significant ontological engagements in a pragmaticist-processual vein include those of Robert S. Corrington (*Nature's Sublime: An Essay in Aesthetic Naturalism* [New York: Lexington, 2013]; *Deep Pantheism: Toward a New Transcendentalism* [London: Lexington, 2016]), Sandra B. Rosenthal (*Speculative Pragmatism* [Amherst: University of Massachusetts Press, 1986]), James Williams (*A Process Philosophy of Signs* [Edinburgh University Press, 2016]), and John Deely, whose magisterial *Four Ages of Understanding: The First Postmodern Survey of Philosophy from Ancient Times to the Turn of the Twenty-First Century* (Toronto University of Toronto Press, 2001) deserves wider recognition. Corrington draws also on another philosopher, whose potential contributions to the objects-processes debate seem to me very promising, yet which are as yet quite untapped: that is Justus Buchler, whose "ordinal metaphysics" attempts to transcend Whitehead's "privileging" of the real and actual over other "natural complexes" — a term that could be fruitfully compared with Harman's notion of the "object." See Armen Marsoobian, Kathleen Wallace, and Robert S. Corrington, eds., *Nature's Perspectives: Prospects for Ordinal Metaphysics* (Albany: SUNY Press, 1991). (I must apologize to a dear friend and helpful reader of the present book, David Brahinsky, for resisting his urges that I explore Buchler in greater depth. In time, I will, but the present book has proceeded without that exploration.)

Comparative studies of process philosophy and Asian thought, whether historical or contemporary, include Steve Odin, *Process Metaphysics and Hua-Yen Buddhism: A Critical Study of Cumulative Penetration vs. Interpenetration* (Albany: SUNY Press, 1984); Nolan Pliny Jacobson, *The Heart of Buddhist Philosophy* (Carbondale: Southern Illinois University Press, 1988); John H. Berthrong, *Concerning Creativity: A Comparison of Chu Hsi, Whitehead, and Neville* (Albany: SUNY Press, 1998); Wenyu Zie, Zhihe Wang, and George Derfer, eds., *Whitehead and China: Relevance and Relationships* (Frankfurt: Ontos Verlag, 2005); Peter P. Kakol, *Emptiness and Becoming: Integrating Madhyamika Buddhism and Process Philosophy* (Delhi: D.K. Printworld, 2009); Hyo-Dong Lee, *Spirit, Qi, and the Multitude: A Comparative Theology for the Democracy of Creation* (New York: Fordham University Press, 2014); and Steve Odin, *Tragic Beauty in Whitehead and Japanese Aesthetics* (New York: Lexington, 2016). Kakol's book and Odin's latter volume are especially recommended. And for a provocative example of a "non-Western" (but Western hemisphere) philosophical system read as a form of process philosophy, see James Maffie's *Aztec Philosophy: Understanding a World in Motion* (Boulder: University Press of Colorado, 2014).

Farther afield, one finds process-relational thinking enlivening many other disciplines and discourses including science studies (Bruno Latour, John Law, Donna Haraway), anthropology (Arturo Escobar, Tim Ingold, Marisol de la Cadena), social and political theory (William Connolly, Brian Massumi, Michael Halewood, Romand Coles), environmental philosophy (Freya Mathews, Brian Henning, Robert Ulanowicz), theory and practice in the performative and media arts (Erin Manning, Mark Hansen, Steven Shaviro, Andrew Murphie, Xin Wei Sha), and the physical and biological sciences (Stuart Kauffman, Lee Smolin, John Dupré, and others already mentioned). A few of these figures are discussed in some detail in this book; to list and discuss all of the others would make this book much longer. Some are listed in the bibliography; others not.

APPENDIX 2

What a Bodymind Can Do: Full Rubik's Cube Version

O = Examples from ordinary experience
M = Examples from meditative or spiritual practice

	OUT	IN
0.	—	—
1. SENSE	**SENSE OUT** **SEE–HEAR–FEEL OUT**	**SENSE IN** **SEE–HEAR–FEEL IN**
Note, observe	Note/observe external states	Note/observe internal states
"This is"	*O: Absorption in sensory activity, "pure" sensing* *M: Sensory-absorptive meditation*	*O: Dream states, absorption in subjective/internal activity* *M: Vipassana (insight) meditation*
2. ACT	**ACT OUT** **SHOW–SOUND–TOUCH OUT**	**ACT IN** **SHOW–SOUND–TOUCH IN**
Respond, intervene	Respond externally / Generate external states	Respond internally / Generate internal states
"I can"	*O: Action in the world, doing (of any kind)* *M: Active meditation, "spirit possession"; Karma Yoga, "good deeds"*	*O: Visualizing scenes in "mind's eye" (e.g., while listening to a story or reading a poem or novel)* *M: Visualization, metta, mantra meditation; Tantra, deity meditation* *SY: "Focus-on-the-positive"*

FLOW	**(SOURCE)**
O: Free activity *M: Nondual flow*	DARK FLOW
SENSE FLOW SEE–HEAR–FEEL FLOW	**VOID** DARKNESS–SILENCE–EMPTI- NESS

Note/observe flow states

O: Intersubjective observation
M: Nondual meditative aware-
ness

ACT FLOW SHOW–SOUND–TOUCH FLOW	**HEART** FLICKER — MURMUR — TREM- OR

Respond in flow with inter-
nal/external world(s)

O: Action with the world,
doing-with, social/collective
action
M: Nondual Tantra/deity
ritual; nondual action (wu-
wei)

3. REALIZE	REALIZE OUT MAP–SPEAK–MOVE OUT	REALIZE IN MAP–SPEAK–MOVE IN
Interpret, understand	Affect/generate understanding externally	Affect/generate understanding internally
"We are this"	*O: Science, logical reasoning (about external world)* *M: Integral science?*	*O: Psychology, Cartesian introspection* *M: Analytical meditation, Jnana-Yoga*

REALIZE FLOW
MAP−SPEAK−MOVE FLOW

MYSTERY
INVISIBLE−UNSPEAKABLE−IM-
MOVABLE

Affect/generate understanding internally/externally

O: Integral, process-relational
ontology
M: Nondual free activity,
enlightened flow, Praxis

List of modalities, by sensory mode and category:

	1 Note/Sense [Void]	2 Act [Heart]	3 Realize [Mystery]
Visual	See [Darkness]	Show [Flicker]	Map [Invisible]
Auditory	Hear [Silence]	Sound [Murmur]	Speak/Convey [Unspeakable]
Feeling*	Feel [Emptiness]	Touch [Tremor]	Move [Immovable]

*Note: "Feeling-Out" includes tactile, olfactory, gustatory, and kinesthetic sensations; "Feeling-In" includes visceral, affective, and emotional sensations

APPENDIX 3

Practices

The following is a selection of exercises derived from ideas and propositions laid out in Part 2 of this book. The idea with these is that they internalize or habituate the concepts fleshed out herein, allowing practitioners to try them on for size and to learn to "in-habit" them if appropriate. They are creative and experimental arts, to be worked with, modified, and mastered over time. The descriptions below are only the most basic kernels of these exercises. Several are derived from longstanding traditions of existential or spiritual practice found across the mystical wings of the world's religions (Buddhism being especially prominent here, and Shinzen Young's system of practical instruction being the most common direct source).

Other exercises can be developed from other suggestions provided in the book. If you are interested in working more directly with any of these exercises described here, please feel free to write the author via my University of Vermont email address or at the blog *Immanence,* at http://blog.uvm.edu/immanence.

Exercise 1: Basic triad practice

(Relevant section: "Philosophy of the Moment")

Choose an activity that does not require your full attention, such as sitting comfortably, walking outdoors, or engaging in a safe physical exercise. Scan your field of awareness and note the distinctly qualitative characteristics (the "firstness") of specific things in it. Select no more than one or a few of these initially, moving from one to another or across several as you gain proficiency for sensing how they feel to you. After a period of time working with firstness, add the "secondnesses" by which you are interacting with one or more of these objects: the force or effort needed to interact with them, the specific resistance they present to you, and the intimately distinctive feel of those interactions. Finally, add the "thirdness," or the meaning and significance, of one or more of these interactions. Keep each of these levels in your awareness over a period of time while engaged in the specific activity. (Note: See the example of the walk in the woods described in this section of the text.)

Exercise 2: Prehension practice

(Relevant section: "Philosophy of the Moment")

Choosing an activity that does not require your full attention, scan your field of awareness and note the distinctly qualitative characteristics of specific things in it that you are encountering as "objects" of your awareness. Select one or a few of these at first, moving from one to another or across several as you gain a sense for how they feel to you. Then, add to your awareness a sense of how you are engaging with those objects — your thoughts, feelings, and reactions to these in your "subjectivation" of these objects. Next, focus on the interactive middle-ground between one or more subjective prehensions and the objects being prehended. For a time, explore this middle-ground to gain a feel for the prehensive encounter itself as it occurs between "you" and one or more "objects" of your awareness. Finally, if and when you feel prepared for this (which may require developing some proficiency with the above practices alone), add the dimension of "withdrawal," that is, the feel of the disappearance of objects from your cognition or capacity to retain, control, or manage them.

Note that in its full form, this exercise is quite advanced, relying on an understanding of concepts explored in depth later in Part 2 of this book. It is recommended that you return to it after reading the entirety of the chapter and trying some or all of the exercises described below.

Exercise 3: Sensory field practice

(Relevant section: "Sensings")

Set yourself a certain amount of time, say twenty minutes, without interruption. Sit comfortably, spine erect but not strained, and choose one or more of the "spaces" or "fields" mentioned in this section: See-In, See-Out, Hear-In, Hear-Out, Feel-In, Feel-Out. Watch what comes up in your awareness of that space, noting things as you observe them (labeling them as such, if it is helpful) and "tasting" their quality, before letting them go and awaiting another thing to note.

If you feel that there is not enough happening, add another layer or space to what you are noticing. If you feel overwhelmed by what there is, reduce the number of things you are noticing, and feel them each a little longer (even staying with each feeling for a certain number of breaths). Find a workable rhythm, perhaps in alignment with your breathing. If you find yourself getting "lost in thought," just come back to what you were intentionally doing. Alternatively, if thoughts or concerns keep intervening, you could decide to work on breaking down and noting the components of one of these intervening strains. For instance, with thinking, label words "hear-in," visual images "see-in," and physical feelings or sensations "feel-in." If musical phrases or random images arise in your mental field, do the same (noting "hear-in," "see-in", and so on). Treat them as anything else that is being noted and then released.

Come back to this exercise on repeated occasions until you have developed a good feel for not only the six different sensory-orientational "spaces," but some of the cross-modal relationships that may arise frequently (for you) between them. For instance, do specific sounds ("hear-out") trigger specific feelings ("feel-in")? Do certain mental images ("see-in") come accompanied by certain physical feelings or sensations ("feel-in")? And so on. If you find yourself emotionally drawn to a particular "space," work with it over time, connecting it to other spaces, until you feel some insight or resolution of whatever the draw in it is for you.

Exercise 4: Advanced triad practice

(Relevant section: "Relatings")

Set yourself a certain amount of time in the midst of some regular activity, such as walking, bicycling, driving to work, eating, taking a shower, listening to music, or browsing the internet. Choose one or more of the eighteen "spaces" or "fields" described so far, that is, the "In" and "Out" variations of any of the following: (1) See, Hear, Feel; (2) Show, Sound, Touch; (3) Map, Convey, Move. Watch how you actively engage with the chosen spaces, labeling any individual event, act, or realization as such and "tasting" its quality, before letting it go and awaiting another to note. Find a workable rhythm, perhaps relating your notings to your breaths.

It is best at first to select the most relevant fields for a given activity. For instance, when walking or bicycling, focus on See-Out, Hear-Out, Touch-Out, and Move-Out. When listening to music, focus on Hear-Out and Feel-In (how the music makes you feel). With time and practice, it is possible to focus more widely. When selecting a wider range of space-activities, you can use more general terms, such as "Sense-Out," "Act-Out," "Realize-In," and so on. (This adds six "gameboard options" to Exercise 3, bringing the total from 18 to 24.)

Treat this as a recurrent practice over time, accumulating insights (or shedding habitual patterns) as appropriate.

Exercise 5: Flow practice

(Relevant section: "How to Make a Bodymind Flow")

Continue working as in the above exercises, but focusing on one or more of the Flow states, either exclusively or in combination with others. This means that to the 24 options mentioned above (18 sensorially distinct options, plus the 6 general options associating with Sensing, Acting, and Realizing in each of their internal and external modes), you are adding at least 12 varieties of Flow: See-Flow, Hear-Flow, Feel-Flow; Show-Flow, Sound-Flow, Touch-Flow; Map-Flow, Convey-Flow, Move-Flow; and the three generals, Sense-Flow, Act-Flow, and Realize-Flow.

In addition, there are variations of Flow states that could be focused on, i.e., "cross-modal" flow, "cross-directional" flow, and "evental-processual" flow. (See descriptions in main text.) It is recommended to spend some time familiarizing oneself with each of these forms of flow, in order to learn to recognize them in any situation.

Exercise 6: Apophatic practice

(Relevant section: "The Apophatic, Inside-out Twist")

These add a further level to the "Rubik's cube," but instead of adding another 24 options, they are best worked with in the following three ways.

Reversal (outline) practice. This works exactly like the regular practice of the triadic gameboard, with the difference that instead of noting the "positive value" of an appearance (sensing), an action, or a realization — for instance, "Hear-In" when noting internal talk, "Sound-Out" when noting the sound one is making, and so on — the focus is on the negative background surrounding that positivity: that is, on the silence surrounding a sound, on the indistinct tremor surrounding one's touch of something, on the unspeakable mystery surrounding one's understanding of what someone else just said, and so on.

Shadow triad practice. Follow the triadic shadows alone, singly or together: that is, on Emptiness, Heart, or Mystery. This is difficult without the practice of the appearances, actions, and realizations, but with time one can develop a "feel" for the three apophatic shadows to the point that a "resting" in the shadows alone becomes possible. These practices alone can provide a profound dimension of experience.

Gap practice. Focus attention on the "jumps" across gaps between zeroness, firstness (sensing), secondness (acting), and thirdness (realizing). Each of the apophatic "shadow" categories fills in one of the gaps: (1) Emptiness comes before the observation of appearances; (2) Heart comes between appearances and the arising of action; and (3) Mystery comes between action and the arising of insight or realization. Focusing on these jumps emphasizes the flow between firstness, secondness, and thirdness in the continual generation of reality from ~~Reality~~.

Exercise 7: Widening and deepening (recollection) practice

(Relevant section: "Toward a Logo-ethico-aesthetics of Existence")

Choose an activity that, for a specified period of time, will not require much active responsiveness from you: for instance, going for a casual walk in a wooded or natural area you are familiar with, riding a bicycle on a familiar bike path, sitting alone in a house looking out a window, and so on. At a relaxed and manageable pace, begin to notice features of the world around you and allow them to "reverberate" in you — for instance, by triggering memories of analogous places or situations you have been in, similar objects you have seen in prior or later stages of their existence, and so on, together with the emotional contours that come with those memories. Allow the memories and sensations triggered in you to resonate in your "depths," such that they elicit a sense of meanings or significances they may have had for you or may hold for you today in the context of your life, your interdependencies with others, your present goals, and your place in time and space (in reference, for instance, to the Anthropocene, the near or distant future, and so on).

Note these widened contexts and the feelings accompanying them, adding an acknowledgment of gratitude for the ways in which they may bring value or meaning to your life. Make space for them in your awareness, perhaps adding an image, keyword, or "hook" by which you may remember them in the future (such as before going to sleep tonight, or in future interactions with others related to those memories and recollections).

ACKNOWLEDGMENTS

This book is written in a more provocative voice than I am accustomed to in my scholarly writing. This is partly due to the milieu from which it grew, which was a set of online encounters with a heterophonic, and sometimes cacophonic, array of interlocutors, with whom I connected through my online weblog *Immanence* (blog.uvm.edu/immanence) and through their blogs and other discussion forums, beginning in about 2009. Many of those interlocutors, whose thinking has served variously as inspiration, instigation, clarification, and (mostly friendly) disputation, have already been named in the preceding pages. Many others have helped along the way.

The kindness and generosity of friends and colleagues who encouraged my writing and thinking, engaged with it in helpful ways, and in some cases invited me to speak and share those ideas and even supported my travels, has been especially important. That varied list, ordered alphabetically, includes Whitney Bauman, Hannes Bergthaller, Dominic Boyer, Rob Boschman, David Brahinsky, Levi Bryant, Vitaly Chernetsky, Sean Cubitt, Shane Denson, Marta Dyczok, Paul Ennis, Andy Fisher, Ted Geier, Alexandre Grandjean, Taras Gula, Olena Haleta, Graham Harman, Natalie Jeremijenko, Ju-Pong Lin, Svitlana Matviyenko, Harlan Morehouse, Tim Morton, Natalia Neshevets, Leon Niemoczynski, Matthew O'Connell, Anatoly Oleksiyenko, Marcia Ostaszewski, Sarah Pike, Patricia Pisters, Jone Salomonsen,

Gabriëlle Schleijpen, James Schwoch, Steven Shaviro, Maria So-
nevytsky, Adrianna Stech, Bron Taylor, Sarah McFarland Taylor, Temenuga Trifonova, Catherine Tucker, Hunter Vaughan,
Christopher Vitale, Janet Walker, John Whalen-Bridge, Michael
York, and Shinzen Young. It also includes numerous friends and
colleagues at the University of Vermont, among them Frank
Zelko, Cami Davis, Mark Usher, and Anthony Grudin, all co-
conspirator Lattie Coor Environmental Humanities Fellows; my
collaborators in BASTA! (Bridging the Arts, Sciences, and Theory
for the Anthropocene) and the EcoCulture Lab including Nancy
Winship Milliken, Cami Davis (again), Al Larsen, Stella Marrs,
Brian Collier, and Tatiana Abatemarco; the "Facing Gaia" reading group; and my many students, especially grad students Emil
Tsao, Finn Yarbrough, and Dan Cottle. There are many others I
could mention, to whom I apologize for any unwitting neglect.

I am deeply grateful for grant, sabbatical, and other support
from the Steven Rubenstein Family for its support of me as Steven Rubenstein Professor since 2016; from the University of
Vermont's Rubenstein School of Environment and Natural Resources and its dean, Nancy Mathews; from the UVM Environmental Program's Enrichment Fund and the program's current
and recents directors, Nate Sanders, David Massell, and Stephanie Kaza; from the UVM Humanities Center and its long-time
co-director, Luis Vivanco; from the Rachel Carson Center for
Environment and Society at Ludwig Maximilians University in
Munich, for a richly rewarding short-term fellowship in 2017;
and from the School of Advanced Research for hosting me and
a group of others at a week-long seminar on science, nature, and
religion in 2011.

Ideas as well as segments of the book have been presented
in various forums, including as conference papers and keynotes
at Oslo University's "Reassembling Democracy" conference, the
"New Materialism, Religion, and Planetary Thinking" Seminar
of the American Academy of Religion, "Under Western Skies
3" at Calgary's Mount Royal University, the University of California Davis and its Environments and Societies Colloquium
Series, Ukrainian Catholic University's Open Access Lecture

Series, the Visual Culture Research Center of Kyiv, CENHS at Rice University, the iCreate Cape Breton iEngage Workshop at Cape Breton University, the "Popular Culture, Religion, and the Anthropocene" symposium at National University of Singapore, the University of Amsterdam's School for Cultural Analysis, the Gerrit Rietveld Academie in Amsterdam, the Munk School for Global Affairs at the University of Toronto, the 11th International Whitehead Conference at the University of the Azores, the Stories of the Anthropocene Festival at the Swedish Royal Institute of Technology in Stockholm, the "Power Dynamics" media and environment conference at the University of California Santa Barbara, the Charles S. Peirce International Centennial Conference at the University of Massachusetts-Lowell, the University of Wisconsin Milwaukee's Center for 21st Century Studies "Nonhuman Turn" conference, Antioch University New England's Environmental Studies Colloquium, Vermont's Gund Institute for Environment; at the universities of Hong Kong, Taichung, Lausanne, Kansas, York (in Canada), and Bucks College, Pennsylvania; at meetings of the American Academy of Religion, the Society for Cinema and Media Studies, the International Association for Environmental Philosophy, the Association for Environmental Studies and Sciences, and the International Society for the Study of Religion, Nature, and Culture; and on the Imperfect Buddha Podcast.

Many segments of the book originally appeared in my blog *Immanence*; they are thoroughly reworked here. Portions have also appeared in the following publications: "Chernobyl, Risk, and the Inter-Zone of the Anthropocene," in *The Routledge Companion to Risk and Media*, edited by Bishnupriya Ghosh and Bhaskar Sarkar (New York: Routledge, forthcoming); "The Event That Cannot (Not) Happen," in *Contemporary Visual Culture and the Sublime*, edited by Temenuga Trifonova (London: Routledge, 2017); "On a Few Matters of Concern: Toward an Ecology of Integrity," in *The Variety of Integral Ecologies*, edited by Sam Mickey, Adam Robbert, and Sean Kelly (Albany: SUNY Press, 2017); "The Art of Morphogenesis: Cinema In and Beyond the Capitalocene," in *Post-Cinema: Theorizing 21st Cen-*

tury Film, edited by Shane Denson and Julia Leyda (Falmer: Reframe, 2016); and my previous book, *Ecologies of the Moving Image: Cinema, Affect, Nature* (Waterloo: Wilfrid Laurier University Press, 2013). I am grateful to the editors and reviewers involved for their help in refining my arguments, and to the publishers for allowing me to re-purpose those materials in this very different form.

I am especially grateful to the remarkable Eileen Joy and Vincent W.J. van Gerven Oei at punctum books, who enthusiastically welcomed my proposal and have made it a delight to publish with them. Open-access is the saving grace for academia's global future; few do it better and more devotedly than punctum.

This book, and most obviously its second part, is inspired in no small part by Shinzen Young's radically innovative teaching of Buddhist mindfulness practice; and more generally by my son, Zoryan, whose presence in my life is such a heartwarming delight. Most of all, however, the book is dedicated with love and gratitude to Auriel, whose support, presence, understanding, and deep companionship have been foundational throughout the years in which the book took seed, germinated, grew, and matured. May our love continue through all the ages.

BIBLIOGRAPHY

Abbott, Pamela, Claire Wallace, and Matthias Beck. "Chernobyl: Living with Risk and Uncertainty." *Health, Risk and Society* 8, no. 2 (2006): 105–21. DOI: 10.1080/13698570600677167.

Albrecht, Glenn. "Exiting the Anthropocene and Entering the Symbiocene." *Minding Nature* 9, no. 2 (2016), https://www.humansandnature.org/exiting-the-anthropocene-and-entering-the-symbiocene.

Asad, Talal. *Formations of the Secular: Islam, Christianity, Modernity.* Stanford, California: Stanford University Press, 2003.

Aslam, Salman. "Facebook by the Number: Stats, Demographics & Fun Facts." *Omnicore,* January 1, 2018, https://www.omnicoreagency.com/facebook-statistics.

Atkins, Richard. *Peirce and the Conduct of Life: Sentiment and Instinct in Ethics and Religion.* Cambridge: Cambridge University Press, 2016.

Badiou, Alain. *Being and Event.* Translated by Oliver Feltham. New York: Continuum, 1995.

Beck, Ulrich. *The Risk Society.* London: Sage, 1992.

Benjamin, Walter. "Theses on the Philosophy of History." In *Illuminations: Essays and Reflections,* edited by Hannah Arendt, translated by Harry Zohn, 253–64. New York: Schocken Books, 1969.

Bennett, Jane. *The Enchantment of Modern Life: Attachments Crossings, Ethics.* Princeton: Princeton University Press, 2001.

———. *Vibrant Matter: A Political Ecology of Things.* Durham: Duke University Press, 2010.

Bilgrami, Akeel. *Secularism, Identity, and Enchantment.* Cambridge: Harvard University Press, 2014.

Birch, Charles, and John B. Cobb. *The Liberation of Life: From the Cell to the Community.* London: Cambridge University Press, 1981.

Bogost, Ian. *Alien Phenomenology, or What It's Like to Be a Thing.* Minneapolis: University of Minnesota Press, 2012.

Bottici, Chiara. *Imaginal Politics: Images Between Imagination and the Imaginary.* New York: Columbia University Press, 2014.

Bozak, Nadia. "Firepower: Herzog's Pure Cinema as the Internal Combustion of War," *CineAction* 68 (2006): 18–25.

———. *The Cinematic Footprint: Lights, Camera, Natural Resources.* New Brunswick: Rutgers University Press, 2012.

Braboszcz, Claire, Stephanie Hahusseau, and Arnaud Delorme. "Meditation and Neuroscience: From Basic Research to Clinical Practice." In *Integrative Clinical Psychology, Psychiatry, and Behavioral Medicine,* edited by Roland Carlstedt, 1910–29. New York: Springer, 2010.

Braga, Corin. "'Imagination', 'Imaginaire', 'Imaginal': Three Concepts for Defining Creative Fantasy." *Journal for the Study of Religions and Ideologies* 16 (2007): 59–68. http://jsri.ro/ojs/index.php/jsri/article/view/425/423.

Brann, Eva. *The World of Imagination: Sum and Substance.* 25th anniversary edition. Lanham: Rowman & Littlefield, 2017.

Brier, Søren. *Cybersemiotics: Why Information Is Not Enough.* Toronto: University of Toronto Press, 2008.

Brown, Kirk W., J. David Cresswell, and Richard M. Ryan, eds. *Handbook of Mindfulness: Theory, Research, and Practice.* New York: Guilford, 2015.

Brown, Wendy. "Idealism, Materialism, Secularism?" *The Immanent Frame,* October 22, 2007, https://tif.ssrc.org/2007/10/22/idealism-materialism-secularism/.

Bryant, Levi R. "Onticology—A Manifesto for Object-Oriented Ontology, Part 1," *Larval Subjects,* January 12, 2010, http://larvalsubjects.wordpress.com/2010/01/12/object-oriented-ontology-a-manifesto-part-i/.

———. *The Democracy of Objects.* Ann Arbor: Open Humanities Press, 2011.

———. *Onto-Cartography: An Ontology of Machines and Media.* Edinburgh: Edinburgh University Press, 2014.

———, Nick Srnicek, and Graham Harman, eds. *The Speculative Turn: Continental Materialism and Realism*. Melbourne: Re-Press, 2011.

Byster, Leslie, and Ted Smith. "The Electronics Production Lifecycle, from Toxics to Sustainability: Getting off the Toxic Treadmill." In *Challenging the Chip: Labour Rights and Environmental Justice in the Global Electronics Industry,* edited by Ted Smith, David Sonnenfeld, and David Naguib Pellow, 205–14. Philadelphia: Temple University Press, 2006.

Cassidy, Eoin G. "'Transcending Human Flourishing': Is There a Need for Subtler Language?" In *The Taylor Effect: Responding to a Secular Age,* edited by Ian Leask et al, 26–38. Newcastle Upon Tyne: Cambridge Scholars Publishing, 2010.

Cassirer, Ernst. *Philosophy of Symbolic Forms,* 3 vols. New Haven: Yale University Press, 1965.

Castoriadis, Cornelius. *World in Fragments: Writings on Politics, Society, Psychoanalysis, and the Imagination, edited by David Ames Curtis.* Stanford, California: Stanford University Press, 1997.

Chown, Marcus. "Mystery 'Dark Flow' Extends Towards Edge of Universe." *New Scientist,* November 14, 2009.

Clarke, Bruce. "Rethinking Gaia: Stengers, Latour, Margulis," Theory, *Culture & Society* 34, no. 4 (2017): 3–26. DOI: 10.1177/0263276416686844.

Connolly, William E. "Deep Pluralism." In *William E. Connolly: Democracy, Pluralism and Political Theory,* edited by

Samuel A. Chambers and Terrell Carver, 85–104. New York: Routledge, 2008.

———. "Europe: A Minor Tradition." In *Powers of the Secular Modern: Talal Asad and His Interlocutors,* edited by Charles Hirschkind and David Scott, 75–92. Stanford: Stanford University Press, 2006.

———. *A World of Becoming.* Durham: Duke University Press, 2010.

———. *Capitalism and Christianity, American Style.* Durham: Duke University Press, 2008.

———. *Facing the Planetary: Entangled Humanism and the Politics of Swarming.* Durham: Duke University Press, 2017.

———. *Neuropolitics: Thinking, Culture, Speed.* Minneapolis: University of Minnesota Press, 2002.

———. *Pluralism.* Durham: Duke University Press, 2005.

———. *Why I Am Not a Secularist.* Minneapolis: University of Minnesota Press, 2000.

Conze, Edward. *Buddhist Scriptures.* New York: Penguin, 1959.

Cooper, John M. *Pursuits of Wisdom: Six Ways of Life in Ancient Philosophy from Socrates to Plotinus.* Princeton: Princeton University Press, 2012.

Corbin, Henry. "Mundus Imaginalis, or, the Imaginary and the Imaginal." *Spring: A Journal of Archetype and Culture* (1972): 1–19.

———. "Prelude to the Second Edition: Towards a Chart of the Imaginal." In *Spiritual Body and Celestial Earth: From Mazdean Iran to Shi'ite Iran,* 2nd edition, vii–xix. Princeton: Princeton University Press, 1977.

Couliano, Ioan P. *Eros and Magic in the Renaissance.* Chicago: University of Chicago Press, 1987.

Coward, Harold, and Toby Foshay, eds. *Derrida and Negative Theology.* Albany: State University of New York Press, 1992.

Cronin, Paul, ed. *Herzog on Herzog.* London: Faber and Faber, 2002.

Crutzen, Paul, and Eugene Stoermer. "The Anthropocene," *Global Change Newsletter* 41 (2000): 17–18.

Curtin, Clara. "Fact or Fiction? Booming Population Growth Among the Living, According to One Rumor, Outpaces the Dead," *Scientific American,* March 1, 2007, http://www.scientificamerican.com/article/fact-or-fiction-living-out-number-dead/.

Davies, Owen. *Paganism: A Very Short Introduction.* New York: Oxford University Press, 2011.

Dawe, Alexandra, and Justin McKeating, et al. *Nuclear Scars: The Lasting Legacies of Chernobyl and Fukushima.* Amsterdam: Greenpeace International, 2016.

Decker, Julie, ed. *Gyre: The Plastic Ocean.* London: Booth-Clibborn, 2014.

deLaplante, Kevin, Bryson Brown, and Kent A. Peacock, eds. *Philosophy of Ecology.* Amsterdam: Elsevier, 2011.

Deleuze, Gilles. *Cinema 2: The Time Image.* Translated by Hugh Tomlinson and Robert Galeta. London: Continuum, 1989/2005.

Deleuze, Gilles. *Pure Immanence: Essays on A Life.* Translated by Anne Boyman. New York: Zone, 2001.

———, and Félix Guattari. *A Thousand Plateaus: Capitalism and Schizophrenia.* Translated by Brian Massumi. Minneapolis: University of Minnesota Press, 1987.

———. *What Is Philosophy?* Translated by Hugh Tomlinson and Graham Burchell. New York: Columbia University Press, 1994.

Demos, T.J. *Decolonizing Nature: Contemporary Art and the Politics of Ecology.* Berlin: Sternberg Press, 2016.

Detienne, Marcel. "The Gods of Politics in Early Greek Cities." In *Political Theologies: Public Religions in a Post-Secular World,* edited by H. de Vries and L.E. Sullivan, 91–101. New York: Fordham University Press, 2006.

di Muzio, Tim. *Carbon Capitalism: Energy, Social Reproduction and World Order.* London: Rowman & Littlefield, 2015.

Dolphijn, Rick, Iris van der Tuin, and Karen Barad. "'Matter Feels, Converses, Suffers, Desires, Yearns and Remembers: Interview with Karen Barad." *In New Materialism: Interviews and Cartographies,* edited by Rick Dolphijn and Iris van der Tuin, 41–70. Ann Arbor: Open Humanities Press, 2012.

Dowden, Ken. *European Paganism: The Realities of Cult from Antiquity to the Middle Ages.* London: Routledge, 2000.

Durand, Gilbert. T*he Anthropological Structures of the Imaginary.* Translated by Margaret Sankey and Judith Hatten. Brisbane: Boombana, 1999.

Dussel, Enrique. *Ethics of Liberation: In the Age of Globalization and Exclusion.* Durham: Duke University Press, 2013.

Eck, Diana L. Darśan: *Seeing the Divine Image in India,* 3rd edition. New York: Columbia University Press, 1998.

Eisenberg, Evan. *The Ecology of Eden.* New York: Vintage Books, 1998.

Electronics Take-Back Coalition. *Facts and Figures on E-Waste and Recycling,* http://www.electronicstakeback.com/wp=content/uploads/Facts_and_Figures_on-EWaste_and_Recycling.pdf.

Emmett, Rob S., and David E. Nye. *The Environmental Humanities: A Critical Introduction.* Cambridge: MIT Press, 2017.

Enfield, N. J., and Paul Kockelman, eds. *Distributed Agency.* New York: Oxford University Press, 2017.

Engberts, Jan. "Immanent Transcendence in Chinese and Western Process Thinking," *Philosophy Study* 2, no. 6 (2012): 377–83.

Escobar, Arturo. *Encountering Development: The Making and Unmaking of the Third World.* Princeton: Princeton University Press, 1995.

Eva Maurer, Julia Richers, Monica Ruthers, and Carmen Scheide, eds. *Soviet Space Culture: Cosmic Enthusiasm in Socialist Societies.* London: Palgrave Macmillan, 2011.

Evans, Nancy. *Civic Rites: Democracy and Religion in Ancient Athens.* Berkeley: University of California Press, 2010.

Faivre, Antoine. *Western Esotericism: A Concise History.* Translated by Christine Rhone. Albany: State University of New York Press, 2010.

Foucault, Michel. *The Hermeneutics of the Subject: Lectures at the Collège de France 1981–1982,* edited by Frederic Gros, translated by Graham Burchell. New York: Picador, 2005.

———. *The Order of Things: An Archaeology of the Human Sciences.* New York: Vintage, 1994.

Frank, Adam. "Is a Climate Disaster Inevitable?" *New York Times Sunday Review,* January 17, 2015, http://www.nytimes.com/2015/01/18/opinion/sunday/is-a-climate-disaster-inevitable.html.

Frey, R. Scott, Paul K. Gellert, and Harry F. Dahms, eds. *Ecologically Unequal Exchange: Environmental Injustice in Comparative and Historical Perspective.* Cham: Palgrave Macmillan, 2019.

Friends of the Pleistocene, "Containing Uncertainty," *FOPnews,* February 24, 2010, https://fopnews.wordpress.com/2010/02/24/containing-uncertainty-design-for-infinite-quarantine/.

Garfield, Jay L. *Engaging Buddhism: Why It Matters to Philosophy.* New York: Oxford University Press, 2015.

Gay, Peter. *The Enlightenment: An Interpretation. Volume 1, The Rise of Modern Paganism.* New York: A.A. Knopf, 1967.

Good, Jonathan. "Crunching the Numbers: How Many People Have Ever Lived?" *1000memories,* May 9, 2011, http://blog.1000memories.com/75-number-of-people-who-have-ever-lived/.

———. "How Many Photos Have Ever Been Taken?" *1000memories,* September 15, 2011, http://blog.1000memories.com/94-number-of-photos-ever-taken-digital-and-analog-in-shoebox.

Gordon, David. "The Place of the Sacred in the Absence of God. A Review of Charles Taylor, A Secular Age." *Journal of the History of Ideas* 69, no. 4 (2008): 647–73. https://www.jstor.org/stable/40208083.

Gorski, Philip S., David K. Kim, John Torpey, and Jonathan VanAntwerpen, eds. *The Post-Secular in Question: Religion in Contemporary Society.* New York: New York University Press, 2012.

Gratton, Peter. *Speculative Realism: Problems and Prospects.* London: Bloomsbury, 2014.

Hadot, Pierre. *Philosophy as a Way of Life: Spiritual Exercises from Socrates to Foucault.* Translated by Michael Chase. Oxford: Blackwell, 1995.

———. *The Present Alone Is Our Happiness: Conversations with Jeannie Carlier and Arnold I. Davidson.* Translated by Marc Djaballah. Stanford: Stanford University Press, 2009.

———. *What Is Ancient Philosophy?* Translated by Michael Chase. Cambridge: Harvard University Press, 2002.

Hampden-Turner, Charles. *Maps of the Mind.* New York: Macmillan, 1982.

Hanegraaff, Wouter. *Esotericism and the Academy: Rejected Knowledge in Western Culture.* Cambridge: Cambridge University Press, 2013.

Harman, Graham. "Aesthetics as First Philosophy: Levinas and the Non-Human." *Naked Punch* 9 (2007): 21–30. http://www.nakedpunch.com/articles/147.

———. *Circus Philosophicus.* Washington: O-Books/John Hunt, 2010.

———. *Immaterialism: Objects and Social Theory.* Cambridge: Polity, 2016.

———. *Object-Oriented Ontology: A New Theory of Everything.* London: Penguin, 2018.

———. *Tool-Being: Heidegger and the Metaphysics of Objects.* Peru: Open Court, 2002.

Hartshorne, Charles. *Creativity in American Philosophy.* Albany: SUNY Press, 1984.

———. *Whitehead's Philosophy.* Lincoln: University of Nebraska Press, 1972.

Harvey, Graham. *Contemporary Paganisms: Religions of the Earth from Druids and Witches to Heathens and Ecofeminists,* 2nd edition. New York: New York University Press, 2011.

———, ed. *The Handbook of Contemporary Animism.* London: Routledge, 2014.

Haynes, Patrice. *Immanent Transcendence: Reconfiguring Materialism in Continental Philosophy.* New York: Bloomsbury, 2012.

Heise, Ursula, Jon Christensen, and Michelle Niemann, eds. *The Routledge Companion to the Environmental Humanities.* London: Routledge, 2017.

Henning, Brian G. *Ethics of Creativity: Beauty, Morality, and Nature in a Processive Cosmos.* Pittsburgh: University of Pittsburgh, 2005.

Herzog, Werner, Roger Ebert, and Gene Walsh. *Images at the Horizon: A Workshop with Werner Herzog.* Chicago: Facets Multimedia, 1979.

Hillman, James. *Archetypal Psychology: A Brief Account.* Dallas: Spring, 1983.

———. "Back to Beyond: On Cosmology." In *Archetypal Process: Self and Divine in Whitehead, Jung, and Hillman,* edited by David Ray Griffin, 213–31. Evanston: Northwestern University Press, 1989.

———. "On Mythic Certitude." *Sphinx: A Journal for Archetypal Psychology and the Arts* 3 (1990): 224–43.

———. *Re-Visioning Psychology.* New York: Harper Colophon, 1975.

Hoffmeyer, Jesper. *Signs of Meaning in the Universe.* Bloomington: Indiana University Press, 1996.

Hutter, Horst. *Shaping the Future: Nietzsche's New Regime of the Soul and Its Ascetic Practices.* London: Lexington, 2006.

Inada, Kenneth. "Immanent Transcendence: The Possibility of an East-West Philosophical Dialogue." *Journal of Chinese Philosophy* 35, no. 3 (2008): 493–510. DOI: 10.1111/j.1540-6253.2008.00493.x.

International Atomic Energy Agency, Division of Public Information. *Chernobyl's Legacy: Health, Environmental and Socio-economic Impacts and Recommendations to the Governments of Belarus, the Russian Federation and Ukraine,* 2nd revised edition. Vienna: IAEA, 2006.

Ivakhiv, Adrian. "Beatnik Brothers: Between Graham Harman and the Deleuzo-Whiteheadian Axis." *Parrhesia* 19 (2014): 65–78.

———. "Chernobyl, Risk, and the Inter-Zone of the Anthropocene." In *The Routledge Companion to Risk and Media,* edited by Bishnupriya Ghosh and Bhaskar Sarkar. New York: Routledge, forthcoming.

———. *Ecologies of the Moving Image: Cinema, Affect, Nature.* Waterloo, Canada: Wilfrid Laurier University Press, 2013.

———. "Nature." In *The Oxford Handbook of the Study of Religion,* edited by Michael Stausberg and Steven Engler, 415–29. New York: Oxford University Press, 2016.

———. "Peirce-Whitehead-Hartshorne and process-relational ontology," *Immanence,* June 9, 2010, http://blog.uvm.edu/ aivakhiv/2010/06/09/peirce-whitehead-hartshorne-process-relational-ontology/.

———. "The Age of the World Motion Picture: Cosmic Visions in the Post-Earthrise Era." In *The Changing World Religion Map,* vol. 1, edited by Stan Brunn, 129–44. London: Springer, 2015.

James, William. *The Principles of Psychology,* vol. II. New York: Henry Holt & Company, 1902.

Jay, Martin. "Modern and Postmodern Paganism: Peter Gay and Jean-François Lyotard." In *Cultural Semantics: Keywords of Our Time,* 181–96. Amherst: University of Massachusetts Press, 1998.

Jensen, Derrick, and Aric McBay. *What We Leave Behind.* New York: Seven Stories Press, 2009.

Jeremijenko, Natalie. "The Art of the Eco-Mindshift." https:// www.ted.com/talks/natalie_jeremijenko_the_art_of_the_ eco_mindshift/transcript.

Johnston, Adrian. *Žižek's Ontology: A Transcendental Materialist Theory of Subjectivity.* Evanston: Northwestern University Press, 2008.

Jones, Judith. *Intensity: An Essay in Whiteheadian Ontology.* London: Vanderbilt University Press, 1998.

Josephson-Storm, Jason. *The Myth of Disenchantment: Magic, Modernity, and the Birth of the Human Sciences.* Chicago: University of Chicago Press, 2017.

Julien, Philippe. *Jacques Lacan's Return to Freud: The Real, the Symbolic, and the Imaginary.* New York: New York University Press, 1994.

Kauffman, Stuart. *Reinventing the Sacred: A New View of Science, Reason, and Religion.* New York: Basic, 2008.

Kearney, Richard. *Poetics of Imagining: Modern to Post-Modern.* New York: Fordham University Press, 1998.

Kearney, Richard. *The Wake of Imagination: Toward a Postmodern Culture.* New York: Routledge, 1988.

Keller, Catherine, and Mary-Jane Rubenstein, eds. *Entangled Worlds: Religion, Science, and New Materialisms.* New York: Fordham University Press, 2017.

———. "Psychocosmetics and the Underworld Connection." In *Archetypal Process: Self and Divine in Whitehead, Jung, and Hillman,* edited by David Ray Griffin, 133–56. Evanston: Northwestern University Press, 1989.

Kent, Beverley. *Charles S. Peirce: Logic and the Classification of the Sciences.* Montreal: McGill–Queen's University Press, 1987.

Kittler, Friedrich. *Gramophone, Film, Typewriter.* Stanford: Stanford University Press, 1999.

Lacan, Jacques. *The Four Fundamental Concepts of Psychoanalysis: The Seminar of Jacques Lacan, Book XI,* edited by Jacques-Alain Miller, translated by Alan Sheridan. New York: W.W. Norton & Company, 1998.

Landy, Joshua, and Michael Saler, eds. *The Re-Enchantment of the World: Secular Magic in a Rational Age.* Stanford: Stanford University Press, 2009.

Latour, Bruno. *An Inquiry into Modes of Existence: An Anthropology of the Moderns.* Cambridge: Harvard University Press, 2013.

———. *Facing Gaia: Eight Lectures on the New Climatic Regime.* Translated by Catherine Porter. Cambridge: Polity, 2017.

———. "How to Be Iconophilic in Art, Science, and Religion?" In *Picturing Science, Producing Art,* edited by Caroline A. Jones and Peter Galison, 418–40. New York: Routledge, 1998.

———. *Politics of Nature: How to Bring the Sciences into Democracy.* Translated by Catherine Porter. Cambridge: Harvard University Press, 2004.

———. "The Puzzling Face of a Secular Gaia." *The Gifford Lectures: Facing Gaia: A New Enquiry Into Natural Religion,* https://www.giffordlectures.org/lectures/facing-gaia-new-enquiry-natural-religion.

———. *We Have Never Been Modern.* Translated by Catherine Porter. Cambridge: Harvard University Press, 1993.

———. "Why Has Critique Run Out of Steam? From Matters of Fact to Matters of Concern," *Critical Inquiry* 30 (2004): 225–48.

———. "What Is Iconoclash? Or Is There a World Beyond the Image Wars?" In *Iconoclash: Beyond the Image Wars in Science, Religion, and Art,* edited by Bruno Latour and Peter Weibel, 14–37. Cambridge: MIT Press, 2002.

———. *What Is the Style of Matters of Concern?* Amsterdam: Van Gorcum, 2008.

Law, John. *After Method: Mess in Social Science Research.* New York: Routledge, 2004.

Lee, A.D. *Pagans and Christians in Late Antiquity: A Sourcebook,* 2nd edition. London: Routledge, 2016.

Lefebvre, Henri. *The Production of Space.* Translated by Donald Nicholson-Smith. Oxford: Blackwell, 1991.

Lefebvre, Martin. "Peirce's Esthetics: A Taste for Signs in Art." *Transactions of the Charles S. Peirce Society* 43, no. 2 (2007): 319–44. https://www.jstor.org/stable/40321187.

Lewis, Simon L. and Mark A. Maslin. "Defining the Anthropocene." *Nature* 519 (March 12, 2015): 170–80.

Lewontin, Richard. "Organism and Environment." In *Learning, Development, and Culture,* edited by Henry C. Plotkin, 151–70. New York: Wiley, 1982.

Lotman, Juri. "On the Semiosphere." *Sign Systems Studies* 33, no. 1 (2005): 205–29.

Lukacher, Ned. "Introduction: Mourning Becomes Telepathy." In Jacques Derrida, *Cinders,* edited and translated by Ned Lukacher, 1–18. Lincoln: University of Nebraska Press, 1991.

Lutz, Antoine, John D. Dunne, and Richard J. Davidson. "Meditation and the Neuroscience of Consciousness." In *Cambridge Handbook of Consciousness,* edited by Morris Moscovitch, Philip Zelazo, and Evan Thompson, 497–549. Cambridge: Cambridge University Press, 2007.

Lyotard, Jean-François. "Lessons in Paganism." In *The Lyotard Reader,* edited by Andrew Benjamin, 122–54. Oxford: Blackwell, 1991.

———. "The Grip (*Mainmise*)." In *Political Writings,* translated by Bill Readings and Kevin Paul Geiman, 148–58. Minneapolis: University of Minnesota Press, 1993.

———. *Just Gaming.* Minneapolis: University of Minnesota Press, 1985.

———. *Peregrinations: Law, Form, Event.* New York: Columbia Unviersity Press, 1988.

Magliola, Robert. *Derrida on the Mend.* West Lafayette: Purdue University Press, 1984.

Marder, Michael. *Chernobyl Herbarium: Fragments of an Exploded Consciousness.* Open Humanities Press, 2016.

Marks, Laura. "Real Images Flow: Mullā Sadrā Meets Film-Philosophy." *Film-Philosophy* 20 (2016): 24–46.

Martin, Luther H., Huck Gutman, and Patrick H. Hutton, eds. *Technologies of the Self: A Seminar with Michel Foucault.* Amherst: University of Massacusetts Press, 1988.

Massecar, Aaron. "The Fitness of an Ideal: A Peircean Ethics." *Contemporary Pragmatism* 10, no. 2 (2013): 97–119. DOI: 10.1163/18758185-90000261.

———. *Ethical Habits: A Peircean Perspective.* New York: Lexington Books, 2016.

Masuzawa, Tomoko. *The Invention of World Religions: Or, How European Universalism Was Preserved in the Language of Pluralism.* Chicago: University of Chicago Press, 2005.

Maxwell, Richard, and Toby Miller. "Greening Starts with Ourselves." *New York Times,* September 24, 2012, http://www.nytimes.com/roomfordebate/2012/09/23/informations-environmental-cost/greening-starts-with-ourselves.

McGushin, Edward F. *Foucault's Askesis: An Introduction to the Philosophical Life.* Evanston: Northwestern University Press, 2007.

McMullen, Ramsay. *Christianity and Paganism in the Fourth to Eighth Centuries.* New Haven: Yale University Press, 1999.

Mearian, Lucas. "Scientists Calculate Total Data Stored to Date: 295+ Exabytes." *ComputerWorld.* February 14, 2011, http://www.computerworld.com/s/article/9209158/Scientists_calculate_total_data_stored_to_date_295_exabytes.

Meillassioux, Quentin. *After Finitude: An Essay on the Necessity of Contingency.* Translated by Ray Brassier. London: Bloomsbury, 2010.

Meyer, Birgit, and Peter Pels, eds. *Magic and Modernity: Interfaces of Revelation and Concealment.* Stanford: Stanford University Press, 2003.

Mignolo, Walter. *Local Histories/Global Designs: Coloniality, Subaltern Knowledges, and Border Thinking.* Princeton: Princeton University Press, 2000.

Miller, Adam S. *Speculative Grace: Bruno Latour and Object-Oriented Theory.* New York: Fordham University Press, 2013.

Mirzoeff, Nicholas. "Autoimmune Climate-Changing Capitalism Syndrome: AICCCS," http://www.nicholasmirzoeff.com/O2012/2012/08/25/autoimmune-climate-changing-capitalism-syndrome-aicccs/.

Mitchell, W.J.T. *What Do Pictures Want? The Lives and Loves of Images.* Chicago: University of Chicago Press, 2005.

Moffett, Mark W. *Adventures Among Ants: A Global Safari with a Cast of Trillions.* Berkeley: University of California Press, 2010.

Moore, Jason W. *Capitalism in the Web of Life: Ecology and the Accumulation of Capital.* London: Verso, 2015.

Morton, Timothy. "Anthropomorphism." *Ecology Without Nature,* December 22, 2010, http://ecologywithoutnature. blogspot.com/2010/12/anthropomorphism.html.

———. *Being Ecological.* Cambridge: MIT Press, 2018.

———. *Realist Magic: Objects, Ontology, Causality.* Ann Arbor: Open Humanities Press, 2013.

Mullarkey, John. *Post-Continental Philosophy: An Outline.* London: Continuum, 2006.

Mycio, Mary. *Wormwood Forest: A Natural History of Chernobyl.* Washington: Joseph Henry Press, 2005.

Needleman, Jacob, and George Baker, eds. *Gurdjieff: Essays and Reflections on the Man and His Teachings.* New York: Continuum, 2004.

Neville, Robert C. "Whitehead and Pragmatism." In *Whitehead's Philosophy: Points of Connection,* edited by Janusz A. Polanowski and Donald W. Sherburne. Albany: SUNY Press, 2004.

Nicolescu, Basarab. "Gurdjieff's Philosophy of Nature." In *Gurdjieff: Essays and Reflections on the Man and His Teachings,* edited by Jacob Needleman and George Baker, 37–69. New York: Continuum, 2004.

Niemoczynski, Leon. *Speculative Realism: An Epitome.* Leeds: Kismet Press, 2017.

Odin, Steve. *Tragic Beauty in Whitehead and Japanese Aesthetics.* New York: Lexington, 2016.

Oppermann, Serpil, and Serenella Iovino, eds. *Environmental Humanities: Voices from the Anthropocene.* London: Rowman and Littlefield, 2017.

Owen, Alex. *The Place of Enchantment: British Occultism and the Culture of the Modern.* Chicago: University of Chicago Press, 2004.

Paper, Jordan. *The Deities Are Many: A Polytheistic Theology.* Albany: SUNY Press, 2005.

Parker, Robert. *Polytheism and Society at Athens.* New York: Oxford University Press, 2005.

Parret, Herman, ed. *Peirce and Value Theory.* Amsterdam: John Benjamins, 1994.

Partridge, Christopher. *The Re-Enchantment of the West,* vols. 1 and 2. London: Continuum, 2005–6.

Peirce, Charles Sanders. "An Outline Classification of the Sciences." In *The Essential Peirce: Selected Philosophical Writings, Vol. 2 (1893–1913),* edited by Peirce Edition Project, 256–62. Bloomington: Indiana University Press, 1998.

———. *Collected Papers.* Vols. 1–6 edited by Charles Hartshorne and Paul Weiss; vols. 7–8 edited by A.W. Burks. Cambridge: Belknap Press of Harvard University Press, 1958–66. Electronic edition edited by John Deely. IntelLex Corporation, 1994.

———. "The Principles of Phenomenology: The Categories in Detail." In *Collected Papers of Charles Sanders Peirce,* vol. 1, edited by Charles Hartshorne and Paul Weiss, 148–80. Bloomington: Indiana University Press, 1958.

———. "The Three Normative Sciences." In *The Essential Peirce: Selected Philosophical Writings, Vol. 2 (1893–1913),* edited by Peirce Edition Project, 196–207. Bloomington: Indiana University Press, 1998.

Phillips, Sarah D. "Chernobyl Forever," *Somatosphere,* April 25, 2011, http://somatosphere.net/2011/04/chernobyl-forever.html.

———. "Chernobyl's Sixth Sense: The Symbolism of an Ever-Present Awareness." *Anthropology and Humanism* 29, no. 2 (2004): 159–85. DOI: 10.1525/ahu.2004.29.2.159.

———., and Sarah Ostaszewski. "An Illustrated Guide to the Post-Catastrophic Future." *Anthropology of East Europe Review* 30, no. 1 (2012): 127–40. https://scholarworks.iu.edu/journals/index.php/aeer/article/view/2005.

Pijanowski, Bryan, Almo Farina, Stuart Gage, Sarah Dumyahn, and Bernie Krause. "What is Soundscape Ecology? An Introduction and Overview of an Emerging New Science." *Landscape Ecology* 26, no. 9 (2011): 1213–32. DOI: 10.1007/s10980-011-9600-8.

Pile, Steve. *Real Cities: Modernity, Space, and the Phantasmagorias of City Life.* London: Sage, 2005.

Polanyi, Karl. *The Great Transformation: The Political and Economic Origins of Our Time,* 2nd edition. Boston: Beacon Press, 1944/2001.

Puig de la Bellacasa, Maria. "Matters of Care in Technoscience: Assembling Neglected Things." *Social Studies of Science* 41, no. 1 (2011): 85–106. DOI: 10.1177/0306312710380301.

Radkau, Joachim. *The Age of Ecology.* Cambridge: Polity, 2014.

Ramey, Joshua. *The Hermetic Deleuze: Philosophy as Spiritual Ordeal.* Durham: Duke University Press, 2012.

Rectenwald, Michael, Rochelle Almeida, and George Levine, eds. *Global Secularisms in a Post-Secular Age.* Boston: de Gruyter, 2015.

Rinpoche, Tsoknyi. *Fearless Simplicity: The Dzogchen Way of Living Freely in a Complex World.* Hong Kong: Rangjung Yeshe Publications, 2003.

Robinson, Gillian, and John Rundell, eds. *Rethinking Imagination: Culture and Creativity.* New York: Routledge, 1994.

Rosenthal, Sandra. "Contemporary Process Metaphysics and Diverse Intuitions of Time: Can the Gap be Bridged?" *Journal of Speculative Philosophy* 12, no. 4 (1998): 271–88. https://www.jstor.org/stable/25670267.

Ruddiman, William F. "The Anthropogenic Greenhouse Era Began Thousands of Years Ago." *Climatic Change* 61, no. 3 (2003): 261–93. DOI: 10.1023/B:CLIM.0000004577.17928.fa.

Ruse, Michael. *The Gaia Hypothesis: Science on a Pagan Planet.* Chicago: University of Chicago Press, 2013.

Sagan, Dorion. "Coda: Beautiful Monsters: Terra in the Cyanocene." In *Arts of Living on a Damaged Planet: Ghosts and Monsters of the Anthropocene,* edited by Anna L. Tsing, Heather Anne Swanson, Elaine Gan, and Nils Bubandt, M169–74. Minneapolis: University of Minnesota Press, 2017.

Sahlins, Marshall. "The Original Political Society." *Hau: Journal of Ethnographic Theory* 7, no. 2 (2017): 91–128. DOI: 10.14318/hau7.2.014.

Said, Edward. *Orientalism.* New York: Pantheon, 1978.

Schmid, Sonia D. *Producing Power: The Pre-Chernobyl History of the Soviet Nuclear Industry.* Cambridge: MIT Press, 2015.

Seznec, Jean. *The Survival of the Pagan Gods: The Mythological Tradition and Its Place in Renaissance Humanism and Art.* New York: Harper, 1953.

Shaviro, Steven. *The Universe of Things: On Speculative Realism.* Minneapolis: University of Minnesota Press, 2014.

Sherburne, Donald. "Whitehead without God." *Process Studies* 15, no. 2 (1986): 83–94.

Shusterman, Richard. *Body Consciousness: A Philosophy of Mindfulness and Somaesthetics.* Cambridge: Cambridge University Press, 2008.

Skholiast. "Eternity and Objects." *Speculum Criticum Traditionis,* June 10, 2010, http://speculumcriticum.blogspot.com/2010/06/eternity-and-objects.html.

Skrbina, David, ed. *Mind That Abides: Panpsychism in the New Millennium.* Amsterdam: John Benjamins, 2009.

———. *Panpsychism in the West,* revised edition. Cambridge: MIT Press, 2017.

Sloterdijk, Peter. *You Must Change Your Life!* Cambridge: Polity, 2013.

Smith, Carl M. "The Aesthetics of Charles S. Peirce." *Journal of Aesthetics and Art Criticism* 31, no. 1 (1972): 21–9.

Smith, Cooper. "Facebook Users Are Uploading 350 Million Photos Each Day." *Business Insider,* September 18, 2013, http://www.businessinsider.com/facebook-350-million-photos-each-day-2013-9.

Social Cognitive and Affective Neuroscience 8, no. 1. Special Issue on Mindfulness Neuroscience. https://academic.oup.com/scan/issue/8/1.

Sørensen, Bent, and Torkild Leo Thellefsen. "The Normative Sciences, the Sign Universe, Self-Control and Relationality—According to Peirce." *Cosmos and History* 6, no. 1 (2010): 142–52.

Stengers, Isabelle. *In Catastrophic Times: Resisting the Coming Barbarism.* Translated by Andrew Goffey. Ann Arbor: Open Humanities Press, 2015.

———. *Panpsychism in the West,* revised edition. Cambridge: MIT Press, 2017. *Cosmopolitiques,* 7 vols. Paris: La découverte, 1997.

———. "The Cosmopolitical Proposal." In *Making Things Public,* edited by Bruno Latour and Peter Weibel, 994–1003. Cambridge: MIT Press, 2005.

Styers, Randall. *Making Magic: Religion, Magic, and Science in the Modern World.* Oxford: Oxford University Press, 2004.

Taffel, Sy. "Escaping Attention: Digital Media Hardware, Materiality and Ecological Cost." *Culture Machine* 13 (2012): 1–28. https://www.culturemachine.net/index.php/cm/article/viewArticle/468.

Tanahashi, Kazuaki. *The Heart Sutra: A Comprehensive Guide to the Classic of Mahayana Buddhism.* Boulder: Shambhala, 2016.

Taylor, Bron R. *Dark Green Religion: Nature Spirituality and the Planetary Future.* Berkeley: University of California Press, 2009.

Taylor, Charles. *A Secular Age.* Cambridge: Harvard University Press, 2007.

Tonder, Lars. "A Secular Age: Spinoza's Immanence." *The Immanent Frame,* December 5, 2007, http://blogs.ssrc.org/tif/2007/12/05/spinozas-immanence/.

Trout, Lara. *The Politics of Survival: Peirce, Affectivity, and Social Criticism.* New York: Fordham University Press, 2013.

Van der Veer, Peter. *Imperial Encounters: Religion and Modernity in India and Britain.* Princeton: Princeton University Press, 2001.

Vitale, Christopher. "The Metaphysics of Refraction in Sufi Philosophy: Ibn Arabi, Suhrawardi, and Mulla Sadra Shirazi." *Networkologies,* May 17, 2012, http://networkologies.wordpress.com/2012/05/17/the-metaphysics-of-refraction-in-sufi-philosophy-ibn-arabi-suhrawadri-and-mulla-sadra-shirazi/.

Walker, Theodore, Jr., and Mihály Tóth, eds. *Whiteheadian Ethics: Abstracts and Papers from the Ethics Section of the Philosophy Group at the 6th International Whitehead Conference at* the University of Salzburg, July 2006. Newcastle: Cambridge Scholars Publishing, 2008.

Weber, Michel. *Whitehead's Pancreativism: The Basics.* Frankfurt: Ontos, 2006.

Weintraub, Linda. *To Life: Eco Art in Pursuit of a Sustainable Planet.* Berkeley: University of California Press, 2012.

Weisman, Alan. *The World Without Us.* New York: St. Martin's Press, 2007.

Whitehead, Alfred North. "Objects and Subjects." *The Philosophical Review* 41, no. 2 (1932): 130–46. DOI: 10.2307/2179771.

———. *Adventures of Ideas.* New York: Free Press, 1933/1967.

———. *Modes of Thought.* New York: Free Press, 1938/1968.

———. *Process and Reality,* corrected edition, edited by David Ray Griffin and Donald W. Sherburne. New York: Free Press, 1978.

———. *Symbolism: Its Meaning and Effect.* New York: Fordham Unviersity Press, 1927/1985.

———. *The Concept of Nature.* New York: Cambridge University Press, 1920.

Williams, James. "Immanence and Transcendence as Inseparable Processes: On the Relevance of Arguments from Whitehead to Deleuze Interpretation." *Deleuze Studies* 4, no. 1 (2010): 94–106. DOI: 10.3366/E1750224110000851.

Williams, Raymond. *The Long Revolution.* Orchard Park: Broadview Press, 1961/2001.

Worster, Donald. *Nature's Economy: A History of Ecological Ideas,* 2nd edition. New York: Cambridge University Press, 1994.

Yablokov, Alexey, Iryna Labunska, and Ivan Blokov, eds. *The Chernobyl Catastrophe: Consequences on Human Health.* Amsterdam: Greenpeace, 2006.

Young, Shinzen. "Five Ways to Know Yourself: An Introduction to Basic Mindfulness." 2011–16, http://www.shinzen. org/wp-content/uploads/2016/08/FiveWaystoKnowYourself_ver1.6.pdf.

———. "Getting the Lingo." *Shinzen Young,* 2006, revised June 2, 2008. https://www.dharmaoverground.org/documents/portlet_file_entry/10128/Getting%2Bthe%2BLingo.pdf/a9a2964c-3f1d-4ee5-b857-bd8e4ed440b4.

———. "What Us Mindfulness? A Contemplative Perspective." In *Handbook of Mindfulness in Education: Integrating Theory and Research into Practice,* edited by Kimberly A. Schonert-Reichl and Robert W. Roeser, 29–45. New York: Springer, 2016.

———. *The Science of Enlightenment: How Meditation Works.* Boulder: Sounds True, 2016.

Zalasiewicz, Jan, Colin N. Waters, Mark Williams, et al. "When Did the Anthropocene Begin? A Mid-20th Century Boundary Level Is Stratigraphically Optimal." *Quaternary International* 383 (2015): 196–203.

Ziporyn, Brook. *Being and Ambiguity: Philosophical Experiments with Tiantai Buddhism.* Chicago: Open Court, 2004.

———. *Emptiness and Omnipresence: An Essential Introduction to Tiantai Buddhism.* Bloomington: Indiana University Press, 2016.

Žižek, Slavoj. "Censorship Today: Violence, or Ecology as a New Opium for the Masses." *Lacan.com* 18 (2008), 42–43.

———. "Human Rights and Its Discontents." Olin Auditorium, Bard College, November 15, 1999, http://www.lacan.com/zizek-human.htm.

———. "Nature and Its Discontents." *SubStance* 37, no. 3 (2008): 37–72. DOI: 10.1353/sub.0.0017.

———. "Of Cells and Selves." In *The Žižek Reader,* edited by Elizabeth Wright and Edmond Wright, 302–20. Oxford: Blackwell, 1999.

———. "The Undergrowth of Enjoyment: How Popular Culture Can Serve as an Introduction to Lacan." *New Formations* 9 (1989): 7–29.

———. "Unbehagen in der Natur." In Žižek, *In Defense of Lost Causes,* 420–61. London: Verso, 2009.

———. *Less Than Nothing: Hegel and the Shadow of Dialectical Materialism.* London: Verso, 2013.

————. *Looking Awry: An Introduction to Jacques Lacan through Popular Culture.* Cambridge: MIT Press, 1991.

————. *The Sublime Object of Ideology.* London: Verso, 1989.

Zong-qi, Cai. "Derrida and Madhyamika Buddhism: From Linguistic Deconstruction to Criticism of Onto-Theologies." *International Philosophical Quarterly* 33, no. 2 (1993): 183–95. DOI: 10.5840/ipq19933327.

Filmography

Austerlitz. Directed by S. Loznitsa, Germany, 2016.

Aftermath: The World After Humans. National Geographic/Cream Productions, Canada, 2008.

Life After People. Directed by David De Vries, History Channel, USA, 2008.

Chernobyl Diaries. Directed by Bradley Parker, USA, 2012.

Pripyat. Directed by Nikolaus Geyrhalter, Czech Republic, 1999.

Return of the Living Dead: Necropolis. Directed by Ellory El-kayem, USA, 2005.

Return of the Living Dead: Rave to the Grave. Directed by Ellory Elkayem, USA, 2005.

INDEX

CPSIA information can be obtained
at www.ICGtesting.com
Printed in the USA
FSHW020016221221
87111FS

9 781947 447875